Advance Praise for *Analysis of Shu Ha Ri in Karate-Do*

Outstanding analysis of *Shu Ha Ri*, the developmental principle in Japanese karatedo that contrasts the philosophical basis of Okinawan karate. Hermann explains how in Okinawan karate functionality is prioritized over perfecting a form, whereas the opposite is done in Japanese karatedo, and how and why *Shu Ha Ri* was applied to the latter during the process that created a fine-art karatedo version of self-perfection on the mainland—which ultimately led to all those consequences of neglecting the logic and reality of fighting.

> —Noel Smith, Hanshi 9th Dan Yamashita International Budo Association; Kyoshi, 8th Dan Shorin Ryu, Shorinkan; head coach for the US karate team (1973 to 1978); USA Karate Hall of Fame Inductee (1976)

Written with unconditional passion and intellectual depth *Analysis of Shu Ha Ri in Karate-Do* presents the reader with a masterful explication of a too-often misunderstood, culturally misplaced concept, vital to the preservation, understanding, growth, and usefulness of Okinawa's unique life-protection arts.

> —William "Bill" Hayes, Hanshi, 10th Dan Shorin Ryu, Shobayashi-Kan; Major, United States Marine Corps (retired); Karate Masters' Hall of Fame and American-Okinawan Karate Association Hall of Fame Inductee; award-winning author of *My Journey with the Grandmaster: Reflections of an American Martial Artist on Okinawa*

Bayer's meticulous research and ability to bridge Eastern and Western thought make this book a valuable contribution to martial arts studies. By offering a comprehensive framework for understanding *Shu Ha Ri*, the author has laid the groundwork for future research and discussions on the evolution and purpose of karate. This work is a complex and wonderful read, which I am sure many of you will enjoy.

> —Dr. James Hatch, Kyoshi, 7th Dan *Chito Ryu, Sichibu Jyuku;* EdD, martial arts researcher, international educator in Tokyo, Japan

Hermann Bayer has created the most thoughtful and complete book on *Shu Ha Ri* in the English language … ever. This book belongs in your library next to *The Bubishi, The Art of War,* and *The Five Rings.*

> —Kris Wilder, 6th Dan Goju-Ryu, black belt taekwondo and judo; USA Karate Hall of Fame Inductee (2018); award-winning author of more than twenty martial arts books, including *The Way of Kata, The Way of Sanchin Kata,* and others

In-depth analysis and very interesting read. I believe that, like me, other karateka will appreciate this work and learn from it.

> —Itzik Cohen, Kyoshi, 7th Dan Shorin Ryu Kyudokan; martial arts researcher; Israel's representative of Kyudokan Kobayashi Shorin-Ryu Karate; author of *Pathways of Karate Development, Karate's Genetic Code,* and others

Hermann Bayer is a distinguished scholar-practitioner and a staunch and convincing advocate for the case of recognizing karate as a cultural heritage of Okinawa. His book on *Shu Ha Ri* gives plenty of food for thought; it is in a way an exercise and execution of this principle and an exhaustive study on the theme, written by an analytical and scientific mind.

> —Professor Dr. Wolfgang Herbert, 6th Dan *Shotokan Karate-Do,* SKIF; professor of Comparative Cultural Studies at the University of Tokushima/Japan; martial arts researcher; author of *Von Shaolin bis Shotokan*

Dr. Bayer weaves historic, socio-cultural, political, philosophical, psychological, and commercial components into a complex analysis that gives a clear picture and that addresses misconceptions and differing interpretations by various groups with their own agenda.

> —Thomas E. Ward, Kyoshi, 7th Dan *Shorin Ryu, Shorinkan;* professional educator

In his latest book, my friend Dr. Hermann Bayer, has taken an in-depth look at the Japanese teaching philosophy known as *Shu Ha Ri*. His enlightening analysis explains how this philosophy is applied and differs between today's martial arts cultures. A worthwhile and highly recommended read.

> —Raymond "Gene" Adkins, Renshi 6th Dan Shorin Ryu, Shorinkan

Hermann Bayer offers us a profound and most valuable reflection on a topic that is as crucial to karate studies as it has hitherto been ignored; namely, how modern Japanese karate appropriated Okinawan karate in the early 1900s by not only simplifying its techniques but also by codifying principles that had previously remained unexpressed.

—Bruno Ballardini, 8th Dan Shorinji Ryu Zentokukai, former professor at the First University of Rome "La Sapienza"; president of the Italian Association for the Study of Ancient Karate, Europe coordinator of International Okinawa Shorinji-Ryu Tode Zentokukai; author of the standing rubric "Karate Archeology" in *Bugeisha* magazine

Analysis of Shu Ha Ri in Karate-Dō

Analysis of SHU HA RI IN KARATE-DŌ

When a Fighting Art Becomes a Fine Art

Hermann Bayer, Ph.D.

YMAA Publication Center
Wolfeboro, NH USA

YMAA Publication Center, Inc.
PO Box 480
Wolfeboro, NH 03894
800 669-8892 • www.ymaa.com • info@ymaa.com

ISBN: 9781594399930 (print)
ISBN: 9781594399947 (ebook)
ISBN: 9781594399954 (hardcover)

This book set in Adobe Garamond and Source Sans.

Copyright © 2025 by Hermann Bayer
All rights reserved including the right of reproduction in whole or in part in any form. Any use of this intellectual property for text and data mining or computational analysis including as training material for artificial intelligence systems is strictly prohibited without express written consent. For permission requests, contact the Publisher.

Edited by Doran Hunter
Cover design by Axie Breen
Photos by author unless otherwise noted
Charts and graphs by author unless otherwise noted

20250324

Publisher's Cataloging in Publication

Title: Analysis of Shu Ha Ri in karate-dō : when a fighting art becomes a fine art / Hermann Bayer.
Description: Wolfeboro, NH USA : YMAA Publication Center, [2025] | Series: Analysis of karate series. | Includes bibliographical references and index.
Identifiers: ISBN: 9781594399930 (softcover) | 9781594399954 (hardcover) | 9781594399947 (ebook) | LCCN: 2024952876
Subjects: LCSH: Karate. | Karate--Japan--Okinawa Island. | Karate--Foreign influences. | Hand-to-hand fighting, Oriental. | Karate--History--Errors, inventions, etc. | Karate--History--Sociological aspects. | Martial arts--History. | BISAC: SPORTS & RECREATION / Martial Arts / Karate. | HISTORY / Asia / Japan. | SOCIAL SCIENCE / Cultural & Ethnic Studies / Asian Studies.
Classification: LCC: GV1114.3 .B393 2025 | DDC: 796.815/3--dc23

The authors and publisher of the material are NOT RESPONSIBLE in any manner whatsoever for any injury which may occur through reading or following the instructions in this manual.

The activities physical or otherwise, described in this manual may be too strenuous or dangerous for some people, and the reader(s) should consult a physician before engaging in them.

Neither the authors nor the publisher assumes any responsibility for the use or misuse of information contained in this book.

Nothing in this document constitutes a legal opinion nor should any of its contents be treated as such. While the authors believe that everything herein is accurate, any questions regarding specific self-defense situations, legal liability, and/or interpretation of federal, state, or local laws should always be addressed by an attorney at law.

When it comes to martial arts, self-defense, and related topics, no text, no matter how well written, can substitute for professional, hands-on instruction. These materials should be used for **academic study only**.

Printed in USA.

Contents

Foreword by Hanshi William R. Hayes — ix
Foreword by Professor Dr. Wolfgang Herbert — x
Foreword by Kyoshi Dr. James Hatch — xv
Foreword by Kyoshi Thomas E. Ward — xvii
Foreword by Kyoshi Bruno Ballardini — xix
Introduction: New Significance of Shu Ha Ri in Postwar Karatedo—or a Mistaken Paradigm? — xxiii

Chapter 1: A Centuries-Old Japanese Fine Arts Principle Finds Its Way into Modern Karate — 1

    Protecting Others and Oneself from Physical and Nonphysical Harm Is the Universal Principle of Okinawan Karate-jutsu That Differs from the Self-Perfection Principle in Japanese Karatedo — 5

    The Japanese Shu Ha Ri Developmental Principle and Its Martial Arts Ramifications — 10

    Though the Shu Ha Ri Concept Is Widespread in Today's Japanese Karatedo, It Is Unknown to Many Karateka — 18

    Shu Ha Ri in the Martial Arts versus in the Fine Arts — 22

    Different Shu Ha Ri Interpretations Are Used in Karate Today — 24

        How Individualism in Western Culture May Impact the Way Shu Ha Ri Is Understood — 25

        The Yardsticks That Measure the Adequacy of Interpretations of Karate Moves — 29

            The Yardstick in Karate-Jutsu Is Measurable Self-Defense Impact — 31

            Subjective Interpretations of Forms in Karatedo Are Not Factually Measurable — 33

            Forms as Defined by Associations Are the Yardstick in Sports-Karate — 34

        Shu Ha Ri, Meditation, Religion, and the Esoteric — 35

    Differing Shu Ha Ri Characteristics Are Found in Today's Karate-jutsu, Karatedo, and Sports-Karate — 43

Chapter 2: Shu Ha Ri Is a Japanese Socio-Cultural Concept, Not an Okinawan One — 45

Okinawa Shows Subcultural Peculiarities That Appeared Inferior to Prewar Japan — 45

Shu Ha Ri Is Not a Traditional Principle of Okinawan Karate-jutsu — 48

    Initially, There Were No Styles in Classic Okinawan Karate-jutsu — 52

    Okinawans Did Usually Not "Break Away" from Their Sensei — 56

    Okinawan Masters May Not Officially See Shu Ha Ri as a Relevant Principle but They Developed Students Beyond Their Own Teachings — 59

Cultural Norms and Social Mechanisms in Japan Support Conformity and Not Breaking Away from Traditions — 61

    Senpai/Kohai, the Social Mechanism That Maintains Traditions — 62

    Giri, the Norm of Conformity and Mutual Obligations — 64

The Initial Shu Ha Ri Understanding in the Japanese Fine Arts (Including the Ikebana Parable "How Jiro Became a Sensei" by Thomas E. Ward) — 65

Chapter 3: Based on Claims of Cultural Superiority, Japan Converts Okinawan Karate-jutsu into Karatedo and Inserts Japanese Philosophies — 71

Prewar Japan's Self-Proclaimed Cultural and Racial Superiority — 72

Based on Self-Acclaimed Cultural Supremacy, Japan Redefines Karate Since Its Okinawan Version Embodied "Backwardness" in the Eyes of the Japanese — 74

    Japan's Redefinition of Karate as Karatedo, a Path toward Self-Perfection, and Its Adoption as a National Cultural Symbol — 76

    Some Major Changes to the Okinawan Conception of Universal Self-Protection in Japanese Karatedo — 79

Formalizing Karatedo into a Japanese Fine Art Allows Shu Ha Ri to Be Incorporated into It and Gives Rise to the Development of Styles — 85

Chapter 4: The Application of a Truncated Shu Ha Ri Concept in Modern Management — 91

Business Consultants Discover Shu Ha Ri — 93

Misunderstandings of Shu Ha Ri in Business Applications — 94

Chapter 5: Misinterpretations of Shu Ha Ri May Allow Excuses for Laxity — 97

Karatedo's Commercialization May Encourage Interpretations of Shu Ha Ri as Breaking Away — 98

Individualism May Turn into Self-Absorption and Narcissism if Shu Ha Ri Is Interpreted as Breaking Away — 100

Transcending in the Ri-Phase and Some Possible Misinterpretations (with contributions by Thomas E. Ward)	103
Shu Ha Ri May Be Used to Sell Fantasy Moves as Genuine Techniques	103
Shu Ha Ri May Be Used to Reinvent the Wheel	104
"New" Karate Styles May Not Be New at All but Rediscovered Traditional Techniques	105
How to Find Instructors in the Kind of Karate One Wants to Learn	107

Chapter 6: Parallels and Differences Between Shu Ha Ri and Western Educational Concepts and Their Probable Mutual Supplementation (with Contributions by Thomas E. Ward) — 109

Modern Western Educational Concepts	110
Limitations and Advantages of Western Concepts Compared to Shu Ha Ri	113

Chapter 7: The Essence of Shu Ha Ri Is Its Coexisting "Trinity of Phases" — 119

Trinity of Coexisting Phases in Shu Ha Ri Instead of Skill Levels	119
Holistic Thinking Overcomes Assumed Contradictions	122
Excurse: Real Fights in Contrast to Consensual Plays	128

Chapter 8: Conclusion and Consequences — 131

Physical, Mental, and Spiritual Development Covers the Totality of Karate Today	137
Integrating a Well-Established Western Educational Concept with Established Asian Teaching Methods May Help Retain Students in Traditional Karate (with contributions by Thomas E. Ward)	140
Classic Karate-jutsu and Old-Style Karatedo Dojos Are Losing Students at an Alarming Rate	141
Instruction Alone Is Not Sufficient for Advanced Learning	144
In a Traditional Western Dojo, Western Educational Concepts Can Support Established Asian Teaching Routines	147
The Necessity of a Yardstick to Formulate Meaningful Learning Objectives	150
The Symbiosis of Eastern and Western Teaching Concepts	152
Excurse: Japan's Cultural Roots of Confucianism and Taoism	153

List of Abbreviations	156
List of Photos and Graphs	157
Explanations of East Asian Terms in Dr. Hermann Bayer's Books	159
References	169
Index	177
About the Author	181

FOREWORD BY
HANSHI WILLIAM R. HAYES

Dr. Bayer's newest book about *Shu Ha Ri*—which means to "follow, transcend, break away"—was both a pleasure to read and to learn from. A skilled researcher and thought leader when it comes to topics such as *Shu Ha Ri*, Hermann also happens to be an active and serious martial artist who has taken this somewhat obscure socio-cultural construct of *Shu Ha Ri* and properly, historically, and practically contextualized it using his well-honed research skills throughout the process. For this we should all be immensely grateful as little clear and useful information has been previously published—or otherwise succinctly transmitted—on the topic.

This book will undoubtedly be of great assistance to students and teachers alike who might muse, "In what ways can I achieve further understanding of the art I have been gifted with?"

Written with unconditional passion and intellectual depth, *Analysis of Shu Ha Ri in Karate-do: When a Fighting Art Becomes a Fine Art* presents the reader with a masterful explication of a too-often misunderstood, culturally misplaced concept vital to the preservation, understanding, growth, and usefulness of Okinawa's unique life-protection art.

Enjoy this book with gratitude just as you might also enjoy your next sunrise.

William R. Hayes
"Old Student"
Hanshi 10th Dan *Shobayashi Ryu*
Major US-Marine Corps (retired)

FOREWORD BY
PROFESSOR DR. WOLFGANG HERBERT

Shu Ha Ri, Bushidô, and Zen-Buddhism as Invented Traditions in Japanese Karatedo

Hermann Bayer is a distinguished scholar-practitioner and a staunch and convincing advocate for recognizing karate as a cultural heritage of Okinawan "karate as a complex and rich art that needs to be preserved in its classic form," as he himself declares. With his two books *Analysis of Genuine Karate: Misconceptions, Origins, Development, and True Purpose* and *Analysis of Genuine Karate 2: Sociocultural Development, Commercialization, and Loss of Essential Knowledge*—which I recommend perusing as a propaedeutic reading—he has already become a distinct voice in the field of karate studies. I deem it an honor to contribute some introductory remarks and additional comments on his new publication about *Shu Ha Ri* in Karatedo, which will be the most comprehensive work on the topic.

To ask the right—and often a simple—question can open the door to exploration and widen perspectives. Now, here is the query: *why is Shu Ha Ri relatively unknown among karate practitioners and when did it start to pop up in writing(s) about karate?* The expedition can begin.

The concept as such is said to go back to a stanza in the scroll "Rikyû dôka" (利休道歌), which describes the way of the tea as celebrated by the master Sen no Rikyû (1522–1591): 規矩作法 守り尽くして破るとも離るるとても本を忘るな *(kuki sahô mamoritsukushite yaburu to mo hanaruru to te mo moto o wasuru na!)* "Do not forget the origin, even when you, after meticulously preserving *(shu* 守*)* the guidelines and etiquette, break away *(ha* 破*)* and even liberate *(ri* 離*)* yourself from those."

It is said that the principle of *Shu Ha Ri* was constructed from this line by combination of the three respective characters in Sino-Japanese. In the original they turn up in their verbal form and Japanese reading. Two points are pertinent here: firstly, this concept of three "stages" of learning and finally mastering an art or a craft originates in the *fine arts* and found its way into other creative activities like music, dance, theatre, poetry, calligraphy and the like. Secondly, Rikyû admonishes us not to forget or neglect the "origin" or basis (*moto* 本, also read: *hon*; it is the *hon* in *kihon* 基本 = basics, fundamentals), thus indicating that as far and yonder as one might go, the foundation remains present and supports one's endeavor. As a well-known Japanese saying goes: 初心忘るべからず *(shoshin wasurubekarazu)* "do not forget the spirit [you had] as a novice," an attitude that Zen-masters like to call the beginner's mind. You always return to the basics and learn afresh. The *Shu Ha Ri* model turns out to be—rather than linear—a *spiral*, as you will be shown in detail in the book at hand.

"Invented tradition" has become a well-known notion and is neatly valid also in the case of *Shu Ha Ri* in the martial arts. I would even like to speak of an "imposed tradition" in cases where a tradition of a dominant cultural strand is grafted upon another marginal one. In the matter at hand it concerns mainland Japanese cultural elements that were transplanted into an originally Okinawan set of skills for self-protection. Only after the transformation of Okinawan karate into a Japanese "martial way," namely *budô*, and its conversion into a fine art for self-perfection, spiritual growth, and character building, the importation of the idea of *Shu Ha Ri* into karate-dô became congruent with this new form of karate as an art of self-cultivation. Hence, the time lag and relative lack of familiarity with the term by many karateka. *Shu Ha Ri*, as Hermann Bayer rightly contends, entered the vocabulary of karate noticeably after WWII. The same phenomenon can be observed in two other cases of imposed traditions: the warrior code of *bushidô* and a rather distorted brand of Zen-Buddhism.

While one of the most influential organizations, the JKA (Japan Karate Association) informs us on their homepage (under "philosophy") that karate is based on Zen and *bushido*, the latter of which *is an invented tradition par excellence* and was originally relevant merely for a marginal part of the population (5 to 7 percent), the class or caste of the *bushi*, the warriors, common Samurai. After the Meiji Restoration and abolishment of the feudal class system, *bushido* was propagated as the core value system of Japan, embodying its "unique soul" *(Yamato damashii)* and to be embraced by every Japanese citizen. Sociologists call this the "samuraization" of Japanese society in order to forge a national identity, conformity, and solidarity, and consequently it was utilized for the all-out mobilization for the wars Japan was going to fight. Loyalty to the Emperor (formerly to the feudal lord), willingness to die for him on the battlefield, absolute obedience, endurance of hardships, frugality, fulfillment of one's duties and obligations were elements of this "imperial" *bushido*, as it was dubbed by the foremost Western authority on the topic, Oleg Benesch. The martial arts and karate were lastingly influenced by this zeitgeist and instrumentalized by the then-extant government and army. Karate came to Japan at a time when the *bushi* have vanished, and *bushido* never had any leverage in Okinawa, thus the two have historically nothing to do with each other. The Samurai did not know anything about karate; their bare-handed method of self-defense was *yawara*, which later evolved into jujutsu and judo. *Bushido and karate are unrelated and an anachronistic mismatch.* The same could be said at least about Okinawan karate and *Shu Ha Ri*. *Bushido* is obsolete, historically contaminated, a fictitious construct that has been imposed onto karate to make it more "Japanese." In my eyes, *bushido* in karate is superfluous and should be kept apart from it.

Since the conscientious studies by Brian Victoria and Christopher Ives we also know how far the Buddhist establishment and notably *Zen-Buddhist clergy have been involved into the ideological mobilization* of soldiers and the populace during wartimes. The Buddhist ontological or metaphysical teaching of the non-existence of a permanent self or "soul" has been perverted into two twisted forms. "No self" was on the one hand interpreted as "self-less" service for country and *tenno*, thus as an act of loyalty in a Confucian ethical prescriptive and moral sense. On the other hand "no self" or "no mind" (*mushin*) in the martial arts was deemed to describe a mental state of total aloofness, alertness, unperturbed by intellectual interference or emotions like anger, angst, or paralysis. Hence the ideal state of mind to fight and strike an enemy and to kill him with no ego, no guilt, and not a trace of empathy. Zen Buddhism was therefore cut off from its ethical and soteriological foundations and instrumentalized as a psychotechnical tool to become a superior swordsman or soldier. The Buddhist values of compassion and not to harm any sentient being were conveniently disposed of. This "warrior Zen" is a pragmatic and reductionist version which was propagated by D. T. Suzuki and brought into connection with bushido by him. He was and probably is the most read author on Zen in martial arts circles. Again, Zen was of not much consequence in Okinawan karate; it was imposed on *hondo* karate in order to align it with the old budo-tradition, in particular swordsmanship, and to sanctify it with a Japanese religio-philosophical tradition.

As Dr. Bayer notes in the first of the above-mentioned books of his, the incorporation of Zen into karate happened in a specific time of social change starting in the late 1960s. Some keywords as reminders: student rebellion, anti-Vietnam-war movement, human rights organizations (anti-racism, feminism, gay/lesbian rights), environmental protection, Woodstock, hippies, Indian gurus, humanistic/transpersonal psychology, psychedelics, New-Age spirituality and much more. Bayer: "New values, evolving from aspirations for peace, from experimenting with self-insight and self-development, from meditation and adoption of Eastern philosophies and their approaches like Zen-meditation, yoga, and tai chi, add an additional layer to the explanation of the broad attraction that the spiritual, health-oriented version of karatedo quickly gained amongst young generations of new disciples in search of a new meaning of life and of the 'way.'" In this context, Zen became topical in karate circles. Since according to D. T. Suzuki's hyperbolic view every aspect of Japanese culture, especially every fine art, was said to be influenced by Zen-Buddhism, it could be that *Shu Ha Ri* was "detected" and transplanted into karate against this backdrop. One of its "Western" interpretations might have been influenced by the search for "self-actualization" (Maslow's term adopted by Dr. Bayer), namely the breaking away from teacher and tradition in order to create something "new."

The scope of Bayer's work is extensive, and he also hints at pathological outcomes of the exegesis of *Shu Ha Ri* when laid claim to by narcissistic personalities or commercially oriented martial arts entrepreneurs. He mentions truncated versions of *Shu Ha Ri* in name only for coaching or the refurbishment of management principles. Funnily, it is in this frame of reference that it readily pops up, if one googles *Shu Ha Ri*. Some use it to fill a market niche or as an exotic and unique selling point for their brand of leadership training.

Dr. Bayer also contrasts *Shu Ha Ri* with Western models of teaching and skill acquirement and looks for a coherent educational approach, where the Asian method of mimicking and modeling, a one-way-only and top-down mode, is complemented with actively involving and stimulating students via assignment of tasks like analysis and reflection upon techniques and their meaning and experimentation on applications. This is followed with deliberations on combining traditional Japanese/Confucian educational concepts with Western methodologies, namely stating clear educational objectives, methods of instruction, and assessment of outcomes. This takes the different (learning) personalities of the students into account and avoids a "one size fits all" and autocratic instructor-centered teaching approach, which dominates "traditional" Asian tutoring.

Hermann Bayer's book gives plenty of food for thought, for safeguarding wholesome traditions *(Shu)*, innovation and personal modifications *(Ha)*, and transcending monocultural contexts *(Ri)* by combining Eastern and Western approaches. This book on *Shu Ha Ri* is in a way an exercise and execution of this principle and an exhaustive study on the theme. It is written by an analytical and scientific mind and is a contribution to understanding how certain notions we are prone to take as a given actually evolved historically and in a particular setting. Such a genealogical investigation also reveals peculiar interpretations that unfold over time and geographical space. Imposed or likewise invented traditions are not spurious per se. To expose them as what they are—as was done here with *Shu Ha Ri*—enables us to reassess them and to decide if we want to accept, adjust, or discard them. All cultures and traditions are hybrid and living entities.

"Habent sua fata libelli" (books have their destiny) goes a saying in Latin, and in this sense I wish for this book to have the fate to become a classic regarding the topic *Shu Ha Ri*.

Dr. Wolfgang Herbert
Professor for Comparative Cultural Studies at Tokushima University, Japan
6th Dan *Shôtôkan Karate-dô*

FOREWORD BY
KYOSHI DR. JAMES HATCH

Shu Ha Ri in Karate-dō: A Bridge Between East and West

Hermann Bayer's *Shu Ha Ri in Karate-dō: When a Fighting Art Becomes a Fine Art* makes a unique and significant contribution to the discourse on the philosophical underpinnings of Okinawan karate. The book is a meticulous exploration of the concept of *Shu Ha Ri*—a cornerstone of Japanese cultural and artistic pedagogy—as it has been applied, adapted, and sometimes misconstrued within the context of martial arts, specifically karate.

Bayer's work is commendable in its ambition to bridge the chasm between the East and West. He deftly navigates the intricacies of translating a deeply rooted Japanese concept into a framework understandable to a Western audience, a task that is particularly challenging given the stark contrasts between Japan's collectivist ethos and the West's individualistic tendencies. The author's success lies in his ability to identify and articulate the core principles of *Shu Ha Ri* while simultaneously acknowledging the cultural nuances that shape its interpretation.

A key strength of Bayer's work is his meticulous tracing of the concept's philosophical roots. By anchoring *Shu Ha Ri* within the broader context of Confucian and Buddhist thought, he provides a rich historical and intellectual foundation for understanding its significance. This approach is essential for appreciating the concept's depth and complexity, as it reveals how it has evolved and adapted over centuries.

Moreover, Bayer's exploration of the concept's application in various artistic disciplines offers valuable insights into its versatility. By demonstrating how *Shu Ha Ri* has been utilized in fields outside of martial arts, the author underscores its potential as a universal framework for learning and mastery. This comparative approach enriches the reader's understanding of the concept and its applicability to diverse human endeavors.

However, Bayer does more than merely provide a descriptive analysis of *Shu Ha Ri*. He also engages critically with the concept, particularly in its application to karate. His astute examination of how the transition from Okinawan karate to Japanese karate-dō has influenced the interpretation and practice of *Shu Ha Ri*, and his highlighting of the potential pitfalls of imposing a Japanese cultural construct onto a different martial tradition, demonstrate the depth of his analysis.

By juxtaposing the collectivist underpinnings of *Shu Ha Ri* with the individualistic ethos of the West, Bayer invites readers to consider the implications of this cultural divide for karate practice. This comparative perspective is essential for understanding the challenges and opportunities of reconciling traditional values with contemporary realities.

In conclusion, *Analysis of Shu Ha Ri in Karate-dō* is a scholarly and insightful exploration of a complex concept. Bayer's meticulous research and ability to bridge Eastern and Western thought make this book a valuable contribution to martial arts studies. By offering a comprehensive framework for understanding *Shu Ha Ri*, the author has laid the groundwork for future research and discussions on the evolution and purpose of karate.

James M. Hatch, EdD
7th Dan *Chito Ryu, Sichibu Jyuku*
Oyamada-machi, Japan

FOREWORD BY
KYOSHI THOMAS E. WARD

Educational Principles Help Instructors to Organize and Systematize Their Teachings

My whole life I've been a karateka and an educator. I've studied *Shorin-Ryu* karate since the age of thirteen, and haven't stopped learning in over fifty years. I taught English and remedial reading in public schools, and, eventually, I pursued a full-time career as a karate instructor and ran my own school for twenty-five-plus years. I never forgot that my main value was the purity of the art and the quality of the teaching that I could provide. I visited numerous other dojos to study, to instruct, or simply as a guest, constantly taking note of the teaching methods and student quality in these schools, and I tried to emulate some of the finer qualities I saw in teachers, and to ensure that the lesser qualities were eliminated from my own school. Many, many hours I spent on evaluation panels for various testing in various schools, where I saw many things I admired, and some things with which I was ashamed to be associated.

Permanently on the lookout for opportunities to improve my own karate teachings, I became aware of the concept of *Shu Ha Ri*, which can be understood as a Japanese andragogical idea, as a way to educate adults. I comprehended it on a basic level, but initially did not give it much thought. Later, in college, I learned about modern educational concepts, like Bloom's taxonomy, and I linked this Western concept to the Japanese one, because as teachers we are always curious about how much our students comprehend at a surface level and how much they actually can apply to their lives outside the dojo doors. Both Bloom's taxonomy and the concept of *Shu Ha Ri* seemed to me helpful methods of measuring a student's understanding in this sense, and the text before you will shed more light on such a thought.

However, what this book delivers to the body of knowledge in our art goes way beyond that. It clarifies why and how *Shu Ha Ri* is a genuine Japanese concept and not an Okinawan one at the birthplace of karate. This distinction seems quite important as conservative Okinawan karate circles adamantly insist on keeping their Okinawan approach separated, unique, and not to be mixed up with Japanese ways. It clarifies further, how *Shu Ha Ri*, as an initial Japanese fine arts principle and not a martial arts principle, was later applied into Japanese martial arts in general, and into karatedo in particular, during a process that converted Okinawa's self-protection art into something closer to a Japanese fine art of self-perfection; that is, into the form that represents today's mainstream karatedo practice. Misconceptions and differing interpretations by various groups with their own agenda during such a process seem unavoidable and created a rather convoluted picture of this *Shu Ha Ri* concept, one not well-known to all karateka in the first place. Fortunately, Dr. Bayer weaves historic, socio-cultural, political, philosophical, psychological, and commercial components into a complex analysis that finally gives a clear picture and that addresses those doubts and questions about ascent or alibi which inevitably arise when an Okinawan self-defense art is changed into a Japanese fine art.

An additional highlight is the inclusion of educational principles and approaches that help instructors to organize and to systematize their teaching approach and to enhance traditional instructor-centered concepts by using approaches that were developed to better reach Western minds.

I met Dr. Bayer several years ago at a *Shorin-Ryu* camp, where I taught educational psychology to my fellow martial arts instructors—what I decided to do after having taught other subjects at various martial arts camps and seminars for a few decades. Later, I discovered that he was a highly accomplished black belt in another karate system, who had started over in *Shorin-ryu* and had worked his way up to black belt ranks there as well. His willingness to do this speaks volumes about his humility and his desire to permanently learn and grow; and his well-rounded academic and professional background qualify him for an analysis that goes well beyond popular, constricted narratives. It seems to me that he understands the martial arts on a deeper level than most, the differing Okinawan and Japanese views of karate in general, as well as *Shu Ha Ri* interpretations in particular, when a fighting art is converted into a fine art. We communicated about several aspects of this socio-cultural phenomenon, which eventually led to me contributing some thoughts to this book.

I am convinced that all readers, martial artists or not, will greatly enjoy Dr. Bayer's analysis, that it will give everyone plenty of food for thought, and, if you're an instructor, that it will allow you to see promising perspectives.

Thomas E. Ward
Kyoshi 7th Dan *Shorin Ryu Shorinkan*

FOREWORD BY
KYOSHI BRUNO BALLARDINI

"Crystalized" Japanese Karate-Do Is the Result of Adopting a Western "Taxonomy"

Hermann Bayer offers us a profound and most valuable reflection on a topic that is as crucial to karate studies as it has hitherto been ignored, namely, how modern Japanese karate appropriated Okinawan karate in the early 1900s by not only simplifying its techniques but also by codifying principles that had previously remained unexpressed. These provisions are to be seen and understood in a broader context of socio-cultural and historic circumstances.

There was a disruptive phase in Japan's cultural history between the end of the Meiji Period (1868–1912) and the early years of the Shōwa period (1926–1989) that coincides with a rush to modernize everything, and with the irresistible attraction of Western ideas in Japan. During this period, Japan not only avidly absorbed Western techniques, technology, and customs, but also Western logic and a new way of organizing knowledge through *taxonomy* (from Greek: τάξις, *táxis*, i.e., "order" and νόμος, *nòmos*, that is "standard" or "rule"). This approach defines a set of rules for the nomenclature and classification of objects, where "classification" means the application of a taxonomic scheme suitable for naming, defining, and categorizing objects of observation and of organizing them into groups and subgroups.

Modern taxonomy was invented by Carl von Linné, born in Sweden in 1707, who published in 1735 the first edition of *Systema Naturae*, in which he outlined such a new system of classification for the sciences. The first contact with his method in Japan occurred when Carl Peter Thunberg, Linné's disciple, stayed there for a year as a doctor for the Dutch Trading House and later published *Flora Japonica*. Thereafter, from the Meiji Period onward, as Emperor Akihito's comprehensive publication on the use of taxonomy in Japan describes, the modernization drive resulted in a widespread adoption of this Western method to rationalize knowledge; it penetrated many fields, including the martial arts. Paradoxically, the first person to apply this method to karate was not Japanese, but the Okinawan master Gichin Funakoshi, who was determined to export the local art to mainland Japan.

It should be noted that the peculiar characteristics of ancient Okinawan karate, which came intact and unaltered until the early 1900s, was that most of its techniques had either no name or were sometimes labeled by the phonetization of a Chinese word. But even if the techniques taught would have had names, it is very unlikely that the masters of ancient karate would ever tell those to their students, deeming it useless, since practice was based on imitation and took place in absolute silence. Funakoshi rationalized the corpus of ancient karate by producing the first taxonomy and nomenclature of karate in a way that appealed to Japan's modern classification trend. He named techniques that had never been named, and he replaced Chinese terms with Japanese terms, although his early classifications of kata created some confusion as Mario McKenna pointed out in 2003, in the first issue of *Classic Fighting Arts* magazine.

Why was it that the Japanese greatly appreciated the application of taxonomy and nomenclature to karate as initiated by Funakoshi? It was because of the attractiveness of Western thought systems in general that were adopted in Japan at that time. In terms of the taxonomy thought system, specifically for Westerners, naming an object was equivalent to knowing it, and thus, in a sense, "owning" it. Within such lines of thought, to appropriate ancient Okinawan karate, Japanese martial arts officials proceeded in the direction pointed out by Funakoshi. They categorized every move and technique, and they applied the same approach to basic principles such as *Shu Ha Ri* as well. In fact, before these principles were codified in Japan, they were rather an implicit consequence of internalizing a practice; they represented a kind of awareness of what the practitioners were expected to acquire along their path of learning. That way, principles were part of the path one proceeds along but does not even need to talk about. Consequently, there is no trace of this concept in the Okinawan masters' writings that have come down to us.

In summation, modern Japanese karate, including its principle of *Shu Ha Ri*, is the result of a new system of organizing knowledge, it is the result of adopting a Western concept of categorizing elements within a subject that was implemented on mainland Japan. Kenji Tokitsu, a sociologist and karate master, was the first researcher to define the consequence of this procedure as "crystallization."

Crystallizing a living art such as early karate amounted to "congealing" its figures and principles in the same way that nineteenth-century Linnean scholars fixed butterflies with a pin inside the frame of a taxonomy, giving the outside observer the illusion of possessing the knowledge of the objects these frames contain, including how they evolved. In doing so, Japanese karate officials were able to impose a modern interpretation of karate and artificially placed it among Japan's so-called traditional martial arts as an "invented tradition"—while actually creating only a new form of mass sport with a martial appearance, perfectly suited to the West and to a now-Westernized Japan.

Bruno Ballardini
8th Dan *Shorinji Ryu Zentokukai*
Former professor at the First University of Rome "La Sapienza"
President of the Italian Association for the Study of Ancient Karate
Coordinator of International Okinawa Shorinji-Ryu Tode Zentokukai in Europe
Author of the standing rubric "Karate Archeology" in *Bugeisha* magazine
Editorial manager of *Edizioni Mediterranee*

INTRODUCTION
NEW SIGNIFICANCE OF SHU HA RI IN POSTWAR KARATEDO—OR A MISTAKEN PARADIGM?

Shortly after the COVID-19 hysteria ebbed and things started settling down to a new normal, an intensive and months-long discussion arose amongst karateka I trained with. In ways surprising and unexpected, new opinions about how to approach our art were brought up, some of which we discussed for months. Not just that, we assessed new views that dared to contradict our decades-long training and teaching routines in long, at times cumbersome, conversations. We debated and tried out new kata applications, and we looked into developing *honto* kata.[1] We reconsidered the fighting benefit of formal *kumite* (sparring) arrangements and especially the lack thereof in some of them, and we examined new, individually created free-fighting sequences. So, what the heck happened here? Why were we suddenly having these talks, which, of course, were not negative as such; it was just that the point in time they occurred came as a surprise, at least to me.

It looks like an unexpected consequence of the COVID-19 lockdowns hit us here: months of quarantine added up to more than a year of imposed isolation during which karateka were forced to study their art individually, to the best of their knowledge, and isolated at home. Those who carried on with their studies that way and did not just abandon their training until it resumed in person used—beyond physical self-training—internet sites, blogs, and print and online publications to continue their education. They tried to figure out deeper aspects of their beloved art by themselves and on their own, without guidance from their sensei (teacher). As a result, not only were new interpretations experimented with, but misunderstandings were born as well, and all that was later brought back to the dojo (school) as new thoughts. Those new thoughts—some productive, some not so much—sparked our constructive and occasionally contentious discussions. The common denominator in these talks was how a specific traditional way

---

1   A *honto* kata is a traditional kata condensed into its fundamentals and core moves, without repetitions or side-mirrored applications, and thus revealing the skeleton of true intent, principles, and meaning of the kata and its techniques (Hayes 2018, pp. 146f).

to learn a karate system can limit a student's growth and exclude other input, thus limiting one's capabilities. Some of these disagreements could not be resolved, and, consequently, a group of students left the dojo and their karate association to establish their own new ways.

As I said, all that happened after the involuntary separation of students from their sensei, a separation which not only took place in the USA, but worldwide. Some sensei tried to bridge the gap by guiding their students' home training with recorded video clips or with online training sessions. That, however, only provided limited support, and it was not done specifically by Okinawan masters and their *honbu dojo* (style headquarters), the custodians of the art's genuine systems at its birthplace. In fact, Japan closed its borders to all foreigners, and for us Western students direct contact with our most senior Okinawan sensei was completely interrupted for almost three years as was contact with our domestic sensei for many months. In summation, all sensei-guided progression became unavailable for many. The related setback in qualification was significant but unavoidable since every practitioner knows how quickly "rust" builds up, neglect starts to set in, and individual idiosyncrasies begin to slip back in unnoticed—not to mention the fact that more than a few dojos lost students during the pandemic, some of which never reopened thereafter. Not all was bad though, because, as I said, in isolation new insights were discovered too and horizons were broadened.

Studying in seclusion myself, I specifically looked at the philosophical aspects of *(budo)* karatedo, at publications concerning topics like realistic fighting logic, surface *(omote)*, hidden *(ura)*, and true *(okuden)* principles in classic kata of *(bugei)* karate-jutsu[2]—and how karateka could grow into a better understanding of all this. In doing that, I realized that the Japanese developmental principle of *Shu Ha Ri* (explanation in next paragraph) was mentioned in modern karatedo publications, starting in the mid-1980s, but not before that time. And, interestingly enough, I did not find it mentioned in the classic karate texts accessible to me, or in the various prewar writings of karate masters. I, of course, cannot claim that there were none, I can only state that I did not find any. This baffled me

---

2   *Jutsu* is a Japanese term that was not in common use on Okinawa. But since the single term "karate" is used today to label different karate versions with different purposes, I use the term karate-jutsu deliberately and as a concession to today's unspecified use of the term karate to distinguish this Okinawan art centered on self-protection from its Japanese karatedo variation that emphasizes the path to self-perfection, and from modern sports-karate (Bayer 2023a, Chapter 1).

and sparked my interest in digging deeper. I started to query whether and when *Shu Ha Ri*, the traditional developmental concept of Japanese fine arts, was incorporated into karate, which I assumed may have happened as a part of Okinawan karate-jutsu's Japanization into karatedo, after the mainland discovered the fighting art of its province and pilfered it. And if that was the case, when, how, and why was it rediscovered for karatedo? The avenues for research from here on became clear to me.

The concept of *Shu Ha Ri* includes the notion that a practitioner's path to mastery goes through the three phases of *Shu* (follow the form, study the fundamentals), *Ha* (digress or break the form, understand its intent and function, apply the fundamentals), and *Ri* (transcend the form, create, and innovate). This path looked somewhat familiar to me, as I, at the same time I was beginning my investigations into *Shu Ha Ri*, was also reexamining the educational concepts I used in my previous academic teaching career in order to optimize my own karate teaching approach. This led to a lightbulb moment where I saw a possible correlation between postwar Western educational approaches and this Japanese principle of development drawn from the fine arts. I started conversations with colleagues to get their opinion on this possibility, conversations which are best summarized as "I never thought of that; interesting idea" in the words of Dr. James Hatch, 7th Dan *Chito Ryu, Sichibu Jyuku*, renowned educator and martial arts researcher. Chapter 6 will pinpoint parallels and disparities between Western educational approaches and Japanese teachings into which the *Shu Ha Ri* principle is woven.

Traditional dojos in the West use (almost) exclusively Japanese teaching concepts; they do not use Western ones. But considering the alarming loss of students in those dojos over the last decade, a decrease that contrasts with increasing student numbers in sports-karate where Western teaching concepts were added and are used, we suggest in Chapter 8 that such a solely Eastern training approach should be rethought. Our Western culture has changed considerably, and so have Western students' mindsets and attitudes. If a social organism, like a dojo, does not adapt to changed socio-cultural environments, it withers and eventually vanishes. Given that fact, and since the traditional karate philosophy is not self-explanatory to today's students, a bridge needs to be built between Eastern thought and those new Western minds and attitudes. Adding a Western teaching concept that reaches these minds could help build that bridge and help to link karate training to students' other learning and leadership experiences in schools, colleges, and workplaces, which may eventually retain them. And, referring to *Shu Ha Ri*, Western teaching methods that go beyond instructor-centered modelling and mimicking seem to be the most promising way of mentoring and coaching advanced students in their *Ha* and *Ri* phases. Adding something Western to what's already there and done in the dojo is not replacing Eastern training routines; it is rather an add-on to ensure their acceptance and internalization in a way that best reaches Western minds.

The text will also explain why some Western martial artists hold a specific interpretation of the *Shu Ha Ri* concept in high regard, not so much because of its beneficial use in general, but because of its implied potential to bring about self-actualization.[3] Whether and how the principle is indeed related to our Western understanding of self-actualization, or whether and how it is not, is a rather complex question, which we will answer in detail and, hopefully, sufficiently.

While diving deeper into the subject, the thought crossed my mind whether *Shu Ha Ri* perhaps could even lie at the root of our above-mentioned controversies about the way we approach our art and our new, often clashing opinions that dared to challenge our decades-long teaching and training routines. Could those new and opposed opinions in the dojo be a form of *Ha* (break the rules), or even *Ri* (transcend the rules)? Possible, yes, but this view did not sit well with me. It felt too simple and like some pieces of a jigsaw puzzle were still missing, and I decided that a better understanding *Shu Ha Ri* is of utmost importance in forming a sustainable opinion. I soon figured out that several considerations I developed in my previous books are related to this subject; those thoughts and background are woven into the text before you and connect all three books into a trilogy about karate's socio-cultural development, classic and modern interpretations of the art, and some possible misconceptions therein.

My suspicion rose that a modern rediscovery of *Shu Ha Ri* after WWII has to do with the modern transformations of self-protection karate-jutsu into a fine-art-like karatedo. To expressing something is the purpose of the fine arts, and artists strive to create original and innovative ways to communicate their personal view of things to

---

3   The psychological concept of self-actualization refers to the process by which individuals reach their full potential. The American psychologist Abraham H. Maslow popularized the concept; he saw self-actualization as fulfillment of one's greatest potential (Maslow 1943).

others. Picasso, for example, differentiated himself from other painters by developing his personal style to articulate his message and his personal views through his paintings. But Picasso, of course, never wrote a manual of practical instruction explaining how his approach could be used for a specific purpose. And this marks exactly an essential difference between a fine art—like painting, calligraphy, poetry, or acting—and an empty-hand self-protection craft like karate-jutsu. Karate-jutsu is not about "expressing something," it is about defending against a (lethal) threat to you or your family. Consequently, when karate-jutsu's purpose is changed and it is stripped of its martial content and turned into an athletic kata dance or into a path toward self-perfection, as was done in modern *budo* karatedo and in sports-karate, then these karate variations turn into fine arts that can be used to articulate a personal message, demonstrate one's individual level of attainment, and be a means for self-actualization.

Therefore, it is understandable, as I soon found out, that *Shu Ha Ri* is not only unknown to many of my fellow karateka but that senior karate authorities, who emphasize karate as a self-protection art and not as a fine art, are unfamiliar with the concept as well. From the standpoint of these masters, a misunderstood *Ri* (transcend the form, create, and innovate) in *Shu Ha Ri* may appear as inappropriately questioning unquestionable basics. The opposing positions here are (a) that continuously practicing and diving deeper into a specific martial arts system equips karateka with all they need to understand what they are doing and to do it correctly in order to survive a lethal threat, versus (b), that at a certain point of their development a specific technique karateka used to train turns into a limitation and that they need to transcend the limits of their style or of their sensei to progress further. In the eyes of position (a) the second position (b) means that those karateka are simply reinventing the wheel, because their so-called new insights are not at all new, they are just new to them; they were included in the system they used to train in, and they'd have found those insights anyway if they'd continued to grow there. Chapter 5 will, among other things, deal with this aspect of possible *Shu Ha Ri* alibis for seemingly new, instead of "not new, just unknown to you," insights.

Nothing could be farther from our intentions than to create conflicts when bringing *Shu Ha Ri* to the karatedo table; the opposite is actually true. In a phone conversation to discuss his thoughts on the subject, Sensei Jason S. D. Perry, 8th Dan, *Okinawa Shorinryu Karatedo*

Kobudo Kensankai, pointed out an important advantage for karateka studying their art today compared to senior karate authorities who did that some sixty or seventy years ago and that is today's abundance of excellent literature and internet resources. Over the past two or three decades, we have had those first-rate sources available, not only in Japanese but actually in our mother tongue. Classic and new texts were translated from Japanese, and plenty of other serious research and inquiry into deeper aspects of karatedo and karate-jutsu are easily accessible. While this makes it easier for us to study these days, it also requires a thorough evaluation of new concepts—well, in the case of *Shu Ha Ri,* not really new but with new significance—and their careful integration into the larger body of knowledge. Not everything new is better than tradition simply because it is newer, and not everything traditional is worse simply because it is older.

Integrating a relatively new construct into the martial arts has become a well-known phenomenon called "invented tradition" by researchers and was already done for karatedo with the concept of *Shin Gi Tai* (mind/spirit—technique—body), which seems to be a modern conception rather than a classic one (Quast 2023), and it was done for *kiai,* which seems to be useful in competition and grading but inappropriate for a secretly taught art that needed to remain undetected and was thus practiced in silence (Motobu 2024). *Shu Ha Ri* also looks like a modern development involving the transfer of a centuries-old Japanese fine arts principle to empty-hand fighting. To evaluate and analyze such a development is exactly what we intend to do here, because, as shown in chapter 5, there are serious pitfalls within the *Shu Ha Ri* concept, which can be used by karateka as an excuse for making mistakes, for reinventing the wheel, and for selling individual phantasies as genuine self-defense techniques. It will be shown further how the *Shu Ha Ri* developmental principle differs in its applications in classic *(bugei)* karate-jutsu for self-protection from its connotation in *(budo)* karatedo, where self-perfection instead of self-defense is pursued, and how both of these versions differ from evolutions in modern sports karate with its focus on competition, where the notion of *Shu Ha Ri* progression is rarely used, if at all.

In this sense, we can distinguish at least two conceptions of the use of *Shu Ha Ri.* One explains a karateka's development *within a karate-jutsu system.* With that understanding we may see the three phases like a crane's development from flapping its wings, to leaving the nest and clumsily starting to fly, and finally to freely fly, swoop, dive, and evade without limitations. *Ri*-transcending *within a karate-jutsu* system would then mean to neither transcend the system as such nor to break away from your sensei. Sensei Jason S. D. Perry explains this progression in terms of a karateka's declining dependence on a teacher: "*Ri* is a state of independence. Where *Shu* is a state of dependence, *Ha* is the state of semi autonomy. *Ri* becomes the state in which the practitioner can learn and grow independent of a teacher. The art itself becomes the source of growth. That does not change the nature of the relationship between student and teacher."[4] The other view, found these days mostly, but not exclusively, in the West, understands the phase of *Ri* as *breaking away from a style or from a sensei*. In other words, the first concept understands *Shu Ha Ri* as perfecting one's capabilities within the traditions of a classic fighting system; the second one understands mastery as an evolution to surpass a sensei and to perhaps invent a new fighting system. The first conception seems philosophically closer to Eastern Confucian roots, and the second one seems closer to Western individualism. The decision as to whether one of those two ways of understanding the concept is a misconception or not, or whether both conceptions can coexist or not, I leave to the reader. My job is to explain the two philosophies to the best of my abilities (though, eventually, I will not hide my point of view on this subject and clearly state my preference).

Now, last but not least: do considerations about *Shu Ha Ri* actually require that writers themselves have reached the *Ri* phase? Should it be "speaking from experience, looking back at the familiar [phase] rather than conjecture and opinion, trying to look forward into the unknown [one]," as Sensei Michael Clarke, 8th Dan *Goju Ryu Jundokan*, put it in one of our conversations about the subject?[5] In my opinion, the answer here is twofold: "no" in one sense and "yes" in another, depending on whether we are considering intellectual comprehension or holistic understanding. In an intellectual, cognitive sense I'd say "no"; to analyze the concept, one need not have experienced *Ri* personally. "You don't have to have cancer to cure cancer" as the saying goes. So, in the sense of intellectual comprehension, there is no need to mystify *Ri* for insiders and to paint it as incomprehensible for outsiders. *Ri* can be

---

4   Email to me on 02/06/2024.
5   Email message to me dated 07/18/2023.

intellectually grasped by everyone, and today it is found verbatim and widely used in areas other than the martial arts, e.g., in the business world, which we will consider as an example in chapter 4. On the other hand, there is a difference between *cognitive/intellectual grasping* and *holistic understanding*. And in this latter sense of holistic understanding, my answer to the above question would be "yes"; I agree that personal competence with *Ri* best equips us to speak about the familiar.

To find our own place within the *Shu Ha Ri* phases, Sensei Michael Clarke suggests that "a large part of where we are in terms of *Shu Ha Ri* depends on what others can see in us" (ibid.). In this spirit, though I dare to write about the concept, my insight remains limited, as it always will be. My thoughts and conclusions are based on my personal level of understanding, and I am in no position to claim that my opinions are as relevant as the ones contributed by anyone else who studied martial arts for several decades. Having said that, I trust that my academic research background and my analytic skills as a scientist—in combination with my current level of understanding—allow some fruitful perspectives, because karateka's general lack of familiarity with *Shu Ha Ri* alone justifies an attempt to shed more light on this Japanese developmental principle's use in karate.

It is my distinct honor to have received helpful feedback and contributions from distinguished karate authorities and martial arts researchers during the ups and downs of diving into the subject before you. I cannot thank all of them enough for their invaluable input, their critiques, and their encouragement. I am not in the position to acknowledge those esteemed experts; I'd rather list their names here alphabetically by last name, as they speak loudly enough for themselves, and I'll add their background when a name is referenced to for the first time. Chris Bates, Lara Chamberlain, Michael Clarke, Steven Franz, Franklin D. R. Hargrove, William R. Hayes, Professor Dr. Wolfgang Herbert, Dr. James Hatch, Terry Maccarrone, Jason S. D. Perry, Dr. Dan Smith, Noel Smith, and Thomas E. Ward, I am deeply grateful for your generous help and support. Thank you.

Dr. Hermann Bayer

Chapter 1
A Centuries-Old Japanese Fine Arts Principle Finds Its Way into Modern Karate

To gain some initial familiarity with the concept of *Shu Ha Ri*, it helps to look at the word itself, Sensei Jason S. D. Perry suggested to me, because we find these three characters in the Japanese language in a variety of everyday words with distinct meanings. "By deconstructing each of the *kanji*, one can further contemplate the building blocks that, when put together, make up the whole of the concept" (Waterfield 2014, p. 1). To do that, since looking at the etymology of Japanese terms exceeds my research skills, I point readers to Sensei Perry's research (Perry 2018, pp. 300–305), and I include here his subsequent explanation of the *Shu Ha Ri* principle as a three-phased process of personal development, where "the first requirement of the student is obedience to strict teachings [*Shu* 守]; second is to overcome the teaching in the strict sense [*Ha* 破]; third is to separate from the rigid form of the art and find his or her way of expressing the art [*Ri* 離]" (ibid., p. 300; terms in brackets were added by me).

Sensei Lara Chamberlain, 8th Dan *Tiida Ryu* All Japan Budo Association, states that "the Chinese character *Shou* [*Shu*] is composed of two parts, 'house' and 'law.' Hence, the house of laws. The character means 'to abide by; to defend.' *Shou* (abide by) *Shi* (time) is being punctual, and *Shou* (abide by) *Xin* (trust) is being trustworthy. *Po* [*Ha*] is composed of two parts, 'stone' and a phonetic part. It means 'to break.' *Li* [*Ri*] is composed of two parts, 'bird' and a phonetic part. It means 'to leave; to depart.'"[6]

Dr. Wolfgang Herbert, Professor for Comparative Cultural Studies at the University of Tokushima/Japan, 6th Dan *Shotokan Karate-do* SKIF, explains that the *Shu Ha Ri* developmental principle is several centuries old and has its twofold origin in the Japanese fine arts. He points out that it is directly mentioned in a text written about *sado* (the way of tea) some five hundred years ago, on the one hand, and on the other, there is indirect reference in a text about the Japanese classic dance theater (*noh*), which was written some seven hundred years ago.[7]

Postwar *aikido* sources allege that *Shu Ha Ri* then found its way into this Japanese empty-hand martial art, which was developed in the 1920s by Ueshiba Morihei (1883–1969) as his self-labeled "art of peace" (Ueshiba 1992). Later, after WWII, *Shu Ha Ri* appears by name in *aikido* texts to explain developmental phases on a path to mastery (Endo 2005, n.p.). It is possible that *Shu Ha Ri* was also referred to by name in *aikido* before WWII; I just could not find any prewar publication using the term.

Referring to karate, it looks like not too many, if any, prewar publications refer explicitly to *Shu Ha Ri* either; otherwise, it would have been easier to locate some. But, again, just because I could not find them does not mean they do not exist, and the lack of records prior to the war should not necessarily lead to the conclusion that the concept was not in use then. But it seems safe to assume that the concept was not broadly discussed, and especially not on Okinawa in reference to the island's local self-protection art karate-jutsu[8] that was based on the

---

6   Message sent to me on 03/15/2024; italicizations in brackets are mine.
7   Email sent to me on 02/22/2024 in which Dr. Herbert wrote that tea master Sen no Rikyû (1522–1591) explains the path of *sado* in the form of a poem in his text *Rikyû Dôka* (利休道歌), where he writes, "Don't forget the origination, even then when you, after preserving the forms and etiquette in every detail (守), separate yourself (破) and even liberate yourself from those (離)." It is Dr. Herbert's opinion, which I share, that this poem includes *Shu Ha Ri* as a spiral of learning that holistically allows all three phases to exist simultaneously. Referring to the second root of *Shu Ha Ri* in *noh*, Dr. Herbert points to the text *Kadensho* (花伝書) by Zeami Motokiyo (1363–1443), where the latter deals with the three steps of prelude-evolution-finale as a universal conception of modulation. I translated Dr. Herbert's German explanations into English.
8   In case you skipped the introduction: *jutsu* is a Japanese word that was not in common use on Okinawa. I use the term karate-jutsu deliberately and as a concession to today's unspecified use of the term "karate" for all its different versions to distinguish the genuine Okinawan self-defense version from its Japanese karatedo variation and from modern sports-karate (Bayer 2023, Chapter 1).

Okinawa-specific, non-Japanese, universal principle of protecting oneself and others from physical and nonphysical harm (see next subchapter).

However, all the terms and most applications we use today in our karatedo practice are not of Okinawan origin anymore but are Japanese inventions and re-creations based on the Japanese karatedo principle of self-perfection. Hence, two differing concepts create a significant contradiction between Okinawan and Japanese karate interpretations, which suggests a broad and early use of the Japanese *Shu Ha Ri* concept on Okinawa as rather unlikely. This situation may, however, have changed over the decades during which there were increasing Japanese cultural impacts on Okinawan karate, even on the Ryukyus themselves. The concept was at least mentioned on Okinawa after WWII, as Sensei Terry Maccarrone, 9th Dan *Shorin Ryu* USKK, recalls: "It is basically a Japanese concept, but Hokama [i.e., Sensei Hokama Tetsuhiro; my addition] did mention *Shu Ha Ri* in deeper philosophical concerns. Shoshin Nagamine also mentioned this. But my sensei [i.e., Ueshiro Ansei, who brought Sensei Nagamine Shoshin's *Matsubayashi Ryu* to the USA; my remark] never used that term as central to Okinawan *Te*."[9] Comparably, Sensei Dr. Dan Smith, the senior *Seibukan* karate authority in the USA, states that "I never heard the reference of *Shu Ha Ri* on Okinawa. I asked Shimabukuro Sensei decades ago about the meaning. His response was that it was difficult to explain in relationship to Okinawan karate."[10] Such a rather cryptic response by Sensei Shimabukuro suggests that the Japanese *Shu Ha Ri* concept was not really relevant for Okinawans and for their way of understanding karate, and it could well be that the concept of *Shu Ha Ri*, and the Japanese way of approaching karate as a whole, conflicts with the Okinawan approach, which is a possibility that will be evaluated further in the next subchapter.

It could well be that the *Japanese interpretation of karate as a fine art*, instead of the Okinawan interpretation of karate as an art for protecting oneself and others, was the entry point for the assimilation of *Shu Ha Ri* into Japanese karatedo. Sensei Perry questions whether "the Okinawans ever did view their own practice as an art that could be defined and therefore subjected to a concept like *Shu?*" and draws out

---

9 Message sent to me on 03/21/2024.
10 Message sent to me on 01/30/2024.

the implication that "if there were not accepted standards of practice, then it follows that *Shu* could not apply until the art was codified and systematized—a process that did not occur until later. So the idea that *Shu Ha Ri* is a foreign construct borrowed from Japan may be true; but then again isn't the karate we practice?"[11] My response to the last question is "yes" for the majority of practitioners, but strongly "no" for an admittedly small but dedicated karateka minority. In my view, karate-jutsu in its initial Okinawan version as the way of protecting oneself and others, still exists in parallel to its systematized Japanese fine-art karatedo version of self-actualization and self-perfection. I do not see those two versions as the "transformation" of the Okinawan craft of karate-jutsu into the Japanese art of karatedo, but I see the creation of the latter as a newly constructed *budo* version in addition to its classic *bugei* or *jutsu* version, thus not representing an evolution or evolvement but embodying the conscious and deliberate generation of a different Japanese thing with its different purpose—newly created and parallel to the still-existing classic Okinawan version.

This classic Okinawan karate version is based on the universal principle of protecting others and oneself from physical and nonphysical harm; it is founded on a subcultural autonomous principle that differs from that Japanese interpretation of the art that an overwhelming majority of karateka practices today. The initial concept of Okinawan karate is not directly related to the Japanese *Shu Ha Ri* principle, which is perhaps one of the reasons why the Okinawans did not accept the latter as broadly as non-Okinawan karateka did. And, finally, while the Japanese *budo* philosophy is well-known, or at least known to more or less all karatedo practitioners, the just-mentioned genuine Okinawan concept of protecting others and oneself from physical and nonphysical harm is not as well-known, especially not in the West. Hence, it makes sense to reiterate it here as it sheds light on some primary reasons that explain the somewhat rare use of *Shu Ha Ri* in Okinawan karate-jutsu, which definitely contrasts with its broader use in Japanese karatedo.

---

11 Email sent to me on 02/07/2024.

Protecting Others and Oneself from Physical and Nonphysical Harm Is the Universal Principle of Okinawan Karate-jutsu that Differs from the Self-Perfection Principle in Japanese Karatedo

Prewar teachings on Okinawa were almost exclusively orally passed down, within close communities, and based on the local language *Uchinaguchi*, which is a separate language, far from the Japanese language, and not just a local Japanese dialect. Okinawan *Ti*, the fighting art for security personnel, and later karate-jutsu, the self-protection art for civilians, was exclusively orally transmitted, at least until the local Okinawan newspaper *Ryukyu Shimpo*, which was founded in 1893, started to publish karate-related articles. Those articles, however, were always heavily influenced by Japanese standards and views. Having no written instructions does not mean at all that Okinawan sensei did not teach based on concepts; they did have concepts and philosophical guidelines, just not in writing.

In this sense, the traditional Okinawan mindset that refers to the well-being of others, especially to that of one's own family, has to be pointed out. Family is a holistic concept of utmost importance on Okinawa, as it is not only composed of living generations but as well of relationships to former generations within the traditional Okinawan belief system of ancestors worship (Matayoshi/Trafton 2000). In a more pragmatic sense, Sensei Ron J. Brookshire Jr., 5th Dan *Seitoshin Kai Bujutsu*, 3rd Dan *Goju Ryu Kodokan*, and black belt in several other martial arts disciplines, says that "if you were the one working or on a stipend, the whole family depended upon you, as well as those in the community. If something happened to you, it affected them. So, in essence, it is not that one fights for their self, they fight for their kids, parents, siblings, etc. If you fight only for yourself … you are using only your own physical power. If you fight for others and for loved ones, [divinity adds its power] and odds shift positively, especially in a just or righteous cause."[12]

My conversations with Professor Emi, a native Okinawan, who was born and raised in a traditional Okinawan family in the meager rural south of the island, confirm that this mindset is still intact in our time and age; she told me that all male members of her family still practice

---

12 Message sent to me on 03/19/2024.

what she calls "Okinawan *Te* to protect us, to protect the family."[13] After WWII, "our family turned inward to mediation, healing the family, harvesting the rice, and everyone had to bring money to support the village … The mission of our family was to feed and to provide for the village."[14] This view of protecting not just oneself but one's entire family, and even the entire community, is of utmost importance in understanding the Okinawan mindset, and it is woven, for instance, into Sensei Asato Anko's view when he justifies making the first move, in contrast to the primarily defensive use of karate "if parents, wife, or children are affronted, if the enemy comes close and compels" (Asato 1914, p. 20).

Referring back to the first part of Sensei Perry's quote above, concerning whether the Okinawans ever viewed their own practice as an art, I don't suppose they saw it as that, as a (fine) art in a Japanese sense. Instead, they saw it as part of a universal conception of protecting family and oneself in order to fend off any harm. That means protection not just from physical threats but from those of a non-physical nature as well, like sickness, damage to relationships (including to their ancestors), unkind mindsets, thoughts, and attitudes. This universal principle of protection requires a healthy lifestyle, positive thoughts, respectful relationships, and overall positive, responsible conduct "from the inside out," which includes the kind of food we eat, the kind of beverages we drink, the way we conduct and present ourselves, the way we think, and the way we treat others. All these components represent aspects of universal protection and are various means to shield oneself and others from harm, and those mental, nonphysical ones unrelated to fighting are as important as the ones providing protection from a physical threat.

Such a concept of protection as a universal principle of life that impacts all aspects of preventing harm contrasts with the narrower concepts in Japanese karatedo of defending only oneself, and of fending off physical threats. Interestingly enough, the priority in Okinawan karate-jutsu is not necessarily to eliminate the threat, but to ensure one's own safety and that of others. These two views sound quite

---

13   I am deeply thankful for clarifying conversations with Ms. Emi, now a college instructor in the USA, who was born and raised in a traditional Okinawan family in the meager rural south of the island. Professor Emi's entire family practices martial arts for generations; its female family members mostly *Tai Chi* and the male members what she calls "Okinawan *Te*," with the reason she denominates as "to protect us, to protect the family." The insights I gained in these conversations greatly helped the me to understand several Okinawan cultural specifics.
14   Email message sent to me by Ms. Emi on 09/25/2020.

similar, but they are not. In Okinawa, the only outcome that counts is that you and others are safe, not whether someone else is hurt. So, in the words of a self-defense expert, "Think less about stopping the bad guy and more about getting to safety … do not lock-in, as many martial artists do, on the thought that stopping the Threat is the best way of achieving safety" (Miller 2011, p. 5). In this view, awareness, avoidance, and de-escalation are at least as important as physical fighting skills. Referring to the latter, to physical altercations, this different Okinawan concept changes the role of causing damage to others as well because damaging others is not a relevant objective in itself, so to speak; it is not a priority, it is rather a possible consequence of pursuing the superior goal of being safe.

To sum it up, in karate's classic Okinawan protection version, there are conceptions in use, not written down or documented as pointed out above, but orally transferred; conceptions that contrast with the Japanese way of standardization, codifying, and systemizing an art. In Japan, "Culture is transmitted and learned through forms; so much so that the Japanese culture has been called a culture of forms" (Endo 2005). Okinawan minds, however, focus on the outcome, on the result of an effort, not on the form itself in which the effort is shaped. In Japanese culture the form is prioritized over the outcome, whereas in Okinawa the outcome is prioritized over the form. For instance, the Japanese tea ceremony exactly defines the way to prepare tea—the way to serve it, the way to hold the cup, the way to drink, etc.—and thus prioritizes the form over how the tea tastes, while Okinawans prioritize the result, a great tasting tea, over the form to get there.

This orally transmitted, unsystematic, pragmatic, and outcome-focused Okinawan way may be characterized by saying that Okinawans might be quite effective in doing but cannot articulate philosophically why that is. As another example, this Okinawan outcome-focused approach shows itself through a different training regimen in Okinawan karate, i.e., by not prioritizing a specific form of training a group of people, but using individual or group assignments depending on training outcomes, which contrasts with those formal, orderly rows and lines with drills and commands that developed out of military training in Japanese karate training. Or, as a third example, it shows itself through different roles of kata in Okinawan karate, where the moves are prioritized over the form, over the kata pattern, which contrasts with the focus on the form, the kata pattern, over *kihon* in

Japanese karate. Such priority of a form goes up to the requirement that in Japanese karatedo a kata has to end in the same spot where it started, which has nothing to do with the fighting intentions of kata moves, and even leads to some ridiculous moves (e.g., hops) to end a kata exactly where it started.

The Okinawan focus on outcome versus the Japanese focus on form profoundly impacts not only how kata is performed but how karate is performed in general. In Okinawan karate-jutsu, the task at hand is determined by an attacker who creates the unique circumstances in a unique situation, where the defender is always behind the curve. Hence, training has to prepare you to accept the task as it comes your way, i.e., with spontaneity. In Okinawan karate-jutsu, you constantly deal with those unpredictable tasks thrown at you. Japanese karatedo, in contrast, assumes that a task is predetermined and that the way of carrying out this task has been identified. That way, in Japanese karatedo, *Shu Ha Ri* can be applied to perfect the execution of predetermined tasks that are put together in kata, whereas in Okinawan karate-jutsu the moves/techniques to spontaneously deal with a task at hand (*waza*) come first, and then later comes kata as a way to sum up moves. Thus, in the Okinawan karate tradition, kata remains unchanged—as kata is kata and *waza* is *waza*—but the latter can be adjusted in the face of the unique circumstances of an attack.[15] For Japanese karatedo, in contrast, the way of carrying out kata as a summation of predetermined tasks—i.e., the way of carrying out those identified tasks—includes different fighting situations and may thus be altered as a result of an individual interpretation.

In addition, again referring to my conversations with Sensei Dr. Dan Smith, *Uchinaguchi* was not the kind of language that could express philosophical conceptions and technical components of karate, which is why Okinawan masters taught through demonstrations, through physically, manually correcting their students' moves and limb placements, complemented by verbal advice like "Do it like that," "Use your hand like this," or "Place your foot there." And even after some Okinawan sensei learned to speak English after WWII, they had only limited options to explain underlying concepts of their art because they'd only learned basic conversational English and were not equipped to bring across either philosophical conceptions or technical matters. Consequently, until the 1970s, Westerners were learning karate by

---

15 Email Sensei Dr. Dan Smith sent to me on 06/10/2024,

doing on Okinawa, and only if someone trained there continuously for a very long time did a karateka have a chance to heuristically "feel" and discover the true content of an Okinawan master's teachings. In other words, to really understand the genuine Okinawan self-protection karate of that time, we have to rely on contemporary witnesses who understood *Uchinaguchi* and who lived on Okinawa for years, meaning as long as it took to establish those kinds of lasting relations with Okinawan masters so that they became trustworthy enough to be taught everything in depth. There are very, very few of those blessed Western sensei still around today who learned Okinawan karate-jutsu that way, in contrast to the limited insight most American soldiers were able to achieve in the 1950s, 1960s, and 1970s, who were stationed on Okinawa for thirteen months (marines), two years (army), or a bit longer (up to a maximum of four years in the air force), and then left. Some, but not many, visited their *honbu dojo* thereafter sporadically, and even fewer, regularly.

In summation, conceptual and philosophical knowledge in genuine Okinawan karate-jutsu was passed on without written references and without a specific terminology for techniques or concepts. It is only conserved as the individual knowledge and wisdom of a few senior karate-jutsu authorities on Okinawa and (even fewer) in the West, and most of what is today promoted as "genuine Okinawan karate" is more speculation and reengineering of what it may have been than anything based on authentic Okinawan teachings.

During its Japanization, the fluid Okinawan karate-jutsu of universal protection of others and oneself changed into static forms. By naming, systematizing, and categorizing all techniques, positions, and moves, the Japan Karate Association (JKA) "created an immense taxonomy thanks to which, for the first time, a definitive name was given to all the techniques of the Okinawan martial art, even those that previously had no name. But by doing so … the result was to 'crystallize' them. An immense but inevitable cultural damage resulting from modernization [sic]. For example, some transitional positions have been interpreted as 'stances' and therefore have acquired a static character that historically they never had, losing their original meaning, that is, the preparation for a technique" (Ballardini 2022, #12, p. 1).

The Japanese Shu Ha Ri Developmental Principle and Its Martial Arts Ramifications

Based on the previous chapter, it seems safe to assume that the explicit use of the term and concept of *Shu Ha Ri* gained more prominence in Japanese karatedo on the mainland than in karate-jutsu on Okinawa. And it seems safe to assume as well that its more detailed explanation through writings and teachings are more often found in the post-WWII era, supposedly related to efforts to articulate mainland Japan's martial arts philosophy to a broader audience.

In his publication about Okinawan kata, Patrick McCarthy notes around 1985 that "famous disciples of great karateka throughout history have made changes in the way they execute certain techniques within the formal exercises, and that is why there are today many variations of the same kata. These adaptions were done according to *Shu Ha Ri*, the principle which has allowed karate to evolve" (1987, p. 68f). He continues to briefly explain the concept as a three-phased path for personal development, an explanation which he, a decade later in the mid-1990s, elaborates and undergirds with his teacher Hiroshi Kinjo Sensei's words, which basically match the explanation at the beginning of this chapter and the following explanation given in postwar *aikido*: "It is known that, when we learn or train in something, we pass through the stages of *Shu*, *Ha*, and *Ri* ... In *Shu*, we repeat the forms and discipline ourselves so that our bodies absorb the forms that our forbearers created. We remain faithful to the forms with no deviation. Next, in the stage of *Ha*, once we have disciplined ourselves to acquire the forms and movements, we make innovations. In this process the forms may be broken and discarded. Finally, in *Ri*, we completely depart from the forms, open the door to creative technique, and arrive in a place where we act in accordance with what our heart/mind desires, unhindered while not overstepping laws" (Endo 2005, n. p.). The concept of heart/mind is a uniquely Asian one and different from Western understandings where heart (or "soul") and mind are seen as separate entities. In Asia, heart/mind can be used to represent the intrinsic spirit of an individual, as well as the relationship between the mind and the body, where "your mind controls your body," as my sensei, Noel Smith, hammers into us to constantly improve our body control. "Therefore, when Endo posits that the practitioner can act in accordance with what their heart/mind desires, he is most certainly implying this mind and body connection resonating within the technique" (Waterfield 2014, p. 3).

My conversations with fellow karateka of all ranks quickly revealed that not too many have heard of *Shu Ha Ri*, and even fewer are actually familiar with the concept. This fact in itself tells us something about the general teaching mindset in mainstream karate, a mindset almost exclusively emphasizing the well-proven learning path from (a) *maneru* (imitate), to (b) *wakaru* (understand), to (c) *nareru* (make a habit). *Shu Ha Ri*, however, adds another dimension of evolution to this learning process. The concept introduces a three-phased growth path from (a) dependently following, imitating, and maintaining the forms/rules of a specific subject, to (b) semi-autonomously detaching oneself from narrow interpretations of forms/rules by beginning to understand their intentions, to (c) unconsciously finding an independent path to intuitively express and apply forms and rules in a way that transcends their narrow application. In other words, this model suggests that karateka move through three phases, from focusing on learning the fundamentals of their art *(Shu)*, to focusing on application of and experimenting with these fundamentals *(Ha)*, to the phase in which they find their own expression and begin to innovate *(Ri)*. This movement characterizes a martial arts journey where the path itself is more important than arriving at a specific goal—more precisely, where no goal can ever be reached, since the three phases are of a perseverative manner (see image 1), as improvements and advanced skills that are gained in a later phase trickle back into what a practitioner did before in a less advanced manner, changing everything continuously in a never-ending circle of development where all phases simultaneously exist.

Applied to kata training, in the first phase of dependence and not departing from a form *(Shu)*, the role of kata is comparable to the one a textbook plays for students in other areas of learning. But learning in the sense of memorizing a kata does not yet mean understanding the kata, just as reading and memorizing a textbook does not yet allow a student to apply theorems to practical situations. Sensei need to further enhance memorization through offering examples of applications, through pointing out parallels, and through guiding their use in as many different situations and challenges as possible. Hence, in the second semi-autonomous phase of departing from a form *(Ha)*, various applications of kata open the mind, enlarge perception, and unveil underlying principles and exceptions to rules. In practical teaching, sensei in my dojo often spoke of this departure using words like, "Up to now we have taught you … [e.g., 'foot then hand']; now we teach you the opposite" (e.g., fist moves before or with foot when ramming/breaking a defense in a fight). Karateka move from reduced singular applications to realizing patterns and common denominators of moves toward an understanding of the intentions behind the moves and toward the creative use of fundamentals. They start to understand the intentions of the kata and use the "common denominators" of clusters of techniques, and also understand the exceptions to the rules. Finally, in the third phase of independence and departing from a form (*Ri*), karateka's perceptions widen even more. They become independent from forms and guidance; nothing is predetermined anymore, and the creative use of fundamentals becomes holistic, automatic, and unpredictable for others.

This third phase (*Ri*), however, is the most problematic one for the development of the art we all love. On the one hand, it opens the door for its evolution, as Sensei McCarthy put it in his quote earlier, and on the other hand it seems to give one license to form new systems and may thus represent a development of "a woefully corrupt misunderstanding of the term '*Shu Ha Ri*'" (Hayes 2018, pp. 93). In other words, *Ri* does not necessarily mean to break away from your sensei or from the karate system you are studying; it rather "means to feel free to experiment with the system we are studying. It means to get out of the habit of only stepping in a certain manner or attacking from a set angle or using a set timing in our techniques" (ibid., p. 95).

This means, in Sensei Perry's interpretation, to become independent of the rigid forms of the art, to see and to understand, in Sensei Chamberlain's words, the exceptions of a rule, and overall to become free of narrow confines so that one can attain a condition where the art itself becomes the teacher. Sensei Perry connects this *Shu Ha Ri* development with a growth path that overcomes the Japan-specific form of relationships based on *amae* (depending on the benevolence of others), which is the behavior of a person attempting to induce an authority figure, such as a parent, a spouse, a teacher, or a supervisor, to take care of them (Doi 1973). As analyzed and explained by the Japanese psychoanalyst Doi Takeo, this Japan-specific form of interrelations, best understood on analogy between children and their parents, provides a general model of human relationships in the Japanese culture—especially when one person is senior to another. In this perspective, *Shu* then represents the phase of a karateka's dependence on forms and on a teacher, *Ha* allows a karateka's increasing autonomy, and *Ri* is the phase of expanding independence from forms and teachers. But again, I must point out that this is a purely Japanese cultural view, and not an Okinawan one.

Supporting the perspective of *Shu Ha Ri* as a karateka's development *within* a system, Master Hong Yi-xiang, the founder of the Taiwanese martial arts system *Yizong Tangshoudao*, uses the beautiful metaphor of a crane's development to visualize progression and the related metaphor that derives from the meaning "bird" in the Chinese character for *Ri*. First, the hatchling flaps its wings; it learns the form (*xing*), the external appearance of something, but it is not able to fly. Then, the fledgling is finally able to successfully flap its wings and to leave the nest. At this stage, it has learned the intent of the form (*yi*) but is not able yet to use it smoothly. Lastly, the mature bird is able to swoop, dive, glide, hunt, and evade; the bird has learned change and adaptability (*hua*) to naturally employ form and intent in any circumstance.[16]

Looking at such a progression from an educational standpoint reveals an evolution of cognitive learning; that is using intellect and understanding which are located in the left hemisphere of our brains in the phases of *Shu* and *Ha;* and increasing senso-motoric learning, which is located in the right side of our brains, in the latter, in *Ha*, as well as in *Ri*, where eventually techniques become subconscious and spontaneous—"second nature," so to speak. In karate-jutsu this is not just the ability to perform *waza* (technique) accurately, but to modify and to adapt them but in a way that the modifications do not lose the purposes and intentions of the originals. This is an understanding of "separation" in the *Ri* phase that does not promote any leaving or breaking away from a system or from a sensei.

There is an important aspect to be pointed out, though, that substantially separates *Shu Ha Ri* and other related Asian developmental principles from the Western understanding of learning and development. In the West, the development of skills is usually understood as climbing a ladder of increasing competence, each rung leading toward

---

16 Metaphor was explained by Master Hong Yi-xiang in part two of a four-part BBC documentary about Chinese martial arts in 1983, and was explained to me personally in an email dated 01/05/2024 from Christopher Bates, 8th level black belt in Burmese Bando, American Bando Association, and indoor disciple of Master Hong Yi-xiang's and Hong Ze-han's *Yizong Tangshoudao*. Chris is the translator of the book that describes, among other things, the creation and development of Hong Yi-xiang's martial arts system Yizong Tangshoudao in postwar Taiwan (Hong Ze-han 2023).

advanced knowledge and skills, as layered levels of capabilities, where at the end disciples arrive at a final stage and are basically done. In contrast, *Shu Ha Ri* is a holistic concept that allows the parallel existence of all three *Shu*, *Ha*, and *Ri* phases. So, in a first approach, it needs to be understood as a circle rather than as a ladder of steps or levels, as shown as the circle in image 1. Improvements and advanced skills that are gained in a following phase trickle back into what a practitioner did before in a less advanced manner, changing everything continuously while all phases continue to exist simultaneously. "A realistic image of human development is that of a circular progression that may shift back and forth as the individuals experience new challenges and develop new skills. Therefore, one may argue that there is potential to shift back and forth between any of these three stages throughout one's development and that the process is never ending in that completing a cycle is to come full-circle and begin the process again. Such is the circle of life" (Waterfield 2014, p. 3).

Image 1: The Circle of the Shu Ha Ri Developmental Principle*

Learning change and adaptability to naturally employ form and intent to any circumstance (phase of independence)	**Ri** 離	**Ha** 破	Learning the intent of the form, the function of a move (phase of semi-autonomy)

Shu 守

Learning the form, the external appearance of something (phase of dependence)

* *Why a circle is used to visualize Shu Ha Ri will be explained in more detail in Chapters 6 and 7, based on the difference between this holistic Japanese developmental concept and the "levels" or "stages" in Western education.*

Chapters 6 and 7 will deal with those parallels and differences between Western educational concepts and *Shu Ha Ri*. The first way of viewing *Shu Ha Ri* development, as a circle, will be expanded with an additional dimension, graphically approximated as a spiral, i.e., as a developing system of revolving circles (images 11 and 12 in those chapters).

At this point, practicing kata may provide an example that illustrates the concept of simultaneous existence of phases. For instance, after a karateka better understands the role of hip movements through the practice of more advanced kata (in the *Shorin Ryu* system I practice, *Kobayashi Ryu*, this could be a *Passai* kata), this insight trickles back into the interpretations and kata practices that were learned earlier (in *Kobayashi Ryu* this could be the *Pinan* series)[17] and it may create those precious light-bulb moments of new ways of understanding those hip movements in *Naihanchi* kata, which then refertilize the interpretation of advanced kata practice, and so on.

Referring back to the crane metaphor, in this way of understanding a karateka's developmental process, there is no suggestion of transcending or breaking away from a specific martial arts system; it is all about growing into the ultimate capacity to effortlessly and habitually use that very system in all circumstances. The widespread Western view of *Shu Ha Ri* according to which martial artists need to study various fighting systems to grow and in that way break with tradition—and that they even want to invent new styles in order to express their own vision of the art—contradicts the Confucian-inspired guiding principles implicated here. And therein lies another issue worth mentioning, because "in the process of 'creating' 'new' systems the founders just happen to appoint themselves 10th Dan, '*Soke*,' '*Hanshi*,' etc., or are recognized as such by groups which have also arrogantly taken such powers unto themselves" (Hayes 2018, p. 94). To avoid a possible misunderstanding here, I want to point out that associations that define ranks and officially promote karateka based on accepted standards are of course an essential component of securing reasonable qualification standards for karate practitioners. And if those associations are linked to and officially recognized by Okinawan organizations for karate-jutsu, or Japanese organizations for karatedo, there should be no raised eyebrows at all. Absent such recognition, it is understandable that a question mark may be raised about rank.

---

17 I am well aware that hip movements were initially to be learned through *Naihanchi* practice, which is the first kata taught in *Shorin Ryu*, where *Naihanchi* initially used to be one single kata. Today, this deeper understanding of hip-movement may be taught—if it actually is taught—in kata other than *Naihanchi* as well, e.g. in *Passai*, as I mentioned in my example.

When karate-jutsu systems are taught as they were intended to be—in other words, when they are based on the reality of a real fight and are taught completely, in a way that covers all their fundamentals of receiving and giving—a practitioner of any of those systems is equipped to succeed in a real fight. An analogy might be how different languages are equally able to precisely express the same thing. The common suggestion that different styles ought to be studied to figure out the "best karate for self-defense" may be explained by the real possibility that a karateka does not have any realistic fighting experience beyond regulated competitions. Missing fighting experience leads to specific teaching and learning priorities, to a different way to express the art, and to keeping the door shut to proven and stress-tested approaches. Thus, a style may be taught incompletely in this sense, lacking those reality-based fighting applications. Such a circumstance would then explain the suggestion, or even request, that another style ought to be studied in order to learn more about fighting. "Breaking away" of practitioners from this style or sensei now seems plausible but still remains a misconception because the style as such is not incomplete; the teachings are.

Again, *Ri* does not have to be seen that way, as breaking away to attain an individual expression of the art, as the crane metaphor in its compelling way illustrates. In an alternative conception of progression *within* a given karate-jutsu system, we can see any style as a system that is complete in itself—with the qualification, however, that this claim is explicitly restricted to the *jutsu* or *bugei* versions of a self-protection art. In this sense, every karate-jutsu system equips its practitioners with everything necessary to succeed in a fight. Every karate-jutsu system with its purpose of universal self-protection is like a language: complete and based on identical fundamentals just as a language is based on comparable linguistic fundamentals and does not need a new grammar to be added by individuals. Instead, all different languages can be used alike to perfectly articulate the same thing; likewise, all karate-jutsu systems can be successfully used for self-protection as they are—if they are taught and practiced with realistic fighting applications. If they are not, the training is incomplete (though not useless as some may call it).

So, it is not important which karate-jutsu system you use to protect yourself; it is only important whether your training prepared you for the difference between a "real fight" and staged dojo scenarios, because such a real fight differs significantly from everything we do, and what we can do, in the dojo. Real assaults confront you with attackers who do want to surprise you and hurt you badly. This reality differs from practice in the dojo; it is coming at you hard with a flurry of attacks instead of the single one that you easily see coming in training, it happens at oddly close distances, and it is usually over in a couple of seconds. Consequently, it is not important how "elegant" the karate system is you use to protect yourself. The only thing that counts is whether your training prepared you to immediately overcome your shock and to receive, absorb, evade, and parry a multitude of blows or stabs, and whether it permits you to respond—without any hesitation or conscious thought—fast, hard, and effectively. Every karate-jutsu system allows you to do the latter; hence, success in such a fight is based more on the psychological factors of being able to snap out of a surprise or a freeze and your own ethics allowing you to seriously injure another human being. It has little to do with whether "my karate is better than your karate."

Referring back to *Shu Ha Ri*, transcending in the *Ri* phase *within* a karate-jutsu system would then mean becoming independent of narrow guidance to naturally (often called *intuitively*) apply form and intent to any circumstance—vicious criminal assaults included. Transcending within a karate-jutsu system would not mean transcending the system as such but to use it whenever and however it is needed and to master its intuitive use after growing through the *Ha* and *Ri* phases of mimicking the teacher, understanding the intentions of the teachings, and becoming the model and then the teacher. "At this stage, the experienced practitioners begin to do things their 'own way' but their own way is still deeply rooted in the traditions they learned when they were still novice" (Waterfield 2014, p. 2).

Of course, karateka will integrate some moves and approaches from other systems into their individual use of their art in the same way that some foreign terms found their way into someone's mother tongue to precisely articulate a specific meaning. But integrating German terms like "kindergarten," "weltschmerz," "angst," or "rucksack" into American English does not change this language into a new one; as in karate-jutsu, the integration of some moves and approaches from other systems do not change the karateka's initial system.

To put it the other way around, a view of *Ri* as "transcending styles," as it is widely understood today, confines the meaning of *Ri* to how it is understood in certain karatedo styles that have undergone transformation from arts oriented toward self-protection into fine arts oriented toward self-development. Such a version of karatedo may also be based on Western individualism, where a karateka's personality can be individually articulated through a path toward self-expression and self-actualization, a path which then can be published as a personal view of a personal karate, or as "how I have bumbled along the way and endeavored to create my own version of *Shu Ha Ri*" (Langley 2018).

Though the Shu Ha Ri Concept Is Widespread in Today's Japanese Karatedo, It Is Unknown to Many Karateka

But why, we have to ask, is this principle not as well known to karateka as other concepts if in karatedo it is an important factor in explaining a karateka's development, as the introductory quotes in Chapter 1 suggest? Why is it not as well-known as "no first attack," "foot then hand," "abdominal breathing," and other principles, just to name a few? As Sensei Michael Clarke assumes, this may be a result of the fact that "even in Japan and Okinawa, such things [i.e., concepts like *Shu Ha Ri* and *Shin Gi Tai*; my clarification] are no longer considered of much importance within karate circles, certainly not in my experience. Mainstream karate (sport and commerce) has no use for such ideas, and without sounding too cynical, that situation will remain as it is until someone works out a way to make money from it."[18]

Beyond Sensei Clarke's not-at-all cynical argument about commerce,[19] in my view the answer lies also in the previously mentioned underlying misreading of the *Shu Ha Ri* concept when it is used as an explanation of, or as an alibi for, any and all changes in karate—for every alteration to the art done by everyone called a master, whether labelled as such by others or calling themselves such. When an argument is used to explain everything, it explains nothing anymore; it becomes therefore unimportant and of no use at all, and it then rather becomes an alibi that glosses over misconceptions.

---

18 Quoted from a personal email to me, dated 07/18/2023.
19 The way to commercialize *Shu Ha Ri* was actually recently found, though not in karate circles, but in the business world, where consultants have applied the concept to management, project management, software development, and other areas since 2010, and where coaches began to use it as their coaching concept starting around 2020. However, in the business world, *Shu Ha Ri* is used as a truncated version of its initial philosophy. That its use by utilitarian pragmatists is blotched with misunderstandings does not come as a surprise. All this will be explained in Chapter 4.

Let me clarify this thought further with a metaphor Sensei Chibana Chosin used to explain changes. Of course, karate changes over time, he says, "because a teacher must continue to learn and add his personality to the teachings. There is an old Okinawan martial arts saying that states that it's much like a pond. In order for the pond to live, it must have fresh water" (as quoted in Chambers et al. 2020, p. 45). In this metaphor, the pond remains the same, though, in spite of new water flowing into it. This is comparable to how changes in Okinawan karate following on the succession of generations of sensei never would change, let alone destroy, the essence or purpose of a form or of a system as an art for self-protection. The form or the style remains the same in its essence, which is universal self-protection, in spite of changes, just like the pond in the metaphor remains the same in spite of new water flowing in. But some Japanizing changes of Okinawan karate, enacted by teachers called masters, did not add fresh water to a style-specific karate-jutsu pond but actually added sand to the initial pond and created a new one, to stay with the metaphor, by changing the essence and purpose of the art from protecting oneself and others to perfecting and expressing oneself and, later, to creating a competitive, sports-oriented discipline. Those masters created something new; they dug out another pond, so to speak, which, because of the complete change of karate-jutsu's initial purpose, no longer represents the original pond. All that happened by way of transforming the genuine Okinawan self-protection art on the mainland into recreational athletics and into a scholarly fine art with its meditative philosophy that supports an individual spiritual way of life, as this guideline from the Japanese Karate Association shows in connection with how to forge a karate mind: "The result of true karate is natural, effortless action, and the confidence, humility, openness, and peace only possible through perfect unity of mind and body. This is the core teaching of *Zen*, the basis of *bushido*, and the basis of the JKA's karate philosophy" (JKA, n.d., tab "Philosophy").

This change and new definition of karate through Japanization is researched, explained, and published plenty and in detail, and thus not repeated here (see footnote 21 for a summary).

As in many other Eastern philosophical approaches, in Sensei Chibana Chosin's pond metaphor for change and constancy we find the dichotomy of two equally important and simultaneously existing contradictory concepts. This is a common concept in the martial arts, states Sensei John Carria, 10th Dan *Uechi Ryu Karatedo Kokusai Kyokai*: "philosophically and literally all things exist in relation to something else. Not so much as stark opposites, but rather as interrelated dualities" (Carria 2022, p. 6). The interrelation of all things is a concept based primarily on Taoist philosophy and Confucian thought. Night and day do not exist without each other, but each defines the other by contrast. The opposites of night and day together form one unit of time, thus constituting an overarching wholeness of mutual determination. Following the same line of argument, the opposites of change and permanence only exist together; one does not exist without the other. Change needs the presence of permanence, of a constant, to become change. The *constant here is the essence of a kata or of a style* as an encyclopedia of moves to succeed in self-protection, which remains constant even if every generation of sensei slightly changes the style or a form:

Image 2: Unity of Constancy and Change in Okinawan Karate-jutsu

Constant	**Change**
Kata/Kihon	Interpretation
Principles	Application
Bunkai	Oyo
Fundamentals	Karate-jutsu Systems

Whether and how kata ought to be changed is not up to us Westerners anyway. In my view, we are simply stewards to the best of our abilities, stewards of a cultural inheritance we are asked to curate and not to transubstantiate. The latter would be up to the owner of that cultural heritage, which are the Okinawan headmasters, and not to anyone else.[20]

---

[20] In all my books (Bayer 2021, 2023a) I express my view that, because karate is a part of the Okinawan (sub-) cultural heritage, no foreigner is in the position to decide on matters important to it, though there may be as many outstanding karate experts to be found outside of Okinawa in the West as on Okinawa itself. This is comparable to the fact that no foreigner is in the position to decide on the status of a monument in Italy as part of Italian cultural heritage, though there may be many outstanding experts on Italian culture to be found outside of Italy. Foreigners may like what Italians do in this sense, or

The principle of change and permanence as a unity allows us to understand *Shu Ha Ri* in karate-jutsu as *individual adaptations of unchanged intents, functions, and fundamentals* and thus parallels the view in the last chapter of the karateka's progression to mastery within a given karate-jutsu system as not transcending that system of self-protection that is complete in itself. That view excludes all those individual innovations and fantasy moves, mostly ineffective in an actual fight, that have been used to create new karate styles aiming at new purposes beyond self-protection and that, in modern times, have been used to create businesses by establishing market niches. Those niches were created by sensei using their own newly invented personal interpretations of classic moves in order to set themselves apart from the competition. Such *Shu Ha Ri* connotations as represented in this modern approach of sensei-specific interpretations were not part of the genuine Okinawan art. These interpretations were later introduced into karate by postwar (often non-Okinawan) generations of sensei during a process of development that started with Sensei Funakoshi Gichin's modification of Okinawan *Shorin Ryu*, which became Japanized *Shotokan* karatedo (Noble 2019 & 2020). Those new alterations to kata and modifications of style and purpose transcended the "allowable differences" (Perry 2018, p. 110), going beyond the accepted individual, physiologically based variations, which were founded on a *Shu Ha Ri* interpretation that did not change karate-jutsu's essence of protection.

Succeeding sensei generations defused or changed original self-defense techniques for a variety of reasons—maybe unknowingly, maybe intentionally to increase Okinawan karate's acceptance on the mainland before WWII,[21] and later, after WWII, because of its acceptance

---

they may dislike it; they may research it, and they may comment on it. But the decision itself should be in the hands of the Italians. The same line of argument applies to Okinawan karate—even if non-Okinawans should claim to come up with a better decision or procedure than Okinawans themselves. This is one of my philosophical, value-based axioms, which may not be shared by everyone, and comparable to the basis of international law, or, in politics, to the doctrine of nonintervention into foreign internal affairs.

21 During and after the Meiji Restoration (1868–1912) Japan altered itself drastically and the role of its martial arts changed completely. Judo was created as a new sports variation of the mainland's traditional martial art of *jiu-jitsu,* and judo spread quickly across the nation. The efforts of Okinawan masters to prevent their beloved art from completely fading into oblivion as martial arts sports variations blossomed on the mainland, are to be seen in this context. Anko Itosu's heavily promoted the inclusion of a "disarmed" version of karate in the physical education program of public schools and as such blazed the trail for the development of the new, non-lethal type of karatedo. This development was

by the US-American occupation force as unarmed athletic gymnastics. New generations of sensei changed karate even more, turning it into competitive showmanship and something spectacular to look at but without any merit in a fight. The sometimes pathetic consequences of kata modifications in this sense of failed fighting applications—not with respect to showmanship or health optimization—are plenty, and some are illustrated with examples and photographs in my earlier books.

To sum up this sub-chapter in terms of *Shu Ha Ri*, some Western karate authorities have heard of the concept, but many have not. But then again, *Shu Ha Ri* is a way to view things and to describe progress; it is an explication of a karateka's development that is neither wrong nor unnecessary. One may practice the art without understanding it in the way that one may drive a car without understanding how the engine works.

Shu Ha Ri in the Martial Arts versus in the Fine Arts

Whereas the *Shu Ha Ri* principle is not too difficult to understand, the practical implications for its use in the martial arts are enormous and more difficult to grasp because the principle gives rise to certain issues that do not occur in connection with the concept in fine arts like acting, painting, calligraphy, the art of tea, and so on. In those fine arts, artists strive to find a perfect form and express their individualized message to others whereas martial artists who use their art as "true

---

furthered by Gichin Funakoshi, who broadly introduced the art on the mainland in 1922 and devoted his life to spread karatedo there by way of transforming it into a form of recreation that was also a physical and spiritual path for everyone. Strong efforts to modify Okinawan karate in the shape of judo followed, which at that time was seen as the benchmark of how to create a new version of a martial art in order to attract new students. This "transition represented the termination of a secret self-defense art that embraced spiritualism and the birth of a unique recreational phenomenon" (McCarthy 2016, p. 147), appealing to new practitioners who were less attracted to fighting capabilities and more drawn by the possibility of personal mental or physical improvements. All this *Japanization of Okinawan Karate* led to the new "disarmed" karate styles of *Shotokan*, *Shito Ryu*, *Wado Ryu*, and a Japanese form of *Goju Ryu* on the mainland, that contrasted with the original Okinawan styles of *Shorin Ryu*, *Uechi Ryu* und genuine *Goju Ryu* (Bayer 2021).

martial arts" *(bugei no bugei)*, as it was intended to be,[22] strive to achieve the specific purpose of self-protection—i.e., to succeed, or at least to survive, in a real fight while using their art in conformity with the law of physics. As I wrote in my introduction, Picasso, Degas, van Gogh, Matisse, Gaugin, and all other masters in the art of painting innovated and differentiated themselves from others by developing their personal way to articulate their message in their paintings. But they never created a manual, an application of their approach to be used in life for a specific purpose. And this exactly marks an essential difference between a creative fine art and an empty-hand self-defense art like karate-jutsu. The latter deals with given determinants of the human body, with angles, distances, leverage, and other practical fundamentals using the laws of physics to avoid, control, or physically eliminate a threat. In lethal encounters there is no room for maneuvers to express oneself, no latitude for fancy new techniques; there is only one successful approach, which is the most direct and effective way to get to safety or to neutralize an attacker as quickly and as effectively as possible; and all this is based on the physiology of the human body and on physical science. Given the realities of anatomy and physics, there is only a limited number of best (and thus "correct") technical-mechanical ways to minimize distance, maximize body-weight-power transfer, and align bones at the moment of impact. Possible deviations by individual karateka from these theoretically best approaches are possible but are also restricted to their individual physiology. Hence, individual deviations from a kata pattern are limited and represent some variation of moves that nonetheless retain, however, the given self-defense purpose of the kata. As soon as we apply the "fighting yardstick" to kata interpretations, there is no room anymore for individual fantasy moves. When adrenaline

---

22 I use the term "true martial arts" as defined by Sensei Matsumura Sokon: *bugei no bugei*, i.e., the use and application of martial arts as a fighting art, as a tool not softened by philosophical restraints. He contrasts this real (in my terminology) karate-jutsu to two other more debatable specifications, namely to the "martial arts of scholars" (i.e., karatedo), which is the martial art of a theorist or a dreamer, one may say, where "the rules of fighting and self-protection against an enemy assault" are unknown, and "dedication to training weakens to become superficial, like a dance" (Matsumura 2020, p. 13). This kind of practice is, in Matsumura Sensei's eyes, as inadequate as "the martial arts in name only" (i.e., sports-karate), which is the art of a player and braggart, where "there is no real ability get things done"; "they debate" and "unsettled, they only talk about victory" (ibid.). Both inadequate martial arts forms have the *common denominator of a lack of fighting experience*, of exercising a version of a martial art without understanding its application in real-life assaults.

levels are off the chart, when vision becomes tunnel vision, and when emotions run high, *kihon* comes into play. Going back to the basics, and unconsciously doing what you trained to do and have ingrained it into what some call muscle memory, creates an opportunity to succeed.

However, when a martial art is stripped of its self-protection purpose and turned into a way to find or to express oneself, then—and only then—is there room to articulate oneself through the creation and invention of individual, sometimes fictional, moves, which can be demonstrated to like-minded spectators and that may work with compliant partners in *kumite* exercises but will not work on the street. These different understandings of karate as, again in Sensei Matsumura Sokon's terms, true martial arts (karate-jutsu), martial arts of scholars (karatedo), and martial arts in name only (sports-karate) suggest that *Shu Ha Ri* will also be differently understood in those variations and will reflect those differing underlying values, purposes, and philosophies within the three karate versions that will therefore not be directly associated with each other.

Different Shu Ha Ri Interpretations Are Used in Karate Today

There are those well-known words attributed to Lee Jun-fan, who is better known as Bruce Lee (1940–1973), which may further illuminate this thought. Bruce Lee developed and taught his extremely successful *Jeet Kun Do* in the 1960s in the USA, and he impacted several generations of martial artists in his short life with his mental/spiritual and physical teachings that reflected the realities of street fighting while promoting the necessity to transcend, and in his logic to unify, styles to reach an overarching fighting concept. His advice to his student Dan Inosanto, appearing in a book dedication, was to "adapt/absorb what is useful, reject what is useless, and add what is specifically your own."[23]

---

23 In an online discussion, Dwight Woods, a long-time *Jeet Kun Do* practitioner who trained with Dan Inosanto, points out that it was actually not Bruce Lee but Mao Tse Tung who created the phrase, and that "the word 'adapt' is not part of the quote … instead the correct word is 'absorb' … Bruce Lee wrote the words in a book dedication to his student Dan Inosanto." https://www.quora.com/What-did-Bruce-Lee-mean-with-Adapt-what-is-useful-reject-what-is-useless-and-add-what-is-specifically-your-own. Retrieved 12/21/2023.

In philosophical terms, this exhortation suggests the superiority of the individual mind to the body of knowledge in a martial art system and thus promotes individualism. It further suggests that karateka are qualified enough to, for instance, distinguish kata moves as "useful" or "useless" instead of digging deeper and discovering possible hidden applications of moves that may at a first glance seem of no good use.[24]

This leads us to another possible misconception in some of today's *Shu Ha Ri* use in the martial arts, a possible misconception that arises from the *differing relevance of individuality in Eastern and Western systems of thought*. Bruce Lee himself was definitely as much impacted by Western culture as he was by Asian culture in his earlier years (Bowman 2010). Hence, a quick look at how the Western cultural value of individualism may impact interpretations of *Shu Ha Ri* seems advisable.

How Individualism in Western Culture May Impact the Way Shu Ha Ri Is Understood

With regards to our subject of karate, we need to understand something about the Confucian and Taoist roots of Japanese culture (see "Excurse: Japan's Cultural Roots in Confucianism and Taoism" at the very end of this text) and its related phenomenon of "groupism," a term used by sociologists to refer to an individual's tendency to conform to the cultural pattern of a group at the expense of individualism and cultural diversity. Such a social orientation and philosophical concept clearly sets itself apart from Western individualism, and it undergirds an aspect of Japanese culture of utmost importance, namely that of representing a culture of conformity (Haitani 1990). It defines an alternative form of togetherness where the reference group—whether the community or the nation as a whole, is valued above the individual, and where an individual's role in the social, political, and economic life of the community is largely determined by his or her membership in a specific ethnic group, class, or caste.[25] This predominant culture of conformity expresses a Confucian-based mindset with its emphasis

---

24 There may be an underlying message beyond individualism here, a message of transcending styles by going back to the fundamentals. This thought will be looked at in the sub-chapter entitled "There Were No Styles in Classic Okinawan Karate-Jutsu."

25 It has to be noted, however, that today there may be another side in the Japanese culture, a private one, contrasting public appearance, as pointed out by scientific research. However, the public version of groupism still establishes the visible norm of everyday

upon the community, its implication of unquestionable authority, its obligations to adhere to longstanding protocol, and its use of the imitative social mechanism of the *senpai/kohai* (senior/junior) system, which will become important later when we look at possible *Shu Ha Ri* interpretations in a traditional Okinawan dojo.

We can now loop this thought (conformity instead of individualism in Japanese culture) back to the above-quoted thought concerning whether it is appropriate for an individual karateka to distinguish kata moves as "useful" or "useless," which represents a notion rooted in our Western value of individualism, but which contradicts, head-on, essential Japanese cultural values of harmony and groupism. Because of this cultural norm, students transcending the borders of their karate system will most likely not find the support either of Japanese masters nor of Okinawan ones. This is the philosophical-cultural argument. But there is another argument too, the logical one, which is to ask whether it's actually possible for an individual karateka to distinguish kata moves as "useless." If we agree that a *bugei* karate-jutsu style (again: not necessarily a *budo* karatedo style) is a complete system that equips a practitioner with everything necessary to succeed in a fight, and that it can be seen like a language, complete in itself, so that you can use different languages to articulate the same thing, why would some parts of that language be "useless"? Why create your own new language, or your own new grammar, when your mother tongue articulates everything perfectly? The only thing that would legitimize a judgment of "uselessness" would be the view that something is more sympathetic to a karateka, or that some move would better fit their individual physiology.

With this metaphor, we can nevertheless illustrate an important and widespread possible misconception of what it is to "transcend the rule" or "break with tradition." Within a language, within a karate-jutsu system, students are guided by their master to their individual expressions of the art, but they stay within their system; there is no break with tradition unless the master's or student's ego get in the way. And any argument along the lines of some newly invented fantasy moves being "more elegant" than the traditional ones, an argument I once heard in a training camp, I deem inappropriate for karate-jutsu: elegance is not a prime criteria in a street fight.

---

togetherness for the Japanese people, including the togetherness of Okinawans (Hasegawa/Hirose 2005, p. 219).

The two contradictory positions implicated here are (a) that continuously practicing and diving deeper into a specific system equips karateka with all they need to understand what they are doing and to do it correctly to succeed in a real-life self-defense situation, versus (b) that at a certain point in their development, the system karateka are training in turns into a limitation and they need to transcend those limits to find competence beyond their style. In the eyes of position (a) the latter position (b) means that such a view of limitations is a misconception; those karateka are now simply reinventing the wheel because their so-called new insights are not new at all. They were already included in the system they used to train in, and they'd have arrived at those insights anyway if they'd continued to grow in the system.

This of course would be a different story if sensei have their own narrow limitations when it comes to understanding the system they teach to their students and thus try to limit students to the level of competence sensei have themselves and are familiar with. That, in fact, would limit the development and growth of their students. To transcend those limitations within a dojo, however, does not require altering a karate-jutsu system, to change a style, or to invent something new; it simply means to find a more qualified sensei and is therefore not an aspect of *Shu Ha Ri* (Chapter 5 will deal with this and other possible *Shu Ha Ri* misinterpretations).

The thought of understanding a karate-jutsu style as an optimized fighting system for self-defense, complete in itself like a language, limits *Shu Ha Ri* in karate-jutsu to *individual adaptations of unchanged fundamentals* and excludes all those unrealistic innovations and fantasy moves that have even been used to create completely new karate styles that aim at new purposes beyond self-defense. In karate-jutsu, students mature within their system without breaking with traditions, and the *Ri*-level allows individual ways to gain full body-weight power and full control based on relaxation, harmony, and complete openness.

Such a view, to put it the other way round, seems to reserve another kind of *Ri* for the scholarly transformation of a self-protection craft into *budo* karatedo—into the fine art of self-development and as a path toward self-actualization. "Talented students who develop a reputation in the arts and who think they've discovered something new after having 'followed' a sensei after a number of years come to think that they've 'transcended' their teacher's understanding and therefore have a right and duty to 'break away' (and invariably form their own 'new' system)" (Hayes 2018, p. 92f).

Right or wrong, it is a socio-cultural fact that the modification of karate-jutsu to karatedo on the mainland had an enormous impact on Okinawa as well and that this pulled the majority of genuine Okinawan karate away from its initial universal principle of self-protection toward a path of self-perfection. Though there are strong efforts and distinguished proponents trying to preserve karate-jutsu in its traditional version today, and though we have seen a remarkable movement back to the original forms over the last two decades, self-protection oriented karate-jutsu has slowly faded after WWII into a smaller fragment of worldwide practice. The reason for its reduced importance is karate's all-embracing and overwhelming Japanization, even on Okinawa itself. This has meant that the precious ancient heritage is slowly being dispersed, although many share the opinion that it is not the eradication of a cultural heritage but its evolution into something more adequate for modern times where the need for hand-to-hand combat no longer exists. We do not share this view; instead, we see the cultural heritage of classic karate as a complex and rich martial art that needs to be preserved in its classic form, which is composed of several complementary disciplines that cannot be simplified. Thus, it is not suitable for everyone and therefore cannot become a commodity for the mass market. It is possible that in some Okinawan schools the most ancient teachings are still handed down to some of the oldest students who are carefully selected by masters who use the same criteria they were chosen by, but there is no guarantee of this.

But then again there is this other connotation of *Ri* in the karate-jutsu tradition that does not involve breaking away from a system, a component of which has to do with a kind of spiritual development that is closer to Confucian origins and that is not based on individualism. It embodies a different kind of "enlightenment and spiritual emancipation" that sets itself apart from self-actualization and rather means to become independent from narrow guidance and to naturally employ form and intent to any circumstance. It means "to break away from the patterns of thinking and 'doing' that we have been taught. It means to feel free to experiment with [and within—my addition] the system we are studying" (Hayes, 2018, p. 95).

The Yardsticks That Measure the Adequacy of Interpretations of Karate Moves

Besides the role of individualism in Eastern and Western philosophies, a second issue in Bruce Lee's quote, "absorb what is useful, reject what is useless, and add what is specifically your own," develops around the individual yardstick that measures usefulness. Useful for what purpose? Useless on what account?

Let's not forget that in our art today we have three established versions with three conflicting ideas and values that leads to three different purposes within those three karate variations, and which defines three corresponding different kinds of "usefulness" to reach those three differing purposes. In another publication (Bayer 2023, pp. 1–16) I characterized those three variations as:[26]

a) The Okinawan *bugei* art of karate-jutsu, a self-protection version for civilians based on *Ti*, which used to be the earlier Okinawan combat art in security circles that was created several hundred years ago.

b) The old-style Japanese *budo* art karatedo for self-perfection and as a way of life (created about one hundred years ago), concentrating on mental, spiritual, and health-related character-development—including newly incorporated philosophical, Zen-based undergirding.

c) Non-martial modern sports-karate for recreational athletics and regulated competition (created about sixty years ago). "During the 1950s, the Ministry of Education [in Japan—my addition] replaced

---

[26] I am glad to see that the terms I suggested are now being used within karate circles and that they are considered "valid at a very abstract and birds-eye view" (Herbert 2024b, p. 14). As Dr. Herbert points out in his following sentence, a closer look at the current reality shows overlaps and blurry boundaries, and I agree. But, since even today the public may think that "karate is just karate," I will briefly summarize this distinction here. Karate may be seen as way of life and a character-building educational system (*budo*), as self-protection (*bujutsu* or *bugei*), as a sport, and as a business. All these views are correct in their specific sense; all these variations are indeed mixed into today's karate practices—they simply address different versions of the art. This creates the unfortunate misconception I've mentioned because the same term "karate" is confusingly used for all these completely different karate types and thereby suggests that differing kinds would be the same. In all other Japanese martial arts, we see different labels for their initial, genuine martial use on the one hand, and for their modern derivatives on the other. For instance, there is the term *jiu-jutsu* for the original empty-hand combat version used by samurai, and there is the different term *judo* for *jiu-jutsu's* modern sports variation. However, we do not see comparable different terms in today's karate; instead, the same term is used without specification for all its versions, which is why I suggest the listed three different terms to better label three differing variations.

the term '*budo*' with the term 'combative sport' in order to gain some distance from prior militaristic connotations … In 1989, the Ministry of Education officially resumed the use of the term *budo* to refer to martial disciplines" (Sanchez-Garcia 2018, p. 77).

In other words, a useful move in a karate-jutsu kata—like the classic, practically effective, small-circled hand and forearm *tuite* move in *Passai Do* used to manipulate, damage, or break an opponent's wrist and elbow joints—may not be known in karatedo and is thus replaced with a simple pull of both hands to the hip in some karatedo styles. Both moves are regarded as not interesting enough for audiences and hence as useless in sports-karate, where they are replaced with a spectacular, big-circled move of both arms, useful for showmanship but without any meaning or purpose in a fight (see image 3), a move we actually may find in some old-style, non-sports karatedo versions like *Doshinkan* as well.

Or, to give another example, karateka emphasize and overextend moves in some karatedo styles, which may be useful for health purposes or as individual representations of full dedication and giving one's best but that can alter angles, release joint-locks, and move the center of gravity, all of which would make them useless for self-defense in karate-jutsu (see image 14 in this text and Bayer 2023, p. 11 for examples).

Those three different karate versions in place today, with their differing purposes, suggest that the way and the benefit of applying the *Shu Ha Ri* developmental principle to them may differ as well. Hence, we do need a benchmark/yardstick to overcome this mix-up. Only such a benchmark allows us to arrive at truths beyond speculation.

The Yardstick in Karate-jutsu Is Measurable Self-Defense Impact
The purpose of karate-jutsu is all-encompassing self-protection, and, looking at physical self-defense, a "correct" move here is the one that most efficiently and directly transfers full body-weight power into an opponent to create enough damage in order to stop the attack and to prevent another one coming from the attacker. That is simple enough, at least in my view, because the result of a "correct" move in karate-jutsu becomes measurable and thus not open to individually differing interpretations (though karateka who never experienced violence may or may not agree with those who have). But since the use and the application of karate-jutsu is exclusively and uncompromisingly

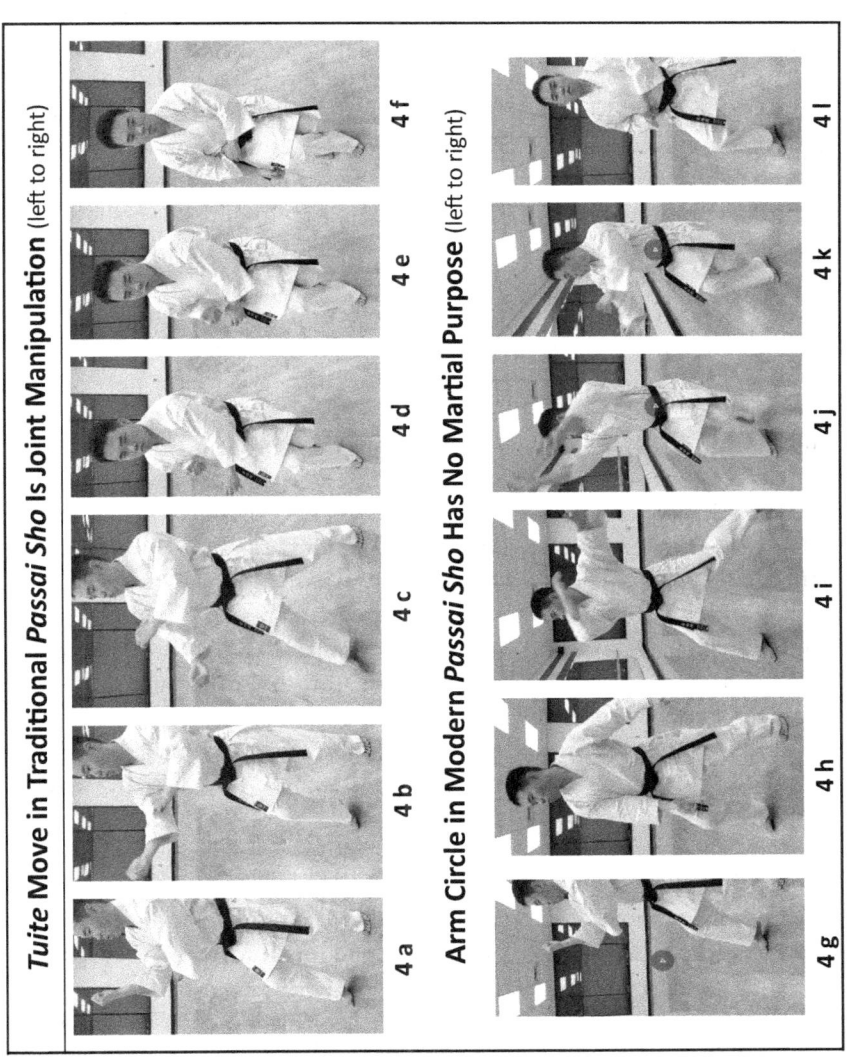

Image 3: Tuite Move to Damage Joints in Traditional Karate-jutsu Passai Sho (4a - 4f) versus Arm Circle without Martial Purpose in Modern Karatedo and Sports-Karate Passai Sho (4g - 4l)

restricted to situations where the life of karateka or of loved ones is threatened, there is no room in those situations for sparring, nor is it an opportunity to engage in the "monkey-dance" (Miller 2011, p. 26ff) like movie actors do; a childish consensus to brawl that in real life may be even unconsciously obtained. There is only the strategy of absorbing/reflecting/receiving an attacker's moves, destabilizing the opponent, and immediately returning force in its most effective form to end the confrontation (Kane/Wilder 2005). In a real fight, he or she will succeed, in the joking words of my Sensei Noel Smith, 9th Dan *Kobayashi Ryu,* "who gives the mostest the fastest."

A yardstick based on the true self-protection aims of genuine Okinawan karate-jutsu allows us to separate effective kata interpretations from wishful thinking. This yardstick measures whether a move follows the logic and reality of fighting in order to stop an attack and to prevent another one coming from the attacker. To ensure a positive outcome, a move or technique needs to be based on the proven fundamental principles of fighting, on a form of combat that in modern times supposedly will be only rarely needed, and hopefully never; but it can occur, of course, for instance as an assault that has to be dealt with—and not only in certain circles or in certain areas. Keeping those kinds of situation in mind, we have to evaluate and to pressure test whether a new (*Ha* or *Ri*) creation is based on the reality and logic of combat and on those ironclad fundamentals that include:

- The shortest distance between two points is a straight line (short and direct moves are faster and thus more effective than "haymaker" or "roundhouse" moves).
- Circular moves best counter straight moves when receiving/parrying and are combined with immediate counters.
- Defending moves can be attacking ones at the same time and vice versa (there is no simple block in karate-jutsu, which would allow an attacker to continue).
- The lower you are the stronger you are (lower center of gravity reduces instability and transfers more body weight into a move).
- No wasted movement means no loss of time (a move explodes from the position a limb is in at that moment; there should be no "winding up" or pulling back).
- All joints are locked at the moment of impact (if not, kinetic energy "escapes" through an unlocked joint instead of being transferred into an opponent).

- Foot then hand (if possible) when stepping while fluidly moving through positions (solid foundations to transfer full body-weight power into an opponent are not inflexible "stances").
- Using hard and soft avenues of approach (soft never means "gentle" but rather "relaxed"; it is "smooth hardness").

As Sensei Steven Franz, 6th Dan *Shorin Ryu Shorinkan*, points out, based on his real life fighting experience of having worked as a bouncer and in other capacities in the security field, many newly created kata interpretations, technique applications, and fighting scenarios presented on the internet are not "pressure tested" in light of the logic and reality of a real fight and do not work in a realistic context as intended and presented by their creators.[27] As already pointed out earlier, those kinds of fights have a viciousness, complexity, unpredictability, and fierceness of their own that differs from most training scenarios in the dojo and especially from *kumite* scenarios with compliant partners.

Subjective Interpretations of Forms in Karatedo are Not Factually Measurable
What has to be measured in the *budo* art of karatedo contrasts with the yardstick in karate-jutsu because much is added there to the classic "textbooks" of self-protection kata and was added for reasons other than for fighting. In karatedo the individual mind is exercised through training of techniques, and ultimately, the spirit is trained that way as well—and through all this the ultimate goal of self-development will be approached. Hence, "true karatedo places weight upon spiritual rather than physical matters," as Professor Dr. Wolfgang Herbert quotes Sensei Funakoshi Gichin in his article about the essence of *Shotokan* karatedo practice (Herbert 2024, p. 32). As a consequence, martial arts applications may now turn into personal Zen-related exercises, into individual expressions of the art, and into subjective interpretations of moves that may be more or less fit for a fight. "Daily practice, self-discipline, physical exertion, intellectual and emotional, are here for personality and omni improvement. Persistent training is connected with the improvement of character" (Cynarski 2017, p. 8).

---

27 Phone conversation on 05/18/2024.

Such a view of kata executions is one result of converting a self-protection art into a fine art that pursues self-perfection and promotes self-articulation. At the same time, self-actualization allows one to "transcend styles" and thus preserves the meaning of *Ri* of "breaking away" from a style or from a tradition for these fine-art versions of karatedo and for the scholarly transformation of a self-defense craft into the fine art of self-development. All modifications may now be considered to be individual articulations, subjectively valid expressions of personal views, which cannot be "wrong" anymore, as they are all individually reasonable creations of articulating oneself. "Fighting techniques with bare hands known today were no longer intended exclusively for combat but were meant to be used to treat and to spiritual improvement … intended primarily for health and religious destiny … This resulted in the synthesis of martial arts therapy and religious self-improvement" (ibid.).

Individual expressions do not have a neutral or factual yardstick but are open to personal interpretations, to individually differing understandings, just as a poem or a painting may denote completely different personal meanings for different poetry or visual art lovers. In this perspective, every interpretation by every individual is subjectively true and thus "individually correct."

Forms as Defined by Associations Is the Yardstick in Sports-Karate
Whereas during karatedo's formation in mainland Japan in the 1920s, Funakoshi Gichin "unequivocally rejected sport competition, his successors introduced karate to the varieties of sports. For as long as Gichin Funakoshi and Shigeru Egami were alive, sport competitions were not organized in their schools, as they were regarded by them as contrary to the spirit of karatedo" (Cynarski 2017, p. 13). That changed considerably, as we all know, after WWII, when Japan's *Shotokan* karatedo association JKA defined the benchmarks for correctness for every technique, move, stance, and step in that style,[28] which can now also serve as benchmarks for correctness in competitions.

---

28 Within the Japan Karate Association JKA, "karate techniques were developed into a complete system. For the first time there emerged a clear, scientific, and practical 'best' form for each *kumite* stance, posture, and movement. There also emerged a clear delineation between the 'correct' and 'incorrect' way to execute each stance, punch, kick, or technique" (JKA "History" tab, n.d., n.p.). However, what happened while categorizing moves and techniques that way was that the fluidity of the art was lost and turned

The complete alienation of sports-karate from its martial source is obvious when "experts" understand their karatedo as a performing art. Now, "a 'karateka' can choose among several types of forms or katas, much like a musician with his or her repertory or a painter occupied in selecting a number of paintings for an upcoming exhibition. This parallelism between karateka and artists, however, is not surprising: even though the main purpose of karate forms is the right transmission of knowledge about blows, tricks, methods to generate power, and many other undisclosed teachings included in them, each karate form has been created also for public demonstrations, in much the same manner as symphonies for concerts and paintings for exhibitions" (Raudino 2007).

The yardstick of correctness here can obviously not be the capability to create enough damage to stop an attack in such a sport discipline that is purposefully stripped of and outlaws all techniques that would do exactly that. Hence, considering moves as correct in sports-karate variations, where performance is actually measured and judged, differs from both approaches and matches neither those in karate-jutsu nor in karatedo. The yardstick used by judges is how close a move and a technique embody a "correct form" as defined by sports-karate organizations. In most cases these are the end positions of a move, e.g., stances and postures after striking or blocking. This contradicts karate-jutsu practice, since the "work" that creates the damage is executed during a move, after its explosion point and within the last third of the move, and not at its endpoint. Hence, there are no static stances or positions in karate-jutsu, only fluid transitions to support a certain technique or application.

Looking closer at modern scoring practice (WKF 2024) reveals that in sports-karate the entire scoring system is based on creating illusions instead of factual applications. It's based on the fact that athletes create impressions. For instance, whereas in karate-jutsu "good" or "correct" is easily validated as "most effective" through the damaging impact a move creates, there is no option to validate "good form," "good timing," or "correct distance" in sports-karate *kumite* other than to compare it to an ideal picture of an athletic dance where correctness is

---

into a chain of stagnant "techniques." Thus, fluid positions as preparations for technique application turned into stances; concepts with multiple application options turned into constricted techniques; and concepts of receiving and giving turned into simple blocks.

defined by the Japanese karate associations as a specific position. The athletes have to create the impression of fighting; they have to create the impression of vigorously hitting—as soon as they would actually hit more or less vigorously, they are disqualified. Hence, in competitions, the winner is not always the better fighter, but it is the one who makes the best impression, as we saw in the 2020 Tokyo Olympics, where knocking out an opponent in sports-karate *kumite* led to losing a fight through disqualification instead of winning it as would have been the case in the sport of boxing.

Shu Ha Ri, Meditation, Religion, and the Esoteric

With its transformation into the "martial arts of the scholars," as Sensei Matsumura Sokon puts it, karatedo opened itself up to new spiritual content, and by applying the *Shu Ha Ri* concept there, some interpretation of redefined karatedo became even prone to enter the gateway of mysticism and the esoteric,[29] where *Ri* is then reserved for insiders and remains incomprehensible for outsiders. Though I use my words carefully here, I need to clarify possible misunderstandings. I am not saying that this connection of *Shu Ha Ri* to mysticism and the esoteric must exist, I am saying that it can sometimes exist. And I am neither saying that practicing mystic and esoteric versions of karate is the wrong thing to do, I am just saying that it is not the way of practice I prefer; others may think differently, which, of course, is everyone's choice and is fine by me.

It is undeniable, however, that through transformation of karate-jutsu into karatedo the initial self-protection focus of karate-jutsu has turned into self-perfection on mainland Japan and possibly into self-actualization to "arrive in a place where we act in accordance with what our heart/mind desires, unhindered" as Sensei Endo Seishiro said (quoted earlier). Or, as explained by Sensei Hiroshi Kinjo,[30] *Ri* is

---

29 "Esoteric is the quality of having an inner or secret meaning. This term and its correlative *exoteric* were first applied in the ancient Greek mysteries to those who were initiated (*eso*, "within") and to those who were not (*exo*, "outside"), respectively... Esoteric in the sense of mystic is also used to describe certain schools of Buddhism." Mysticism on the other hand is explained as "the practice of religious experiences during alternate states of consciousness, together with whatever ideologies, ethics, rites, myths, legends, and magic may be related to them" (https://www.britannica.com/ retrieved 1/16/2024).

30 Hiroshi Kinjo (1919–2011), who is characterized as a living encyclopedia on karate and *kobudo* history, was one of Sensei Richard Kim's and Sensei Patrick McCarthy's teachers. Sensei Kinjo was born in Shuri on Okinawa and trained there under several masters until

"commonly referred to as enlightenment or spiritual emancipation. Provoked by relentless austere conditioning, philosophical assimilation, and protracted meditation, the intermittent flashes of penetrating wisdom become more frequent as one ascends to the portal. Passing through the portal of the 'world within,' one is absorbed into its abyss and emerges reborn. Those who fail to enter remain forever unfamiliar with the true essence of karatedo and mastery of the 'world without'" (Hiroshi Kinjo in McCarthy 1994, n.p.). This sounds indeed a bit esoteric, like there is some secret inner meaning that can only be found by initiates through mystic experience.

To be clear again, my intention is not to say anything against those approaches. All I am saying is that the substance of those approaches has to be transparent; it has to be named in general philosophical and cultural terms as it is instead of veiling it as secret way for martial artists to attain extraordinary capabilities. In other words, there is a difference between incorporating Zen philosophy as a self-developmental path into karatedo (Herbert 2021) versus mystifying that path into a religious experience "for initiates." To clarify a bit further, "Zen has no theory; it is an inner knowing for which there is no clearly stated dogma. The Zen of martial arts deemphasizes the power of the intellect and extols that of intuitive action. Its ultimate aim is to free the individual from anger, illusion, and false passion" (Hyams 1979, p. 10). Thus, Zen in martial arts provides avenues to achieve spiritual serenity, mental tranquility, and abiding self-confidence.

Zen meditation can be connected to karate-jutsu's core purpose of self-protection to open up a path toward overcoming one's own emotional limitations and aberrations in order to be a better defender: "the inward journey advocated by Zen philosophy might seem at odds with the aggressive nature of karate training; however, these seemingly disparate paths complement one another, enabling karate practitioners to confront fear and accept the uncontrollable aspects of hostile conflict. By acknowledging and embracing what lies beyond our control, we attain mental clarity, allowing us to respond effectively and decisively

---

he moved to Tokyo in 1939, where he was awarded an instructor's license from Sensei Toyama Kanken to teach at the latter's *Shudokan* (not to be confused with Sensei Gichin Funakoshi's *Shotokan*). Holding a PhD, Sensei Kinjo was a prolific researcher and author of many karate publications. He became one of the two vice presidents at the Japanese All Japan Karate Federation under Toyama Kanken in 1950 and continued to teach *Shudokan* until his retirement in 2011 (Quast 2012, n.p.).

in challenging situations" (McCarthy 2023, p. 294). In contrast, in its mystic interpretation, kata performance is turned into a purpose in itself, into a meditative dance without connection to fighting, where "practitioner and practice fade away. 'It' exercises the kata without any difference between form as inherited template and the practitioner's concrete movements" (Meissl 2021, p. 55, my translation). So, whereas the first quote actually connects Zen meditation to karate-jutsu's core purpose of self-protection, the latter approach does not do that and converts a fighting art into a meditative art form for scholars to achieve mystic enlightenment through kata dances. And since mystics do not experience or perceive an objectively existing unity but formulate their own experiential unities in different ways, the bridge from here to self-actualization and individualism is not difficult to build.

Several scientific studies shed light on Eastern mysticism in martial arts and point out that in order for karateka to find their preferred version of karate: "it is important to know for every practitioner whether his trainer or sensei views the martial art as a form of recreation, aiming to promote it as such, with modern training methods, or if there is a mystical approach to training with religious elements prevailing" (Mijatov 2014, p. 84). A closer look at karatedo in this study shows that "while it could be said for judo that it is completely rational, certain authors find a dose of mysticism and religiousness in karate. In its extreme, *aikido* represents a religion, with its teachings and a Prophet" (ibid., p. 92).

I want to separate the issue of Zen's incorporation into karate, which parallels the way Zen is included in the classic art of Japanese swordsmanship (Herbert 2021 and 2023), from religious interpretations of karate practice and from divine interventions, as postulated by some practitioners, which I will discuss in a moment. Zen meditation is a belief system that does not worship God, as there is no God in Buddhism; instead, it centers on an emptiness/void that can be reached mentally after holistically comprehending the caducity of all being. Somewhat opposed but related is the concept of universal energy to which everything in existence is connected as a part of this system from which it derives and into which it is reabsorbed after perishing in its material form. Practitioners aim to reach a state that can be interpreted as enlightenment of body and spirit as a unity (*ming*), which is a notion with a long tradition in Chinese philosophy. A thesis at Beijing University concerning this matter concludes that "despite the fact that enlightenment is a broad concept by itself, my research has shown that *ming* ... can be interpreted as *enlightenment excluding religious or sectarian interpretations, but in the sense of knowing nature* ... it is through knowing the nature of one's own body ... to knowing the nature of all things" (Karpov 2021, p. 60; *italics* are mine). In other words, even a concept like "spiritual enlightenment," a term that does suggest a bridge to esotericism and religion, can be interpreted with philosophical, nonreligious Daoism without those religious or esoteric connotations and can be understood as deep insight into nature through physical and mental practice instead.

Connections of karate with transcendental powers are often related to "mind over matter" thought systems that postulate the superiority of the mental and spiritual over the physical. And indeed, an example I witnessed at a training camp is convincing, where four strong karateka were not able to lift up Sensei Douglas Perry, 10th Dan *Shorin Ryu Okinawa Shorinryu Karatedo Kobudo Kensankai*, who is not a big person at all, when he focused on his *hara* (energy center in the abdomen) and its connection to the ground (actually, to the center of the earth). Those four karateka could lift him up easily when he was not focusing that way, and I do know this with certainty because I was one of those four karateka. This phenomenon does not require an explanation in terms of the supernatural, though, as we know about the superiority of focused minds in many areas (e.g., in management and at the workplace) and the psychological effect of willpower in social and competitive situations. Even pragmatic self-defense instructors point out that "you are fighting a mind, not just a body" (Miller 2011, p. 159). Greater concentration defeats the lesser strategically and tactically, just as an axe better splits wood than a sledgehammer.

A different set of religious approaches that explicitly refer to God and to divine interventions through karate practice is found when karatedo is combined with Christian belief systems. Such a combination surprises me, and, in my opinion, may be either a product of the human propensity to see connections that aren't actually there, or may be used as a pragmatic vehicle by churches to attract and to evangelize kids and teens. It sounds strange to me that Christianity would be philosophically connected to a lethal fighting art based on a philosophical thought system that conflicts with its own. Moreover, if a martial art that originated on a far-away eastern continent is indeed related to religion, it's a non-Christian one like Buddhism, Shintoism, Taoism, and ancestor worship.

Referring to Christianity, I personally know many karateka with strong Christian faith, who keep their religion separate from their karate practice. They read the bible regularly, they practice their Christianity, and some even serve as ministers, but none of them combines their religion with their karate. However, we find more than a few organizations in the USA, and even internationally, that do exactly that in their effort to evangelize. They label themselves as "Savior Martial Arts," "Karate for Christ," "Christian Karate," "Faith Fighters Martial Arts," "Totally Christian Karate," or use other flowery labels. Unfortunately, in too many cases, neither the qualification or international recognition of instructor ranks, nor the versions of the arts taught seem to reach high standards in those Christian karate organizations (Franz 2016). I personally was able in 2024 to witness rank testing events in such an organization, where black belts were issued to preteen kids and to young teens like candy. The criteria for earning these promotions were unclear to me; my conversations with parents and some instructors, who were teenagers themselves, could not clear that up (the adult head instructor was "busy" and avoided talking to me), so, I assume it was based on the time of their attendance and on their devotion; it could not be the less-than-mediocre performance many kids gave during those testing events as compared to the minimum black belt requirements for teens in other associations I am familiar with (side note: in those organizations black belts are not issued to preteen kids).

These examples go hand in hand with the long-standing tendency to infuse mysticism and religiosity into karatedo and thereby associate it with almost (if not outright) supernatural powers, especially in the *Ri* phase, where it is not uncommon for practitioners to give themselves divine airs. However, the philosophical foundation of *Shu Ha Ri* (where *xing* is the form, the external appearance of something; *yi* is the intent of the form; and *hua* is adaptability to all situations and circumstances) does not need esoteric, philosophical, or religious undertones to be comprehended, and neither does the art itself to be practiced, and used—and it definitely does not support a modern Western concept of karatekas' self-actualization in their *Ri* phase. All it needs is an "empty mind" that overcomes fear and other emotions that hinder action, and that opens up perception to give access to the complete range of fighting alternatives and applications stored in the mind of the practitioner.

In this way, empty mind, non-religious enlightenment, and Zen meditation (or other forms of meditation) are closely related.

Increased spiritual connotations of *Shu Ha Ri* can be seen as an outcome of the transformation of *koryu* (genuine old-school) martial arts with their combat purpose into the *budo* arts of self-perfection on mainland Japan. However and interestingly enough, this development changed how karate is viewed by some on Okinawa itself as well as how it is generally seen in postwar times. In mainstream Okinawan karate, we no longer find the official promotion of a protection art for oneself and for others, at least not when presented to foreigners. Instead, we find the promotion of a character-building, self-perfecting, nonviolent interpretation of the art. It is now endorsed as "a 'martial art of peace' that emphasizes the training of the body through severe discipline, the refining of the mind, and the respect of courtesy" (ODKS message by the chairman). This understanding is no longer directly related to the initial universal Okinawan principle of protecting others and oneself from any kind of harm; it rather comes closer to what *aikido* developed into. In this sense, "karatedo aims at shaping a psychologically and socially mature personality of its disciples … *budo* karate training affects human development as a whole, including all factors, both intrinsic and extrinsic … The spiritual component … constitutes a factor of an individual's moral, or even spiritual, maturation and growth" (Ambrozy/Piwowarski 2013, pp. 49–50). "A possible difficulty here is that such views face the charge of over-emphasizing the 'philosophical' aspect of martial arts" (Holt 2013, p. 6).

Referring back to the initial theme of this subchapter, starting in the *Ha* phase, and particularly when entering the *Ri* phase of *Shu Ha Ri*, the connections of karate with spirituality in its non-esoteric, non-religious sense are related to the notion of "mind over matter" that postulates the superiority of the mental and spiritual to the physical. These concepts are also connected with non-esoteric "spiritual enlightenment" that allows one to understand nature in its totality by deeply understanding the nature of one's own body, just as the totality of the universe may be seen by understanding the structure of an atom; in Laozi's words "without going outside you may see the whole world" (Lao Tsu 1972, Chapter 47). These concepts include the nonreligious understanding of an "empty mind" that allows one to fully focus and to act correct on an intuitive level without any distraction.

Image 4: Swastika Is a Religious Symbol in Many Asian Cultures

It may come as a surprise to find a swastika on a statue of the Buddha on Okinawa, because in the West this symbol is widely recognized as a symbol of the German Nazi Party before and during WWII. However, Asian religions use it is as a symbol of divinity and spirituality, and in Buddhism it represents positivity. The difference between this ancient cultural/religious symbol and its later version in Germany is that in most versions of the swastika in Buddhism the arms are bent counterclockwise to the left whereas the Nazi symbol shows the arms bent clockwise to the right and it was tilted 45 degrees.

However, *if spiritual references and components are overemphasized and become the sole center and purpose of practice*, a version of karatedo may approximate esoteric and sectarian approaches. Only then, "engaging in martial combat, whether for military, self-defense, or cultivation purposes, is taken to sensitize practitioners toward existential issues which in turn enliven potential religio-spiritual experiences and awakenings" (Brown et.al. 2022, p. 36). Such "religio-spiritual experiences and awakenings" are the exceptions though and are only exhibited by certain personalities who have an esoteric understanding of a martial art. They are not the rule.

Differing Shu Ha Ri Characteristics Are Found in Today's Karate-jutsu, Karatedo, and Sports-Karate

Based on the perspectives presented in this chapter, it is now possible to tentatively integrate the different connotations of *Shu Ha Ri* from those three current karate versions of karate-jutsu, karatedo, and sports-karate into one overarching whole as represented in image 5.

In *bugei* karate-jutsu, *Ri* is not understood as transcending your style or as breaking away from your sensei. This is not needed to achieve karate-jutsu's essential purpose of universal self-protection and to neutralize an attacker as quickly and as efficiently as possible. Karate-jutsu styles were introduced as systems that are complete in themselves and that equip their practitioners with everything necessary to succeed in a fight. Every karate-jutsu system for self-defense is like a language, which is complete, based on comparable linguistic fundamentals, and not in need of innovative additional grammar to fulfil its purpose. With that understanding we may see the three phases like a crane's development from flapping its wings to eventually leaving the nest to freely fly, swoop, dive, and evade without limitations. *Ri*-transcending *within* a karate-jutsu system then means to gain independence from narrow guidance and to transcend one's own limitations but not to transcend the system as such or to break away from the sensei.

This is different in the *budo* art of karatedo, a redefined version of a fighting craft as a fine art with its new purpose of self-development. Martial arts applications may turn here into personal interpretations, into individual expressions of the art, and they may be more or less fit or unfit for the reality of fighting. This reserves *Ri* in its interpretation of "transcending styles" for this scholarly interpretation of a self-defense craft as a fine art of self-development. There, karateka may reach their full potential in its psychological sense of self-perfection through expressing oneself and through individual paths toward self-actualization.

Finally, there is no systematic spiritual evolution as a specific purpose in sports-karate, neither toward community-related Confucian values, nor toward Western individualism. Indirectly, however, the "educational process in sport or in the physical education can also be a source of improvement of personality. The condition is here, however, adherence to the noble principles of fair play … tough competition for the results brings the risk of pathology" (Cynarski 2027, p. 13). Hence, personal ambition, hopefully mediated by non-violent ideals, fair play, and (perhaps) learning how to lose well, seem to be the driving values of progression in this karate version, which leads to a *Ri* understanding of "breaking the form" by inventing spectacular fantasy moves and individualized kata rhythms not suited for combat but breathtaking to look at as well as intentional interruptions to the flow of kata that would be counterproductive in a fight but make sense as emphasizing positions and demonstrating body control for judges and spectators.

Image 5: Tentative Shu Ha Ri Interpretations for Today's Three Main Karate Variations

	Karate-jutsu	*Karatedo*	*Sports-Karate*
Shu *Dependence*	Physical self-control Learning the **external appearance of classic forms** [created as self-protection "textbooks" for **fighting moves**] is **LEARNING THE FORM**	Physical self-control Learning **the external appearance of modified forms** [created as "textbooks" for **non-combative athletics**] is **LEARNING THE FORM**	Physical self-control Learning the **external appearance of modified forms** [created as "textbooks" to **impress judges** and **spectators**] is **LEARNING THE FORM**
Ha *Semi-Autonomy*	Comprehending underlying [*ura*] fundamental principles of receiving and giving and adapt to various self-defense challenges Using bodyweight-power and mental self-control Comprehending and adapting the **intention of forms** and **the function of moves** is **BREAKING THE FORM**	Comprehending the face value [*omote*] of moves and their use in prearranged kumite Using bodyweight-power and mental self-control Individualized fluid **kata performance for physical and mental health** and grasping "the way" is **BREAKING THE FORM**	Using the face value [*omote*] of moves in kumite and kata as speedily as possible Using speed, mental self-control and a winner-mindset for competition Individualized speedy **kata performance for audiences and judges** with subjective timing and understanding is **BREAKING THE FORM**
Ri *Independence*	Naturally employing true [*okuden*] intent and fundamentals to any self-protection circumstance Self-control, control of others, and control of the entire situation Effortless use of *hara* and full bodyweight-power for [*okuden*] fight-effective moves **Empty mind** and **independence from forms** and **from guidance** is **TRANSCENDING THE FORM**	Aiming for harmony of mind, technique, and body Kata performance with individual-specific alterations is effortless and may become a meditative process Effortless use of *hara* and bodyweight-power for individually interpreted moves **Empty mind** and perhaps **breaking away from the style or its master** is **TRANSCENDING THE FORM**	No obvious spiritual evolvement Values may be competitive attitudes and positive values of sportsmanship. **Inventing spectacular fantasy moves** not suited for combat, as well as **kata-flow interruptions to emphasize positions** is **TRANSCENDING THE FORM**
	SELF-PROTECTION	**SELF-PERFECTION**	**WINNING**

Chapter 2
Shu Ha Ri Is a Japanese Socio-Cultural Concept, Not an Okinawan One

Though Okinawa is of course part of the Japanese nation, there were, and there still are, significant cultural peculiarities to be found in the local subculture of the Ryukyu islands, which, among other things, include different understandings of karate in the latter's traditional circles. Japan, the "karate-reproducing" country, however, is—and used to be—the superior political power governing the "karate-inventing" and culturally autonomous region of Okinawa and aimed at integrating the local self-protection art into the mainland's cultural traditions.

Okinawa Shows Subcultural Peculiarities That Appeared Inferior to Prewar Japan

Okinawa shows a dichotomy between culture and citizenship (Meyer 2007). On the one hand, Okinawa is, since the Satsuma invasion in the 1600s, a part of the Japanese nation, and on the other, it is an island far away from the mainland, with its own cultural roots, traditions, customs, and symbols; all of those developed while simultaneously serving the Chinese, Japanese, Korean, and Indonesian empires as their trading hub for centuries (Kerr 2018). During those centuries, Okinawa established its own subcultural identity. Within this subculture, its local fighting system, *Ti,* is a paramount cultural symbol for Okinawan subcultural identity, and thus *Ti* was an important target for mainland Japan's efforts during the Meiji Period and in the following decades before WWII to create cultural homogeneity across the nation. In this integration process, the local Okinawan civilian self-protection art (which I call karate-jutsu) that developed out of *Ti* (which was initially a combat art for aristocratic security circles), was converted, "Japanized," into the *budo* art kara-te-do and reinterpreted with the Japanese philosophical *budo* framework as a means of character development and recreation. As a result, this new karatedo matched mainland Japan's other "*budoized*" martial arts in terms of purpose, structure, etiquette, and general philosophical approach.

The sociological/social borders of cultures and subcultures and their unique symbols, cultural assets, and heritage do not necessarily match the political borders of governments, and until today the Okinawans have not 100-percent assimilated into Japanese society (Hein/Selden 2003), which did not consider Okinawans as equal and that perpetuated a mindset of superiority even after the Ryukyus were no longer a colony and became a prefecture. But even at that time "Japanese rule in Okinawa had a touch of colonialism, particularly during the first two decades. Although nominally a prefecture, Okinawa remained under a separate system of administration. Most of the government agencies and institutions, starting with the prefecture office, were manned by appointees from Japan. Japanese merchants took control over the local economy and monopolized trade with other prefectures. Paternalism and arrogance characterized Japanese expatriates' attitudes toward the local people" (Meyer 2020, n.p.).

In spite of considerable efforts by Japan to assimilate the autonomous Okinawan subculture, including the Japanization of its subcultural symbol karate-jutsu (Johnson 2012), a wall remains up to this day, a dichotomy of culture and citizenship, and nothing indicates that it will disappear in the future (Meyer 2007). This means, that an Okinawan subcultural heritage and symbol does not necessarily represent the overarching culture of the nation—or, in other words, the subcultural symbol karate-jutsu may from the outside be incorrectly interpreted as the traditional national Japanese cultural symbol karatedo, which it is not (Bayer 2022). There is no traditional Japanese karate, only a traditional Okinawan one (Swennen 2006), because (1) the Japanized karatedo versions on the mainland were developed less than a hundred years ago—which is a rather short period of time in the millennia-old history of martial arts; and (2) karatedo was, in fact, pilfered from Okinawa, then redefined, altered, and forced into mainland Japan's cultural framework in a such a way that it can only be factitiously called "an 'authentic' *Japanese* martial tradition through a series of historical contingencies and elective affinities," (Tan 2004, p. 187), i.e., through political maneuvers and not because of similar Japanese and Okinawan martial arts traditions.

The Okinawan socio-cultural situation remains complex. Though politically moving from Japanese colony to prefecture in 1879, "in light of nearly two decades of resistance from the Okinawan aristocracy, Japanese administrators long remained distrustful of Okinawan locals, frequently reproaching them for their allegedly pro-Chinese sentiments. When Okinawa Prefecture was finally granted suffrage in 1912, the 'uncivilized' islands of Miyako and Yaeyama remained excluded from the electoral system, and Okinawa received only two seats in the Diet—fewer than other prefectures with the same population" (Meyer 2020, n. p.).

Nevertheless, a large group of Okinawans then and today want to be both Japanese and Okinawan. In many aspects of daily life this cannot be consolidated and results in an overwhelming impression of Okinawa representing an essentially Japanese culture, expressed in cultural symbols like the language spoken, the food eaten, the educational, administrative, and governmental systems implemented, the money and banking system used, the visible presence of Shintoism and Buddhism, the politics that determine society, and the policies that govern it. As such, Okinawans are subject to the same state canon and mindset that originated on the mainland. This official and public mindset represents, beyond all dichotomy of culture and citizenship, an overarching culture of conformity. The impact of the Confucian values of harmony and mutual obligations that governed Okinawa for several hundred years is undeniable and created the prevalent, all-embracing culture of group conformity, including its components of not questioning authority and of adhering to longstanding protocol.

"The Japanese government was winning the campaign to have Okinawans to think of themselves as Japanese subjects, but in general there was little done to overcome the widespread Japanese sense of superiority toward the Okinawans as an 'out-group,' a minority of rather second-class country cousins" (Kerr 2000, p. 448), which may explain

Okinawans' strenuous efforts to maintain and conserve their local symbols. So, underneath that visible Japanese culture, another unofficial and private set of aspiration can be found: to preserve genuine Okinawan roots and conserve the island's distinct subculture. One identifying symbol of that is Okinawan *Ti*, mostly in its current modified form as a self-protection art for civilian use, which I call karate-jutsu, but sporadically as genuine *Ti* as well. Though the latter is only taught to selected students in the very few schools that preserved the old ways.

In its genuine version, this is a complex art, not a simple one, composed of several martial methods beyond simple punching. It includes grappling, limb and head manipulation, throwing, joint locking and joint straining, nerve striking, and more—in addition to the unity of its martial, mental, and spiritual components. Not just *Ti* but karate-jutsu was not, nor is, freely and completely shared with non-Okinawans. Specifically, those outwardly "small" nuances in moves, which make all the difference to success in a fight, were not taught to all—not in the past and not today.

Shu Ha Ri Is Not a Traditional Principle of Okinawan Karate-jutsu

Thus, we still have to interpret socio-cultural developments on Okinawa in light of the incongruity between official Japanese culture and unofficial Okinawan subculture, which results in a modification of Japanese thought when integrated into local circumstances. Referring to Okinawan karate and the use of *Shu Ha Ri* in this sense, the possible use of such a Japanese philosophical concept is likewise filtered through the Okinawan cultural dichotomy. "Something Japanese" is not just integrated as-is but is adapted and modified by those specific Okinawan sub-cultural interpretations. Sensei Lara Chamberlain points out in this context that "all Japanese cultural concepts that were brought up by my teachers had to be seen in context, it was *champuru* in nature [*champuru* is an Okinawa word, originally denoting a dish, but now means 'mixed up' or 'stirred together'—my explanation]. The Okinawans are so rooted that while they may blend or mix in other ideas seamlessly, in order to fully understand you have to understand the nuances between their root culture and the others mixed in."

This last thought implies the use (restricted at best) and the limited acceptance of a Japanese concept like *Shu Ha Ri* on Okinawa. Let us remember that karatedo was basically unknown on mainland Japan before 1922, and that it is believed that the art was originally introduced to the mainland as a "disarmed" variation that did not represent the entire original Okinawan empty-handed self-protection art. Only parts of a larger whole, namely kata, were adopted by mainland Japan, and even those not in their initial self-defense version but changed and disarmed, missing entire moves or parts thereof, and only showing their most obvious surface applications (*omote*) that can even be seen by untrained karate laymen without revealing hidden (*ura*) and true (*okuden*) applications. In addition to this loss of hidden applications of kata moves, the Japanized versions of karatedo lacked the secret practices of *tegumi* (grappling) and *torite* (seizing and controlling), as well as the art of using pressure points and nerve strikes (*kyusho jutsu*) (Bayer 2023a, pp. 62ff). Other things were added into karatedo on the mainland, especially new spiritual and philosophical components that were not included in classic Okinawan self-protection karate-jutsu before, but which became the scholarly component of all *budo* arts on the mainland, and which became essential in support of Japan's nationalistic hegemonic policy from the Meiji Period (1868–1911) until the end of WWII, when the *budo* arts of kendo, judo, and karatedo became militaristic vehicles to produce an able body and a dauntless fighting spirit.

The connection of karate practice with Zen occurred as well after the art's transformation into karatedo in the 1920s, that is, after seven centuries of independent and pragmatic *Ti* and karate-jutsu on Okinawa. But now, the predominant meditative basis of Japanese martial arts that turned Japanese swordsmanship (*kenjutsu*) into its *budo* version kendo, its empty hand fighting system *jiu-jutsu* into judo, and *aiki-jitsu* into *aikido,* was applied to the alteration of karate-jutsu into karatedo, to gain insights and enlightenment on an individual way (*do*) while pursuing a path of self-development through the meditative practice of athletic moves (Herbert 2021). Now, Japanese karate-texts explicitly mention karatedo as a medium for Zen meditation to gain new insights, and, specifically after WWII, *Shu Ha Ri* is mentioned as its implicit developmental principle. Since the new self-perfecting, meditative, and health-related athletics of karatedo contrast considerably with the classic, pragmatic *bugei* practice of karate-jutsu on

Okinawa, it sounds reasonable that the philosophical principle of *Shu Ha Ri* can be found mostly on the mainland, where the self-protection art became interrelated with spiritual self-perfection. It sounds reasonable as well that therefore the further spread of a rather academic conception like *Shu Ha Ri* was concentrated in Japanized karatedo versions on the mainland and not on Okinawa. And it finally makes sense that some senior US-karate authorities of Okinawan styles, who started training in Okinawa in the 1960s, and who I have conversed with, either never, or at best occasionally, have heard of *Shu Ha Ri* there. Their Okinawan masters focused on the "true martial arts" in Sensei Matsumura Sokon's term, on (*bugei*) karate-jutsu, as my Sensei Noel Smith remembers: "Training was always based on the mindset of fighting an actual fight, and it produced a deep understanding of body-weight-power transfer into direct, short, hard, effective moves. The reality of combat and its logic were the leading ideas for every training session in O'Sensei Nakazato Shugoro's dojo and in other Okinawan dojo at that time" (Smith in Bayer 2023, p. VII).

There is another piece of the socio-cultural background that supports my opinion that the *Shu Ha Ri* principle was not broadly used in Okinawan karate, and that is the character of formal education on Okinawa before, during, and after WWII. Formal education would be needed to learn, discuss, and apply sophisticated scholarly conceptions to a martial art. That did not occur on Okinawa, which was due not to the intellectual capacities of Okinawans but to limited or no broad access to formal education. During Okinawa's colonial centuries, formal education was a very limited privilege reserved for the few descendants of a small class of Okinawan gentry; more advanced scholarly education, centered on Chinese language and Confucian philosophies, was only offered to a fraction of them. The vast majority of Okinawans, except those few royals and gentry, were illiterate, formally uneducated, and unable to read or write. Even later, when Okinawa was established as a Japanese prefecture, this situation hardly changed on the Ryukyus; when it did, in some administrative centers on the island, it changed very slowly and only in terms of primary education. Tokyo was opposed to open schools above the primary educational level in its new prefecture, and for the few new schools at that level "it was not easy to persuade parents to enroll their children and to keep them there … the peasants were reluctant to send children to school and did not trust the new government" (Kerr 2000, p. 413).

Consequently, an overwhelming majority of the two or three generations of sensei who taught on Okinawa before and after WWII were not formally educated; the vast majority of them did not even have the opportunity to finish what we in the West would call grade school or primary school. They embodied rather another holistic, non-academic martial arts sort of attainment, one developed and hardened through fighting experience, combined with their down-to-earth wisdom obtained through hardship, life-threatening experiences like natural disasters, economic meltdowns, devastating battles, as well as through their pain and suffering during the occupations of their homeland by foreign forces.

This educational situation was completely different for martial artists on mainland Japan. There, besides combat training with weapons and empty-handed, every *bushi* (member of the warrior class) received a scholastic and literary education. "At first … it was Buddhism and its teachings that attracted their allegiance; but later on, as Chinese became the classical language of the country, the Confucian Classics, the 'Four Books' and the 'Five Canons' took the place of the Sutras, and so continued to do until the advent of European ideas" (Norman 2012, p. 4f). Hence, the traditional Japanese warrior was academically educated, and this tradition continued to impact mainland Japan's understanding of martial arts as the "way of the warrior and the scholar" until modern times. At the end of the day, this understanding of martial arts contributed to the tendency of mainland Japanese *budo* practitioners and officials in the early 1900s to look down on Okinawan karateka, who they viewed as backward and unsophisticated, even though the latter embodied true karate-jutsu that far outperformed the karate-do of their Japanese cousins.

Shu Ha Ri is a scholarly concept that can best be understood at a philosophical level. It goes well beyond any intellectual conception a student would have encountered in the course of his primary education in prewar Okinawa as well as in the early postwar period, and it is doubtful that the few Okinawan sensei, who had the advantage of higher education in studying on mainland Japan or attending Japan's military academies, would find it useful to discuss philosophical and fine arts developmental principles at a time when the nation was engaged in several military campaigns. Hence, *Shu Ha Ri* would be easier and more broadly understood by mainland Japanese martial artists and perhaps by those Okinawan masters who moved to the mainland to study and to teach there. Again, this is not a question of the intellectual capacities of Okinawan sensei but rather a question of the decades-long lack of access to formal education for most. That was a socio-cultural given, which had the effect of keeping Okinawan karate-jutsu down to earth, prioritizing self-protection, and placing spiritual and intellectual components of the art second.

Initially, There Were No Styles in Classic Okinawan Karate-jutsu

Sensei Toyama Kanken pointed out in the 1930s that "a name is just a name; all styles are the same in principle, no matter under what name they are known" (Toyama 2007, p. 56). So, when considering *Shu Ha Ri* in its (modern) connotation of eventually breaking away from a style, it has to be underlined that Okinawa's legendary karate authorities did not promote a distinction of the art into styles but rather promoted its overarching purpose of forging individuals capable of both defense and offense. "There is no reason to have different styles of karate … Even with countless variations there is one and only one orthodox style of karate; much the same as there is only one 'style' of sumo wrestling and boxing" (ibid.). It was, however, not uncommon for early karateka to honor their masters' memories and to pay homage to their families by using their name to immortalize their teachings, a practice that labeled some branches growing out of their unifying trunk *Ti* and later karate-jutsu, which thereafter, later in history, were called styles.

Ti, the ancient Okinawan professional combat art, and later karate-jutsu, the Okinawan civilian self-protection art, used to be a complete and unified lethal art, secretly taught to selected individual students or to small groups as offensive and defensive moves with their *bunkai* and *oyo,* before it was summed up into those textbook-like kata as a new teaching method for larger groups and to make it easier for many students to remember the moves taught.

So, in classic Okinawan karate-jutsu the fundamental moves and techniques (*kihon, waza*) were first, then came kata. This concept of prioritizing *kihon* over kata is still practiced today in traditional Okinawan dojo, though some (maybe many) dojo there changed their teaching over time and now match the Japanese karatedo way of prioritizing kata over *kihon*.

We do not know with certainty what Okinawan karate-jutsu looked like before it was taught through kata. It would be awesome to have documents beyond the famous *Bubishi* showing or describing what Okinawan karate-jutsu may have looked like before kata were introduced. Unfortunately, not only because of the complete destruction of valuable documents during battles and natural disasters but due to the fact that the Ryukyuan people's language, *Uchinaguchi,* is not a written language but was only used orally, karate-jutsu teachings were conducted only verbally, in *Uchinaguchi,* and not through texts. Consequently, much of Okinawan karate history before the development of kata is speculative, and much of the information that has been shared about it is conjecture and not based on firsthand knowledge that comes from the Okinawans themselves.

It seems reasonable to assume that karate "styles" were introduced in the decade preceding WWII for a variety of reasons, a request for styles by mainland Japan's martial arts officials and the effort to not offend them politically being one of those. Hence, avoiding any possible reference to Chinese influences on Okinawan karate-jutsu at a time when those references were not welcome, Okinawan karate masters explained the kata demonstrated to visiting Japanese royalties, martial arts officials, or political dignitaries by simply naming the hometowns of the presenting karateka as their "styles." Now, suddenly, three Okinawan town-specific *Te*-styles were born (*Te* being the Japanese word for *Ti*). Demonstrations were assigned to karateka from the town of Shuri, and what they presented was now called *Shuri-Te*; presentations by karateka from Naha were called *Naha-Te*; and what those from Naha's port village Tomari showed was called *Tomari-Te*.

There were more than a few famous karate-jutsu masters practicing and teaching their art in other Okinawan towns as well, the most prominent of them being the city of Itoman, which is located to the south of the island and so far away from the governmental centers of Shuri and Naha that it could only be reached after a long and cumbersome journey. Supposedly because they practiced so far away from the central area the Japanese royals and dignitaries visited, Itoman masters were not appointed to perform there and were thus never named as the representatives of a town-specific style.

With Japan's growing impact on Okinawan karate-jutsu came its first attempts to codify and politicize the practice of the art, as shown, for instance, in the emerging use of the term *ryu* (connoting school or style), which on the mainland "provided a sense of familial identity and lineage pervaded among the various *kenjutsu* and *jujutsu ryu* that traced their genealogies to premodern feudal Japan" (Tan 2004, p. 181). In addition to the three town-specific terms for styles on Okinawa, two other style-related terms were mentioned, *Shorin Ryu* and *Shorei Ryu*. The former had presumably emerged from the *Te* styles that had developed around the districts of Shuri and Tomari, whereas the latter stemmed from the Naha locality. The moves in those two approaches are rooted in two related but separate ways to learn and perform karate-jutsu with somewhat different emphasis on moves, body conditioning, and calisthenics, but with similar purposes and intentions. There were efforts to assign specific kata to these two paths, for instance by Sensei Funakoshi Gichin (Funakoshi 1973, p. 8) and to call them styles, but, as Sensei Hokama Tetsuhiro, 10th Dan *Goju Ryu Kenshikai*, points out, a classification of kata into these two avenues of *Shorin* and *Shorei,* seems inconsistent (Hokama 2000, p. 69). Whereas the term *Shorin Ryu* is still widely used today for a tradition within the array of karate systems practiced in the Shuri area, the term *Shorei Ryu* became insignificant.

On the other hand, the three town-specific karate categories of *Shuri-Te*, *Naha-Te,* and *Tomari-Te* are still in use today to categorize practice and kata, and they entail *Shorin Ryu*, *Goju Ryu,* and *Uechi Ryu,* which became a couple of years later the three officially recognized umbrella karate styles in Okinawa until today, where more than a few Okinawan kata, however, are not practiced in just one of those three Okinawan styles but, sometimes with different names, in either two or in all three.

Organizationally speaking, all three official Okinawan karate styles are today united in Okinawa Dentou Karatedo Shinkokai OKDS, the local association for the Ryukyus' traditional empty-hand and *kobudo* arts (which use farming and fishing tools as weapons).[31]

Hence, once again, this time in terms of introducing styles into Okinawan karate-jutsu, a substantial change to the Okinawan self-protection art is the result of mainland Japan's martial arts officials' political power. Without going into the details of karate-jutsu's further

---

31 This association was founded in 2008, in opposition to the powerful karate associations of the mainland (Bayer 2021, pp. 21ff), thus simultaneously integrating and uniting three previously independent Okinawan organizations.

development into about a dozen sub-systems[32] within the three umbrella styles on Okinawa, it has to be mentioned that, in contrast to the situation on Okinawa, on mainland Japan an estimated two hundred wannabe karatedo styles were active in 1955,[33] the majority of which were taught by self-acclaimed instructors, many without sufficient qualifications (Kotek 2016, p. 61). Though some years later Japanese karatedo was condensed into four official umbrella styles of *Shotokan, Wado Ryu, Shito Ryu*, and a Japanese version of *Goju Ryu*, this development on the mainland contrasts with the one on Okinawa quite considerably. There, karate-jutsu continued to be understood as a united and holistic art, of course showing different nuances, but still united in its overall purpose of universal self-protection instead of breaking away into dozens of styles of self-development or into avenues for self-expression.

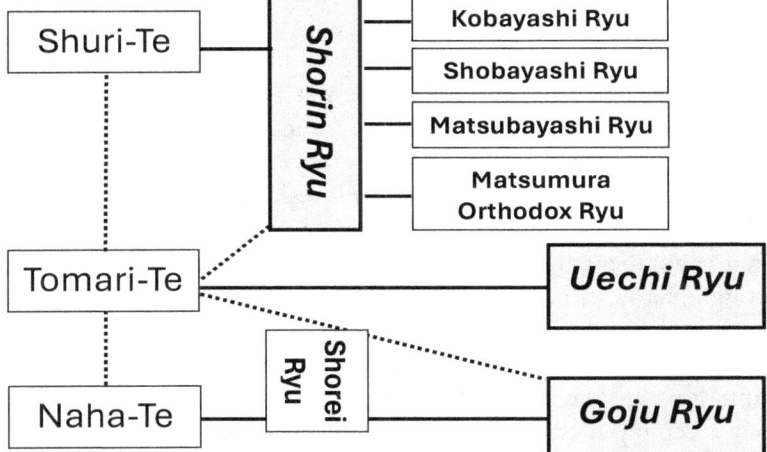

Image 6: Today's Three Non-Japanese Umbrella Karate Styles on Okinawa

---

32 The 2023 Day of Karate was the first time thirteen Okinawan style headmasters demonstrated essential kata; all the years before it was twelve headmasters.
33 The figure of two hundred karate styles in 1955 on mainland Japan comes from Masatoshi Nakayama Sensei, the famous Shotokan karate master who helped establish the Japan Karate Association (JKA).

Okinawans Did Usually Not "Break Away" from Their Sensei

Referring further to our subject of *Shu Ha Ri*, Okinawan *senpai* did usually not break away from their sensei; they rather observed their Confucian socio-cultural duty of passing on tradition based on their understanding of their art as self-protection. For instance, in the Okinawan system I train in, my sensei Noel Smith never broke away from his sensei, Nakazato Shugoro, who never left Sensei Chibana Chosin, who himself never left Sensei Itosu Anko. And in the holistic karatedo system I practice, which is related to the birthplace of karate through his Okinawan creator Toyama Kanken, Sensei Fujimoto never broke away from Sensei Ichikawa Nabuo and his predecessor Ichikawa Isao, who never left O'Sensei Toyama Kanken. They all continued the tradition and preserved the system.

Nevertheless, after WWII breaking away happened occasionally, but even then, it was an exception, not the rule. "When such a thing did happen, it caused major disruptions. When my teacher's older brother—Shimabuku Tatsuo—announced the creation of *Isshin-Ryu* karate-do in the 1950s, there were not only widespread chaotic ripples within the karate community on Okinawa, but within the Shimabuku family as well."[34] Such a development was very unusual for an Okinawan dojo, where, up to the 1970s, "students became members of something akin to a nuclear family—they were, generally speaking, too close, figuratively, to even consider 'breaking away'" (ibid.).

Hong Yi-Xiang, the founder of *Yizong Tangshoudao* mentioned earlier, uses another telling metaphor to illustrate how martial artists grow through phases without breaking with tradition: "Take a big tree as an example. New students with different talents and gifts are like the roots of a tree … however … everyone will converge within a single big tree trunk, learning the same art. At the same time, as one is simultaneously accepting these restraints, one directly progresses to the very top of the tree … From the convergence at the roots to the unification and promotion in the trunk, to the opening and dispersing of branches, flowering and fruiting, this is a complete learning process" (Hong 2023, p. 384). His son, Hong Ze-Han, adds to his father's conception of a school and transmission of the system as like a tree: "the tree produces fruits that eventually drop off the tree [*Ri*] and sprout, naturally

---

34　Email sent to me on 01/19/2024 by Sensei Hayes, 10th Dan *Shobayashi Ryu*, and long-time disciple of Sensei Shimabukuro Eizo.

creating a new tree."³⁵ Notably, this kind of development creates a new tree of the same kind; it does not create a new species. Thus, the tree metaphor visualizes the evolution within a unified martial art as maintaining its tradition without breaking away from it.

Perhaps because it seemed to imply that breaking away was an option, some Okinawan sensei were in fact not in favor of using *Shu Ha Ri* at all as their guiding principle, as witnessed by Sensei Bill Hayes, who told me that, his Okinawan Sensei Shimabukuro Eizo, "and a number of his colleagues, viewed the term somewhat negatively, from an organizational and cultural standpoint—especially with regard to its generally recognized Japanese origin and with respect to American service members and the potentially attendant troubling meaning of the third character '*Ri*'… My teacher's major concern focused on the ease with which some of his students felt they could 'break away' once they returned to the States—several thousand miles away from their sensei—and the adverse impact of doing so on the overall life and growth of his association and art as a whole. It became too simple for some to start new organizations (and 'new' systems in some cases), based on Dan grades and tournament records alone."³⁶

The last part of this statement refers to the unfortunate fact—well, unfortunate for the preservation of the art but, I suppose, financially beneficial for the actors—that many American service members who returned home after their rather short deployment considered themselves ready to create their own style, at least concoct their own interpretation of the "traditional karate" they learned while stationed on Okinawa for thirteen months as marines, two years as army soldiers, and somewhat longer as air force personnel. A minority visited their *honbu dojo* sporadically thereafter, and even fewer did so regularly. But many of these soldiers were combat experienced, all were equipped with a strong mindset, and many were eager to fight and to compete. This set them considerably apart from the majority of today's karateka, who intend to learn something about themselves while doing athletic kata dances, and, perhaps, want to learn a bit about self-defense too. Those US marines and other soldiers in the 1950s and 1960s were a different breed. They fought in wars, they saw and experienced violence, they had the mindset and competence needed to fight and to

---

35 Email sent to me by Chris Bates on 01/08/2024.
36 Email sent to me on 01/19/24.

compete, and they wanted to do just that. Many made karate their business after they returned home—they opened their own schools, and they held seminars and training camps—but something changed there with regard to karate principles. Suddenly, the number of attendants and the revenue generated in a school or at a camp became the most important criterion discussed amongst more than a few American sensei.

While they were building up and presenting their competence and authority not on years of continuous studies with an Okinawan master but on success in competitions, on financial success, and on mutual recognition by rewarding each other high dan ranks, it is easy to comprehend how *Shu Ha Ri* provided a welcome avenue for karateka sharing this kind of mindset. It allowed them to break away from the Okinawan, and also from Japanese, roots so that they could create their own personal interpretations, associations, and styles.

On Okinawa, you never stop following your sensei. Beyond physical fighting skills, you continue to learn about the unity of physical, mental, and spiritual development through high-level training, and you study the true conceptions, functions, and intentions of karate-jutsu as a universal path of self-protection. Success in competition and receiving high ranks from like-minded colleagues as legitimization for breaking away does not come close to those kinds of insights—and it generates different kinds of personalities. The contrast between those approachable, humble, open, and friendly Okinawan masters who went all the way in this sense, versus some aloof, self-absorbed, and attention-seeking masters we sometimes encounter in the West, gives a telling picture of this contradiction. In Sensei Michael Clarke's words: "Beyond an internal awareness that I felt when I was in the presence of a small number of *budoka*, I have never been able to quantify what it is ... Meeting someone for the first time who is considered a 'great master' of karate ... Shoshin Nagamine Sensei, Eiichi Miyazato Sensei, etc... . it felt different than meeting other karateka who were considered by many to also be 'great masters.' I've often wondered, when I did meet sensei who had something 'different' about them as human beings, was this '*Ri*' I was experiencing ... who knows?"[37]

Dr. James Hatch sums all this up perfectly with his rhetorical question, "Is the *Shu Ha Ri* as currently in vogue not simple wishful

---

37 Email to me dated 07/18/2023.

thinking by Westerners (especially those from heavily individualistic societies) who want to believe they are ready for *Ha* and *Ri* when they have not truly grasped *Shu?*"[38]

But, as elaborated on earlier, there is another connotation of *Shu Ha Ri* in place as well that explains development as maintaining traditions instead of breaking away from them. This interpretation views the three *Shu Ha Ri* phases as a path of becoming increasingly independent from forms and narrow guidance, a path that understands a karateka's development within the traditions and framework of a classic karate-jutsu system without breaking away from it or from a sensei. It seems like this is the conception that is in fact used in postwar karatedo on mainland Japan, where karateka with the officially recognized rank and title of *Shihan* are officially allowed to leave a sensei and to open their own school but carry on the tradition and continue to teach the same karate system. A comparable conception may be used on Okinawa too without being labeled as *Shu Ha Ri*, and certainly not as obviously in use as is the case with the official regulation on the mainland mentioned above. In Okinawa, it is a long-standing tradition for high Dan ranks who want to open their own school to ask their sensei for permission, which is usually not just given but encouraged. So, a proven and tested protocol for leaving one's sensei without creating conflict and based on mutual respect is woven into the way Okinawan masters teach right up to the present day: mimic the teacher, understand the intentions of the teachings, become the model, then become the teacher.

Okinawan Masters May Not Officially See Shu Ha Ri as a Relevant Principle but They Developed Students Beyond Their Own Teachings

The arguments and facts presented in the previous subchapters make the case that the concept of *Shu Ha Ri* was not an official concept in the Okinawan karate community. But the way the old masters taught their art based on the Okinawan principle of universal self-protection could be seen as indirectly and implicitly following a comparable development path. "Tales of early Okinawan *Ti* practitioners are replete with accounts of storied, accomplished teachers sending their students to fellow teachers to develop the student's abilities. This is just one

---

38 Email to me dated 09/30/2023.

expression of how the concept of *Ri* was encouraged in the Okinawan tradition" (Perry 2018, p. 304f). It is, in my opinion, proof as well that all of karate-jutsu was seen and understood as a unified art of self-protection, a unified art that develops karateka capable of defense and offence that goes beyond styles. "When the master felt that the student was mature, it was the master himself who urged him to go and take lessons at the dojo of another master who was a friend and colleague of his, because the other master had something different to teach and the first master felt that knowledge, that learning, was of vital importance to his student's growth. This approach existed until Funakoshi's time." (Ballardini 2022, #15, p. 11). I can confirm that this developmental approach continued to be practiced in the decades after WWII as well. Sensei Dr. Dan Smith of *Seibukan*, for instance, told me that his teacher, Sensei Shimabukuro Zenpo, sent him to Sensei Nakazato Shugoro to learn the latter's *Kobayashi Ryu* approach in the early 1970s. It could be, however, that such a journeyman opportunity, so to speak, was only offered to the very few Western students who lived on the island for a long time and that it, with the passage of time, became the exception rather than the rule.

Nevertheless, the initial understanding of karate-jutsu as the united "trunk of a tree" in Hong Yi-xiang's earlier tree metaphor, or Sensei Toyama Kanken's argument that there are no styles at all in karate as there are no styles in sumo wrestling or boxing (Toyama 2007, p. 56), support the interpretation of Okinawan karate-jutsu as an entity for self-defense where different masters' approaches are united into the one universal principle of physical and nonphysical self-protection.

Since then, however, monetary, economic, and political considerations became increasingly so important that "today this idea of *Ri* is difficult to imagine with associations vying to gain and retain followers" (Perry 2018, p. 305). It is, nonetheless, still maintained to a certain degree in Okinawan karate, though at a more rudimentary level. Two examples may explain this. First, when Sensei Nakazato Shugoro was asked to present karate at the 1996 Olympic Games in Atlanta,[39] he would have been free to demonstrate some kata from the *Shorin Ryu* system that he teaches and represents; instead, he created and then

---

[39] I personally find it quite interesting that the powerful karate associations on the mainland asked an Okinawan master to represent karate and did not name one of mainland Japan's masters.

demonstrated *Gorin* kata, i.e., a system-combining kata into which he merged moves and techniques from all three Okinawan karate-jutsu systems of *Shorin Ryu*, *Goju Ryu*, and *Uechi Ryu*, thus respecting and integrating all three local umbrella styles into an overarching Okinawan way of self-protection.

Second, when thousands of Okinawan karateka present their art on the Day of Karate every year, they all start by exercising one *Fukyu* kata out of those *Fukyu* kata that were created for the three Okinawan karate-jutsu systems, at least one in each system, to teach the specific basic techniques (*kihon*) of that system. In other words, alternating every year, a *Fukyu* kata of a major Okinawan karate system will serve as the opening kata for all karateka on Karate Day. In 2019, the last time Karate Day was celebrated in public before the nation's COVID-19 shutdown, I witnessed how a *Fukyu* kata of *Goju Ryu* was demonstrated simultaneously by all karateka. In 2023, after reopening the event to the public, my friend Peixu Wang and I were honored to participate as invited guests to demonstrate a *Fukyu* kata of *Shorin Ryu*, together with 2,000 fellow karateka (Bayer 2023b). Hence, still today, there is this "unifying something" in Okinawan karate, the reminiscence of the purpose of universal self-protection, that unites all three major Okinawan karate-jutsu systems under one overarching purpose.

Cultural Norms and Social Mechanisms in Japan Support Conformity and Not Breaking Away from Traditions

In contrast to Western societies, which are based on individualism and where different individuals or groups may pursue opposing interests that create conflicts, Confucianism tends to create a social order where differences harmonize into reciprocal obligations. Hence, in Japan's norm and core code, clashing desires and interests of the governing and governed, between children and parents, husband and wife, older and younger siblings, supervisor and subordinate, colleague and colleague, friend and friend, melt into a moral relation of reciprocal obligations that dissolve into one single mutually shared interest. That way, diverse interests may melt together as obligations balance each other. Giving is balanced by receiving, resulting in a state of social harmony, at least ideally.

Grounded in such Confucian values, Japan developed its prevalent, all-embracing culture of group conformity, including its norms of not questioning authority, of adhering to longstanding protocol, and of using an imitative social mechanism, the *senpai/kohai* system, to maintain those existing cultural structures. This social mechanism is not just closely related to, but is actually one expression of, the important Japanese norm of *giri*, which may be loosely translated as "duty and respect." Both concepts, the *senpai/kohai* system and the social norm of *giri* are explained in the following two sections.

Whereas those sections deal with the socio-cultural consequences of Japan's traditional thought systems in reference to our topic of *Shu Ha Ri*, the Excurse at the end, after the last chapter in this book, gives an account of Japan's cultural roots in Confucianism and Taoism for interested readers by summarizing the original philosophies themselves.

Senpai/Kohai, the Social Mechanism That Maintains Traditions

One social mechanism to implement and preserve long-standing traditions, practices, and routines in the social system of Japan is the *senpai-kohai* mechanism. It represents a mainly informal hierarchical interpersonal relationship of seniority in administrations, associations, clubs, businesses, schools, and many other social institutions and organizations, including families, neighborhoods, and social gatherings. The status of *senpai* seniority is based on time of membership in an organization, which sometimes—for instance, in families—correlates with age, and sometimes doesn't. The concept has its roots in Confucian teaching, but it has developed a distinguished Japanese style over the centuries and ultimately became a defining part of Japanese culture, impacting public and private social life and even some legislative norms.

The *senpai's* obligation is to care for the *kohai*, to give directions, to set the tone, to personify an ethical, professional, and behavioral benchmark. A *senpai's* authority is not questioned and provides comprehensive guidance and advice benefitting the organization as well as the *kohai*. The *kohai's* reciprocal obligation is to follow the *senpai*, to learn and to imitate, and to develop matching skills and abilities. This interpersonal social process leads to the assumed identity of individual goals between all parties involved, *senpai*, *kohai*, and group. It is understandable how such a social mechanism on the one hand perpetuates the status quo and on the other hand confers on seniority the status of unquestioned authority. *Senpai* seniority is, as mentioned, based on time of membership in an organization (which in a family of course translates into age) and thus on the amount of time it takes to become familiar with specific internal social conditions and specific knowledge and experience.

It seems quite plausible that the Japanese-specific concept of *amae*, which was introduced in Chapter 1, comes into play within the *senpai/kohai* system as well: the concept of juniors shaping relationships with formal and informal seniors in such a way that their actions and behavior earn the latter authority figure's goodwill. The Japanese psychoanalyst Doi Takeo analyses and explains how in this Japan-specific form of interpersonal relations the behavior of one person—here, of a *kohai*—attempts to induce an authority figure—here, a *senpai*—to take care of this person. It provides a general model of human relationships in the Japanese culture, especially when one person is senior to another (Doi 1973).

Knowing of *amae* helped me personally to understand why an Asian-born and socialized friend and fellow karateka of mine never independently arrives at a decision, not even with a suggestion, when someone senior is around, whether inside or outside of the dojo, and whether the decision be as insignificant as what restaurant to hit for lunch, or at what time to meet for a drink. His standard response is rather a "What do *you* want?" This evasiveness, which completely contradicts my friend's behavior in his other roles of successfully running his business and of teaching *kyu* ranks as a black belt, became over time somewhat annoying to my Western mind until it clicked for me, and I understood his interpretation of my role in relation to him. He obviously sees me as a *senpai*, since I had already trained in the dojo for several years before he joined. Now, with a better understanding of each other's cultural values, we can be both friends and fellow karateka, as well as *senpai/kohai*.

Relating this social mechanism to the *Shu Ha Ri* developmental principle, it seems unimaginable that *kohai*, who will actually remain in their junior status in relation to their *senpai* and sensei on a lifelong basis, would break away from the latter in the Japanese culture. This strongly supports the contrasting view, suggested earlier, of another—not just Okinawan, where *Shu Ha Ri* is not in use, but Japanese view too—interpretation of *Ri* than of breaking away; this latter interpretation seems to be based on Western individualism and neglects, even dishonors, one's teachers and traditions.

This thought is even more supported by *giri*, by the norm of conformity and group orientation in the Japanese culture.

Giri, the Norm of Conformity and Mutual Obligations

In its essence, *giri* (duty) encompasses a sense of obligation and social responsibility. It represents an underlying ethic in various aspects of Japanese life, as it influences relationships, decision-making, social expectations, and—last but not least in relation to our topic—the student-teacher relation in a learning environment. It represents not so much a morality that is enforced from above or by authorities but rather the voluntary realization of honor and dignity in one's motives and of mutual respect in human relations in general.

Thus, *giri* requires one to balance one's fulfillment of personal desires with fulfilling one's social obligations at the same time. In this regard, *giri* is closely related to Confucian teaching with the latter's emphasis on social order, hierarchy, stability, and responsibilities to each other. The conception of *giri* was a way to articulate the complex network individuals have, this web of mutual social responsibilities and obligations toward their families, neighbors, colleagues, communities, the society as a whole, and the nation.

Understanding that norm in the Japanese culture renders an interpretation of *Shu Ha Ri* based on Western individualism unimaginable. Such an interpretation of breaking away from a style, school, or teacher, and thereby indirectly neglecting, perhaps even dishonoring, one's traditions, is as unimaginable in the traditional Japanese culture as it is for the *senpai/kohai* relationship.

Bringing it all together, my answer to James Hatch's question, "Is *Ri* not ultimately about respect for the lesson (i.e., *giri*) which our teachers want for us?"[40] is "yes." Or in Sensei Noel Smith's words, which he spoke in more than one training session when addressing black belts, "I want you to find your own way beyond what I am teaching you. Add your individuality. Every sensei wants that. Just stay on the road. When you become independent, do not forget where you came from. Do not forget who taught you to become independent."

---

40 Email sent to me on 09/30/2023.

The Initial Shu Ha Ri Understanding in the Japanese Fine Arts

The previous look at some of Japan's cultural roots and the social mechanisms, norms, values, and ethics that grew from them strongly supports the contention that the interpretation of *Shu Ha Ri* as implying that a karateka's self-actualization is to be achieved through breaking away from a teacher—and finding one's own path that way—is highly unlikely to be embraced in Japan as well as in Okinawa particularly. How such an interpretation would contradict traditional Okinawan socio-cultural codes was laid out earlier—leaving aside the fact that the *Shu Ha Ri* concept itself was supposedly not in use there—but now we see a strong possibility that this view is not a familiar one on the mainland either. Thus, we need to seriously consider the possibility that this specific view of *Ri* (karateka achieve self-actualization through breaking away from a teacher) is based on Western individualism and may represent a misconception, or at least a specific reinterpretation, of the traditional *Shu Ha Ri* understanding in the Japanese fine arts.

The other question—why a Japanese fine arts principle was incorporated into karatedo—will be answered in the next chapter. At this point, the interpretation of the *Shu Ha Ri* developmental principle with three phases ("mimic the teacher—understand the intentions of the teachings—become a model, and then become a teacher") can best be explicated by looking at its original use in the Japanese fine arts. An example is the fine art of arranging flowers (*ikebana* or *kado*), a Japanese fine art that dates back to the first millennium of our common era. The term *kado* (the way of flowers) depicts this practice as a fine art that includes a way or path (*do*) to perfection with never ending dedication, and thus shows the very concept of continuous improvement characteristic of all Japanese fine arts. The following fable illuminates such an *ikebana* path, and it especially exhibits *Shu Ha Ri* in that the artist is to become independent under a sensei's guidance without breaking away as in the earlier-depicted Western (mis)understanding.[41]

---

41 Another example displaying *Shu Ha Ri* phases and competencies, an example referring to the fine art of calligraphy, can be found in Sensei Jason Perry's book about his father (Perry 2018, pp. 300–307).

Shu Ha Ri in the Art of Kado (Ikebana): How Jiro Became a Sensei
by Thomas E. Ward*

It seems there was a young man named Jiro, who wanted to become a flower arranger. He dreamt of the accolades he might receive and the glory of producing a beautiful arrangement, even though he wasn't sure what that might entail. One day he encountered a true *kado* master and sought his instruction. The master was reluctant; he was unsure Jiro had either the background, pedigree, or the temperament for such a life-long study. Finally, the master acquiesced, and plans were made for the first lesson.

Jiro arrived early for his first lesson. He was filled with excitement, yet a bit anxious not knowing what the lesson might teach him. Finally, the master appeared. He carried with him all the necessary items for a flower arrangement. He also brought with him his own arrangement. Jiro glanced at the arrangement and silently dismissed it as basic. Jiro thought that the master obviously was unaware of his latent talent, but he was happy to show him what a prodigy he would become in his first lesson.

The lesson was brief and surprisingly simple. The master simply said to Jiro, "Copy my work," and left him. Jiro, anxious to prove his mastery, quickly copied the master's arrangement and waited patiently for his return. As he waited Jiro noticed his arrangement didn't quite match the master's, but surely these small inconsistencies wouldn't matter. It was art for art's sake.

The master returned and took a cursory look at Jiro's copy. He showed Jiro one small deviation between his own piece and Jiro's copy then quickly disassembled Jiro's work with the simple admonition, "Do it again." Before those words were even silent in Jiro's ears, the master was gone. Jiro went straight to work, trying to reassemble his copy and to fix the small deviation the master noted. Try as he might, the master's work had a feeling about it that Jiro couldn't replicate. There was just something else that seemed natural and beautiful in the master's work. Even when he thought he had duplicated the deviation the master pointed out, Jiro noticed his work didn't seem the same. Over and over Jiro attempted the arrangement and over and over he failed.

Eventually, the master returned. He took a quick glance at Jiro's work, tore it apart, and said calmly, "Do it again." Jiro was crestfallen. How could he receive all the praises he had dreamt of if he couldn't do this basic arrangement? He wasn't sure what he was missing, and he seemed to be getting little help from the master. Perhaps it was the master's fault? Perhaps the master wasn't much of a teacher at all. If only Jiro could find a great true master, then he could advance. Unfortunately for Jiro, there was only one *kado* master anywhere near his home, so he would simply have to work around this obstacle.

He returned to the next session, determined to overcome even the poor teaching of his master. He made attempt after attempt to duplicate the arrangement only to fail every time. Finally the master entered. Jiro watched as the master replaced just one flower; he looked closely at his technique and discovered something in the way in which he placed the flower that he had overlooked before. After the master left, Jiro attempted to use the same technique the master had used. He felt awkward and unnatural, but the result was closer than he had ever seen. Proudly, Jiro waited for his master to return. The master, once again, tore Jiro's arrangement apart and said simply, "Do it again." This time, however, the master spent extra time with Jiro showing him techniques and principles of flower arranging that had eluded him before. Jiro counted these moments as precious and enjoyed the master's attention and instruction.

This type of monotonous repetitive training went on day after day. Almost without knowing it, as he was practicing arrangements, Jiro was honing basic techniques. Almost without realizing it, Jiro was learning. His arrangements were slowly, gradually becoming more and more like the master's, but something was still missing. When he sat his own arrangement side by side with the master's it was clear whose was whose. It was as if the master's arrangements were somehow speaking to the viewer, while Jiro's arrangements were simple copies.

One day, while working on an arrangement, Jiro took notice of the way the shadow of a stem highlighted the color of the leaves of the flowers. He noticed that if he turned the stalk, that shadow seemed to make things more natural. He also began to notice the smell of the flowers and the greenery, and how that smell brought his mind to a meadow. He sometimes found himself far away walking in nature and observing the flowers growing along the path. His mind would wander to these little flights of imagination and yet his body was still in a room placing flowers in a vase. Upon arriving to inspect his pupil's work, the master would point out little discrepancies in his work, small places where Jiro had missed a detail or changed the arrangement unintentionally. He was always brusque, but more often now he was reassuring in his words. Jiro took heart, but wondered if the master was just very picky on him for details that no one else would notice.

One day, while Jiro was busy assembling an arrangement and cleaning his workspace as the master insisted, Jiro realized he felt more at home working on flowers than he did anywhere else. He was surprised to discover that he felt more comfortable under the eye of his master than he did with his own family. While he sat, he realized that being at his workplace made him confident in who he was and what his purpose might be. He looked forward to the challenge of arranging flowers and even began to enjoy the master's criticism of his work. Jiro went on with his work with an almost imperceptible smile. Once again, the master entered, briefly looked at Jiro's work, and took it apart piece by piece only to leave with the familiar words, "Do it again."

One day, Jiro was working on a familiar arrangement. He noticed that, if he altered the master's work only slightly, a new picture emerged. It was the same vase, the same flowers, the same greenery, yet there was the very slightest of variations in the overall effect. That variation seemed to evoke a whole new emotion. Jiro liked the variation and decided to leave it. The master entered and walked around Jiro's creation. He circled the arrangement several times and for the first time ever in Jiro's acquaintance with him, the master smiled. It was a small quick smile that was gone in an instant. The master looked at the student and said, "Maybe you're starting to understand." With those words he took the arrangement apart piece by piece and said briefly but almost politely, "Do it again."

Years passed as Jiro continued to work on his technique and his understanding of flower arranging. Always under the watchful eye of the master, Jiro began to make no longer just copies of the master's work, but he developed works of his own. He became adept at matching colors of flowers, vases, and greenery. Jiro began to understand the relationships between his work and his other world, and how the flowers he placed symbolized more than just simple adornments or centerpieces.

One day, while walking home, Jiro realized that the way he felt while assembling arrangements was how he was feeling more and more in his everyday encounters with others. The calmness and centeredness he felt when approaching an arrangement was creeping through into every task that he undertook. While shopping for food, cleaning his home, or dealing with others, Jiro realized that his flower arranging was more than just an occupation or a hobby, but it was who he was. He realized then that the calmness and equanimity he felt working on flowers made his entire life better. The centeredness he knew from producing arrangements allowed him to approach any situation with that same feeling. He was no longer just comfortable while arranging flowers, he was comfortable living his life.

Many years later Jiro found himself with an apprentice who was trying to learn what he knew of flower arrangements. After what seemed like countless attempts by his apprentice to copy even the simplest of arrangements, Jiro saw himself dismantling his student's work piece by piece and saying to him that familiar phrase, "Do it again."

*Thomas E. Ward is a professionally trained educator and 7th Dan *Shorin Ryu Shorinkan*, who used to run one of the US dojo within O'Sensei Shugoro Nakazato's worldwide *Shorin Ryu Shorinkan* association in Sensei Chibana Chosin's *Kobayashi Ryu* version. He unknowingly planted one of the seeds for this book in 2018 when he held a lecture entitled "Applying Modern Educational Concepts to Teaching Traditional Karate" at a training camp I attended.

Chapter 3
Based on Claims of Cultural Superiority, Japan Converts Okinawan Karate-jutsu into Karatedo and Inserts Japanese Philosophies

Although being a colonial possession of Japan since the early 1600s, Japan's occupying Satsuma aristocrats insisted that Okinawa was a foreign and barbarian land and forbade Okinawans from wearing Japanese clothing or adopting Japanese names. "For the following centuries mainland Japanese viewed Okinawans as second-class citizens and found them to be so different from themselves that they would challenge any assertions of a common identity" (Hein/Seldon 2003, p. 9). Even after the Ryukyu's political status was changed from colony to prefecture, the Japanese did not see the Okinawans as on a level with the Japanese, whether politically, socially, or culturally. "Although nominally a prefecture, Okinawa retained a semi-colonial status for two decades after its annexation in 1879. Despite the fact that Okinawan people accepted Japanese rule with little resistance, which ultimately turned into active support for the assimilation policy, Japanese policy makers never lost their distrust of Okinawan people. Similarly, Japanese society did not fully embrace them, perceiving them as backward and inferior, and even questioning their Japanese-ness" (Meyer 2020, n.p.).

Beginning in the Meiji Period (1868–1912), Japan's government sought to assimilate Okinawa Prefecture politically, ideologically, and culturally. The official rationale was that Okinawans needed to abandon all those aspects of their culture that kept them in their "backward," inferior status and to embrace the superior culture of mainland Japan (Rabson 2012, p. 6), thus representing an attitude that would heavily impact karate's development in the following years. Because karate was such an important symbol in Okinawan subculture, Japanizing this local self-defense art became a priority, not just for militaristic purposes, but also for the purpose of creating some kind of cultural homogeneity across all of Japan.

Prewar Japan's Self-Proclaimed Cultural and Racial Superiority

What were the grounds for such an attitude of cultural and racial superiority, one might ask? Whereas the answer to this question is relatively well known for Nazi Germany—which was its ideology of an Aryan-Germanic super-race, and its quest to cure the world of racial mixtures that were supposed to be degenerative aberrations—the answer is not as well known for Japan. Hence, I will briefly summarize the findings of scientific research into where such beliefs about Japan's cultural and racial superiority may come from. Researchers have identified the following factors:

a) *The view of the Japanese race as unique and isolated,* having no known affinities with any other race. This view is promoted by most Japanese scholars, who classify Asian culture into the four areas of Islamic, Indian, Chinese, and—as a separate category on the same level as the other three—Japanese. In contrast, non-Japanese historians use three categories to classify Asian cultures, namely Islamic, Indian, and Chinese and see Japan not as a separate category but as a participant in Chinese civilization (Bellah 1965, p. 573).

b) *The ancient mythological belief that Japan was created by divine beings* and that the Japanese are their descendants and thus indirectly linked to and protected by divinity. The concept gained further stature when the Mongols attempted twice to invade Japan but were routed both times by the "divine" intervention of seasonal typhoons.

c) The widespread assumption that, because of its century-long isolation as an island state, *Japanese culture developed into something unique and different from all other cultures.*
d) The fact that the *Japanese language is supposed to have a unique grammatical structure, vocabulary, and connotations* that are unparalleled in other languages. This is actually not completely true and represents an interesting switch of cultural beliefs in prewar Japan, after, for centuries, the Chinese language and philosophy used to be seen as the very benchmark for academic education.
e) A *specific Japanese psychology*, where mutual interdependence of wishes and duties create a unique reciprocal form of human relationship in which boundaries between self and others become fluid, where on that account individualism cannot properly exist, and groupism will always prevail.

In summation, Japan has a history of self-acclaimed superiority that led to strong nationalism, which cumulated during and after the Meiji Restoration when Japan aimed to catch up with the Western powers. This superiority-based nationalism played a significant role in the project of unifying and strengthening the nation as well as in the justification of invading and occupying Pacific islands and large parts of Southeast Asia. The official ideology was that it was Japan's calling to a "righteous crusade" (Kerr 2018, p. 462) to (a) free this region from the influence of Western imperialists, from the barbarians who took advantage of Asia only to enrich themselves, and (b) to lift Southeast Asia's oppressed civilizations up to the standard of modern Japan through temporarily occupying and governing them, thereby reforming their systems, educating their populations, and releasing them into their new elevated self-regulated independence thereafter, closer to Japan's superior level. The Sino-Japanese War (1894–1895), the Russo-Japanese War (1904–1905), the country's participation in WWI, the preparation for the second war with China, its initiation in 1937, and Japan entering WWII by attacking Pearl Harbor in 1941—all represent facets thereof.

This political mindset of supremacy changed considerably after World War II and Japan's surrender, a change further hastened by deliberate attempts to politically distance the country from its prewar aggressive nationalism and militarism. So it is important to point out that Japan today is a diverse country with a wide range of attitudes and beliefs among its population. Though even in this time and age we find some publications indirectly supporting those prewar views of racial superiority,[42] it would be inaccurate to claim that this translates into a widespread attitude of supremacy. A better term than superiority, or even supremacy, for characterizing the attitude of many Japanese is that they are convinced of their own cultural "uniqueness." That very attitude of uniqueness, however, is still today widespread. At a time when Japan surprised the world with its economic success after WWII, this attitude came in handy and was broadly used to further fertilize the nation's endeavors. "It is almost an article of faith amongst Japanese that their culture is unique, not in the way that all cultures are unique, but somehow uniquely unique, ultimately different from all others ... Japanese are constantly persuaded of the specialness of their nation in schools and corporations and through the media and speeches by functionaries, whenever an opportunity arises for comparison with the outside world" (Van Wolferen 1990, p. 14).

Of course there are scientific studies debunking this component of Japanese self-understanding as unfounded—see, for instance *The Myth of Japanese Uniqueness* (Dale 2011)—but as always in history, politics, and life, it is not the facts as such that determine decisions, attitudes, or actions; all of these are rather determined by what people believe in, by their perceptions, and by their interpretation of facts that create their subjective "truth," which may or may not correspond to objective reality. An entire library can be filled with psychological studies proving that beliefs determine human behavior, not facts.

Based on Self-Acclaimed Cultural Supremacy, Japan Redefines Karate Since Its Okinawan Version Embodied "Backwardness" in the Eyes of the Japanese

In the prewar period, Japan's self-acclaimed cultural superiority was the official ideological basis of the nation's militaristic regime. Consequently, after karatedo was introduced to mainland Japan during that time, Japanese officials representing that kind of mindset insinuated the necessity to elevate the Okinawan self-protection system into the refined "art" of

---

42 For instance the one titled "Why the Japanese Are a Superior People—The Advantages of Using Both Sides of Your Brain" (De Mente 2009), which, though it is a layperson's psychological and neurophysiological speculation, was uncritically promoted in the newspaper *Japan Today* https://japantoday.com/category/features/why-the-japanese-are-superior-people.

karatedo that aligned with the cultural standards of the mainland. Okinawan karate in its original version "embodied backwardness" (Feldmann 2021, p. 196) to the Japanese eye, and it was considered socially acceptable only after its conversion into a Japanized form based on *budo*. Though such cultural arrogance was not only in place in relation to the Okinawans, this attitude of Japanese officials toward their distant, uneducated, and poor fellow citizens was especially significant for the development of Japanized karatedo in the prewar decades.

Martial arts did not exclusively start in Japan—there were indigenous traditions in China, Thailand, India, and in other Asian countries—but it is undisputed that" Japan was instrumental in giving the martial arts a recognizable form/shape as they were transformed from a local set of practices to a global aspect of physical culture" (Sanchez-Garcia 2018, p. 76). Sociological research shows how in this historic development the Japanese martial arts transformed—from their initial and authentic form as martial methods and techniques—into a philosophically based, character-building way of self-perfection, based on *budo*, which in the early 1900s carried strong militaristic undertones.

It was a time in which the military, in the name of the emperor, wielded the actual power and heavily impacted all aspects of life and of course the development of all *budo* arts. *Bu-do*, the martial (*bu*) way (*do*), was formed as a new philosophical synthesis of (1) *bu-jutsu*, the martial craft or skills (*jutsu*), which describes the Japanese martial disciplines in their original function as arts of war, with (2) *bushido*, the code of conduct and chivalry that guides warriors' conduct (Benesch 2011). Instead of solely focusing on the art of fighting, on the craft of combat and war (as *bu-jutsu* does), *budo* widens this thought system into a philosophy of the comprehensive development of body, mind, spirit, and character and as such denotes the process by which the study of *bu-jutsu* becomes a means of self-development, self-actualization, and developing that all-embracing warrior spirit the nation needed for its military campaigns.

At the time Sensei Funakoshi Gichin introduced karate to the mainland in 1922 (Funakoshi 1983 p. 85f), Japan's preparations for its second war with China had already started. "For every lack in physical equipment and manpower the military leaders attempted to compensate by developing fanatic spirit" (Kerr 2018, p. 461). For such a psychological and educational campaign, the nationwide spread of *budo* arts, including the Japanized version of Okinawan karate,[43] became the crucial vehicle. In this way Japan's officials killed two or even three birds with one stone, so to speak. First, they transformed the Okinawan self-perfection art into their Japanese *budo* art; second, they further encouraged cultural homogeneity between the Ryukyus and the mainland; and third, they supported the military's educational campaign.

Hence, all martial arts were integrated into one organization placed in charge of cultivating *budo* with its utilitarian emphasis on warrior spirit, i.e. the Dai Nippon Butoku-Kai, at that time an essentially nationalistic organization with close links to the emperor and to the military. The entire educational system was reformed to adopt *budo*, led by the Dai Nippon Butoku-Kai, in that way promoting Japan's nationalistic-militaristic enthusiasm and warrior spirit in all educational institutions, schools, and universities. As part of this educational campaign, karatedo, introduced by Sensei Funakoshi Gichin as a new and modified (Japanized) version of Okinawan *Shorin Ryu*, quickly spread across the nation and became, in conjunction with judo, the core educational vehicle for spreading *budo*.

Japan's Redefinition of Karate as Karatedo, a Path toward Self-Perfection, and Its Adoption as a National Cultural Symbol

In the 1930s Okinawan karate's Japanization was well and irrevocably underway, and the Okinawan subcultural symbol and cultural heritage of universal self-protection was, quasi-unopposed (Bayer 2023a, pp. 33ff), turned into a means of recreational self-perfection. Karate was overtaken by the mainland as a cultural symbol of Japan and soon evolved further, together with judo, into a symbol of Japan's national cultural identity. Today, "karate, together with judo, is commonly regarded as a Japanese national sport symbol" (Swennen 2006, p. 1). Mainland Japan claiming karate as a Japanese martial art—though correct in terms of the governmental sphere but incorrect in terms of subcultural heritage—denies proper credit to Okinawa, the region that

---

43 Some are of the opinion that Itosu Anko Sensei's support of this Japanization by bringing karate to the public and to create the foundation of modern training methods for physical education in the school system was not to promote Japan's military endeavors but was instead the only way to save and uphold an art that otherwise would have faded into historic oblivion (Swift 2019).

invented and cultivated the art; it questions subcultural identity and lacks acknowledgement of cultural traditions. Such a socio-cultural development has comparable developments in other cultures, e.g., mistaking the local festival of "Oktoberfest" for a national German cultural symbol instead of a regional subcultural one in the German state of Bavaria, as explained in my earlier books (Bayer 2021, pp. 78ff and Bayer 2023, p. 35).

As a result, the original Okinawan karate-jutsu concept of self-protection underwent the well-known and aptly described revisions that distinguish Japanese karatedo considerably from its Okinawan karate-jutsu origin; it matched karatedo to the way judo was structured and taught, and it generated the change of purpose from universal self-defense, protecting oneself and the lives of others, into self-perfection. The loss of ancient knowledge in this Japanization process—knowledge about *bunkai* in general and about nerve strikes and using pressure points in particular—was considerable.

Karatedo became a recreational and meditative activity that now prioritized spirituality, health, and character development over self-defense, where most of the lethal fighting applications were eliminated, and moves and kata now served another purpose than fighting "through a considering of the rich arsenal of movement available in the martial arts not as ways of harm, but potential ways of healing" (Jennings, n. d., p. 3).

The (mainland) Japanese Karate Association illustrates this transformation accurately: "True karate is based on *bushido*. In true karate, the body, mind, and spirit—the whole person—must be developed simultaneously … Our aims through karate training are the mental and physical well-being of our members and improving one's character … The result of true karate is natural, effortless action, and the confidence, humility, openness, and peace only possible through perfect unity of mind and body. This is the core teaching of Zen, the basis of *bushido*, and the basis of the JKA's karate philosophy" (JKA tab Philosophy, n.d.; n.p.). Though Japanese officials thus label their karatedo version as "true karate," it is not true karate in the sense of "genuine" (Okinawan) karate, as explained not only by me throughout this text and in my previous books, but as well by other karate authorities and martial arts researchers. It is neither genuine Okinawan karate in terms of purpose, applications, and authentic moves, nor in terms of philosophical undergirding.

As stated in the above quote, mainland Japan's meditative karatedo approach is linked to Zen-Buddhism. However, classic Okinawan karate-jutsu developed independently from religious belief systems, as already pointed out by Itosu Anko Sensei who, in his introductory words to his famous "Ten Articles" on karate training, unequivocally states that karate did not descend from Buddhism or Confucianism. Instead, "Zen in karate ... was 'imported' through 'Zen-inspired' swordsmanship. This happened in the process of 'budozation' of karate in the 1930s after its introduction on mainland Japan" (Herbert 2021, p. 18; my translation). Since then, the philosophical undergirding of Japanese karatedo contrasts with classic Okinawan karate-jutsu's philosophy and principles. Those newly integrated *budo*-specific, Zen- and health-related ideas became more important in today's Japanese karatedo than the art's original purpose of universal self-protection. The practice itself is turned into "applied philosophy" (Lloyd 2014) (specifically Japanese Buddhism and Zen-philosophy, I want to add because Okinawan karate-jutsu's principle of universal self-protection used to be, and still is, an applied philosophy as well).

Image 7: Pairs of Ferocious Warriors (Nio) Protect the Buddha

At many Buddhist temples in Japan and other east Asian countries, we find two wrathful warriors guarding its entrance and protecting the Buddha. The two statues pictured here are displayed at the National Museum of Asian Arts in Washington, DC.

Some Major Changes to the Okinawan Conception of Universal Self-Protection in Japanese Karatedo

One significant consequence of reinterpreting karate as a *budo* art of personality and character development, a consequence whose profound impact is not always fully understood, is the Japanese way of formalizing and standardizing a fine art and by prioritizing form over outcome. At first glance, this seems to be a good thing; after all, the art can now be broken down into elements, those elements can be connected to learning objectives, and the execution of elements can be compared to benchmarks. At second glance, however, this Japanese method of systematizing karate techniques completely and irreversibly changes the genuine Okinawan understanding and approach.

Firstly, Okinawan outcome-focused approaches impact profoundly how karate is performed in general. The task at hand in Okinawan karate-jutsu is determined by an attacker in a unique situation, where the defender is always behind the curve. In contrast, Japanese karatedo assumes a task is predetermined and that the way of carrying out this task is identified and can thus be standardized. That way, in Japanese karatedo, *Shu Ha Ri* can be applied to perfect the execution of predetermined tasks that are put together in kata whereas in Okinawan karate-jutsu the moves or techniques to spontaneously deal with a task at hand (*waza*) come first, and then kata come later as a way to sum up moves, which results in the "principle of never-changing kata" (Bayer 2021, pp. 124ff) whereas *waza* can be adjusted. In Japanese karatedo, the way of carrying out kata as a summation of predetermined tasks—i.e., the way of carrying out those identified tasks—may be altered as a result of individual interpretation.

Secondly, Japanization condensed the initial Okinawan karate-jutsu principle of universal self-protection into the narrower concept of defending primarily against physical threats, which excludes all those nonphysical components of Okinawan karate meant to maintain well-being at every level by avoiding health issues, egoism, laziness, bad habits, low morale, and a generally unhappy life (see "Protection from Physical and from Nonphysical Harm Is the Universal Principle of Okinawan Karate" in Chapter 1). Those Okinawan nonphysical components were replaced with Japanese *budo* and *bushido* values.

Thirdly, in Japanized karatedo, the continuous practice of techniques to fend off physical threats is based on—or at least connected to—a meditative, Zen-related way, which can open up karatedo to Japanese religious and esoteric influences that were not part of the Okinawan tradition. Karatedo training related to Zen Buddhism is now turned into a fine art of self-development, where the mind is exercised through the techniques, and the spirit is trained through meditative athletics, both, in combination, oriented toward attaining the ultimate goal of self-realization or self-actualization.

And finally, the systematization of karatedo separated and categorized Okinawan karate-jutsu's initial fluid physical responses to attacks into a series of separated techniques. In the words of the Japanese Karate Association, "Through years of training and experience, we've developed a unique and unrivalled system of *kihon* techniques. We put tremendous focus on the fundamentals, teaching scientifically and step-by-step the proper posture, balance, and angle of each specific movement" (JKA n.d., "Techniques" tag). That sounds reasonable, of course, but in reality this specific underlying Japanese philosophy—namely, the philosophy that prioritizes forms over effect in all Japanese fine arts—comes to life here and stands in contradiction to the Okinawan way of karate-jutsu that prioritizes effect over form. "Crystallizing" everything, says Sensei Bruno Ballardini, 7th Dan *Shorinji Ryu Zentokukai*, university professor and president of the Italian Association for the Research on Ancient Karate, "did quite a disservice to the art and caused immense cultural damage" (Ballardini in *Bugeisha* #12, 2022, p. 9). The fluidity of the art was lost and turned into a chain of stagnant techniques, where fluid positions as preparations for the application of technique turned into stances, concepts with multiple options for application turned into rigid techniques, and concepts of receiving and giving turned into simple blocks and counters.

Modern, Japanized *kumite* (one-on-one training exercises), in comparison to its original form on Okinawa, may further illustrate this difference. In classic karate-jutsu, one-on-one fight training was done in the form of *tegumi* (a term that actually is *kumi-te* with switched syllabi), as a two-person training method that linked basic techniques to defensive applications. This purpose of *kumite*, the one-on-one practice setting of classic Okinawan karate-jutsu, was Japanized as part of Japanizing the entire art; it was redefined from practicing fight-ending technique applications (outcome focused) to one-on-one *kihon waza* drills with a partner (form focused):

a) *Ippon kumite* is the practice of receiving one attack while simultaneously responding with an attack technique. The specific interpretation of this exercise in Okinawan karate-jutsu is to teach concepts of successfully receiving and interrupting attacks, while creating immediate damage, i.e., receiving in a way that prevents opponents from continuing their attack. Hence, *in Okinawan* karate-jutsu, Ippon kumite *is training how to immediately end a fight*. The widespread reinterpretation in today's karatedo practice, however, is the view of *Ippon kumite* as just another drill form to learn basic techniques, comparable to all the other drills used in modern training—here, just with the modification of executing those drills not on one's own, isolated, but in a two-partner-setting.

b) *Renzoku* or *yakusoku kumite* are prearranged, scenario-based partner drills. This training approach did not exist in Okinawa until the early 1970s and was as such not a part of classic Okinawan karate-jutsu training. Relying on *yakusoku kumite* to prepare oneself for self-defense will set karateka up for failure in a real fight, as using this training format exclusively carries the risk of developing a mindset formed by regulated sequences of moves and compliant training partners. Attacks in real life do not conform to predetermined scenarios; only attackers know in advance what they intend to do. Security professionals and as well as research both point out how thinking in "if-then" scenarios "promotes a view that self-defense skill development is linear. These foci ultimately will limit … effective skill development for practitioners who need to be able to cope with complex dynamics of real-world violence" (Staller et al. 2020, p. 157). The reality and logic of fighting are not predictable and require, using standard terms of Okinawan karate, "receiving" and immediately "giving" moves that are adequate to fit most of those nonlinear, complex situations, without the necessity of first reaching a decision about how to react. *Yakusoku kumite* practices alone cannot achieve their goal of sufficiently preparing a student for self-defense and are exclusively used in karatedo styles that reject sparring as a training method. In short, solely practicing *yakusoku kumite* is more closely related to scenario partner drills meant to facilitate learning basic techniques than to any sort of training that prepares one for actual self-defense.

c) *Jiyu kumite*, a third approach to *kumite* common today, is often also called free fighting. If trained in its genuine form, not limited by competition rules, it is indeed a way of practicing the art that comes close to the reality of a real-life fight, though it lacks an attacker's vicious determination and disregard for the victim's life. This last component cannot be sufficiently simulated in a dojo, and as mentioned, a realistic preparation for a fight through *jiyu kumite* cannot be achieved in the regulated competitive format of modern sports-karate, where all damaging, fight-ending techniques are ruled out.

In classic Okinawan karate-jutsu it was quite common for karateka to test their fighting skills in *jiyu kumite* settings, long before sports competitions were developed on mainland Japan. Students participated individually in consensual fights as challenge matches (*kakedameshi*). The aim of these matches was for them to find their own weaknesses to further work purposefully on their skills. The better fighter limited himself to the other person's level and neither of the fighters tried to deliberately injure the other (Swennen 2009, p. 30). Today, the fighters mostly wear protective gear. In the old days, the Okinawans did not, but there were and are guidelines for controlling your moves and not injuring your partner.

On the master level, challenge fights could be serious combat, in rare cases fought to the bitter end. In addition, many karateka tested their skills—or were forced to prove their skills—outside of the dojo, e.g., in nightlife scenarios or in encounters with criminals. Some examples of these kinds of fights involving Matsumura Sensei, Itosu Sensei, Asato Sensei, Kyan Sensei, and Motobu Sensei were orally handed down.

Many modern dojo no longer teach based on the logic and reality of a fight. The entire attitude of younger karate student generations toward violence and fighting has changed, and karatedo with its modern orientation toward self-perfection is aimed at different kinds of students than karate-jutsu was, with its classic concept of universal self-protection. The modification of Okinawan karate-jutsu into a recreational, health-oriented athletic activity created new karate versions with their own characteristics and that aim at consumers who are interested in physical exercises, in self-improvement, and in spiritual enlightenment rather than in achieving fighting capabilities.

One of the so-called "Original Seven" black belts sent to the USA by Nakazato Shugoro Sensei in the 1970s to promote Chiba Chosin's *Kobayashi Ryu* tradition through his *Shorin Ryu Shorinkan* there, Sensei Frank Hargrove, 9th Dan *Shorin Ryu Nakazato-Ha*, summarizes his experience with today's karateka in these terms: "Today, people don't want to get touched anymore. They don't want to fight anymore. Training changed completely compared to how we used to train; it became artificial ... and what they show today in tournaments, both kata and *kumite*, does not have any fighting application whatsoever."

Image 8: Sensei Frank Hargrove and Sensei Noel Smith in the Late 1970s

To be successful in a self-defense situation, one cannot assume how an attacker will move, in many cases not even if they'd telegraph their intention to physically attack. Most criminal attacks tend to involve close proximity, be of short duration, and require instantaneous responses. Since only the attackers know in advance when and how they will attack, preparing oneself through scenario training (*yakusoku kumite*) leads to practicing how to fail. A defender's mind needs to be open and not fixated on trained scenarios, and their receiving-giving response needs to be immediate, effective, and match a multitude of attacking scenarios. Responses can be controlling, immobilizing, or damaging but must all be fight-ending. Such instantaneous responses come from "mindless" *jiyu kumite* training, not from preoccupied minds only familiar with formalized *kumite* scenarios.

Not every sensei today can count on having his or her own realistic fighting experience to pass on. Experiencing the logic and reality of a fight is not just about receiving and giving, about the techniques and physical moves; there is more: you have to reckon with the huge psychological difference between a situation where you know with certainty that you could be badly hurt and even lose your life, and a training situation where you know with certainty that your partner does not intend to hurt you at all, at least not badly. Sensei who have experienced the emotional challenge of the reality of fighting will teach the mental and spiritual components of the art in ways other than how sensei without that experience will teach them; the latter will rather guide you on an athletic-meditative path toward self-perfection, self-expression, and self-actualization, or toward playing games in competitions.

Which one of these ways individual karateka might prefer to pursue depends on their personal goals and how they want to practice the art. Neither way is good or bad, or better or worse than another. The advantage for today's karateka is that they have almost unlimited options to choose from and can practice that version of karate that best fits what they want to achieve. They may prioritize universal self-protection and practice *bugei* karate-jutsu in a version as close to its classic Okinawan origin as possible; they may prioritize self-perfection and practice *budo* karatedo in a version as close to old-style Japanized karatedo as possible. They may prioritize physical exercise and competition and practice a modern sports-karate version—or they may combine those approaches, study diverse versions, study more than one style, and switch between versions.

Though I personally prefer a specific version of practicing the art, which I imagine shines through in the way I articulate my thoughts, it is not at all my intention to criticize any other karate version—leaving aside the fact that I myself continuously practice two versions of the art, Okinawan *Shorin Ryu* karate-jutsu and Japanese *Doshinkan* karatedo, and that I used to compete in tournaments, and still do every now and then.

The parallel existence of karate-jutsu, karatedo, and sports-karate and their evolution over the last decades are socio-cultural facts, so to speak, facts that are neither good nor bad but are just reality. Period. My intention is simply to characterize those versions, to point out their underlying purposes and philosophies, and to analyze their socio-cultural evolution. In this sense, this subchapter showed major changes to the Okinawan conception of universal self-protection as part of karate-jutsu's "*budozation*" into karatedo, i.e., during a process of formalizing, standardizing, and undergirding the art with Japanese philosophies on the mainland. The Japanization of Okinawan karate represents one consequence of Japan's self-acclaimed cultural superiority at that time, a political ideology that after WWII came to have a corresponding mindset of cultural specialness and that is still occurrent today in the mainland's assumed cultural uniqueness which regards itself as not just distinct from all other cultures of this world but as somewhat better than the traditional Okinawan subculture.

Formalizing Karatedo into a Japanese Fine Art Allows Shu Ha Ri to Be Incorporated into It and Gives Rise to the Development of Styles

An important consequence of the Japanese way of formalizing and standardizing an art is that now, after karatedo's systematization, the latter is turned into a fine art, and Japanese fine arts allow the insertion of specific philosophies and purposes for their disciples, namely those purposes of self-expression and self-articulation. Hence, as a fine art, karatedo opens itself up to individualized *Shu Ha Ri* interpretations and applications. As long as karate was not systematized, formalized, or standardized and was practiced as a fairly loose construct on Okinawa, a principle such as *Shu Ha Ri* would not apply to that "something" that could not be standardized, defined, and thus subjected to a concept like *Shu* (follow and practice the form), *Ha* (break the form), and *Ri* (become independent from the form). There was no "systematized form" in Okinawan karate-jutsu where the outcome justifies the means, so to speak, though there were, of course, outcome-focused kata and moves. But you need a defined form to follow a form, you need a defined form to break a form, and you need a defined form to become independent from it. Thus, a concept like *Shu* could not apply until the art was codified and systematized, which was only accomplished during the process of its Japanization, and which therefore could not have happened before Sensei Funakoshi Gichin introduced karate to mainland Japan in 1922.

But again, to avoid a possible misunderstanding here, I am not saying that classic training in Okinawa took place without forms, rules, or regulations. We do know that Okinawan masters created kata themselves, and that they imported kata from China at least three sensei generations before Sensei Funakoshi and mainland Japan opened karate training up to non-Okinawans. So of course there were forms on Okinawa; they were just not prioritized and were not practiced in a systemized way that would allow the definition of this local fighting method as a fine art in its Japanese sense. Long before kata, there were the moves and techniques, then came kata as an encyclopedia of moves to make it easier to remember them. Both approaches prioritized the outcome over the form, i.e., the effect over the way to get there. So, what I am saying is that on Okinawa, karate-jutsu training was based on the principle of universal self-protection, which followed those wider standards that prioritized the outcome over the form, and that did not meet the well-defined criteria of a Japanese fine art. This, among other things, was, one of those important reasons why Japanese martial arts officials frowned upon their Okinawan brethren's practice and saw them as inferior, embodying unrefined backwardness in comparison to the sophisticated and philosophically undergirded (fine) martial *budo* arts on the mainland.

That all changed after karate's Japanization with its redefinition, formalization, and systematization of Okinawan practice into the Japanese fine art of *budo* karatedo. Now, karatedo aligned with the philosophical concepts of other Japanese fine arts like *ikebana*, *sado*, calligraphy, etc., and it followed the evolutionary lines of Japanese *budo* arts like judo, aikido, kendo, and their underlying philosophies, one of those being the *Shu Ha Ri* developmental principle. We can distinguish how two conceptions of this *Shu Ha Ri* developmental principle are used in the Japanese *budo* arts and hence in the art of karatedo:

a) One explains a karateka's development within a karate-jutsu system. With that understanding we may see the three developmental phases like a crane's development (an analogy offered previously) from flapping its wings to leaving the nest to freely fly, swoop, dive, and evade without limitations. *Ri*-phase-transcending within

a karate-jutsu system would then mean to become independent from narrow guidance, to employ form and intent unconsciously and spontaneously to any circumstance—without attempting to transcend the system as such, or to break away from your sensei.
b) The other view understands the phase of *Ri* as breaking away from a style or from a sensei in order to create one's own version and, perhaps, one's own style.

In other words, the first concept understands *Shu Ha Ri* as perfecting one's capabilities within the tradition of a system while the second one understands mastery as an evolutionary process of breaking away from a style and its sensei up to the point of inventing a new style. The first conception seems philosophically closer to Confucian roots, the second one seems closer to Western individualism. The first conception, moreover, seems closer to its use in Okinawan karate-jutsu (if the *Shu Ha Ri* principle is actually used there occasionally), while the second one can be found on mainland Japan as individual versions but is especially used after WWII in the West for the creation of new styles.

Based on his own research, Professor Dr. Wolfgang Herbert confirms my view and sees both *Shu Ha Ri* interpretations as valid and in use; namely, the interpretation of the principle as a karateka's evolution within a style, as free development of the individual and his or her creative potential, as well as the other interpretation of the principle as breaking away from a system and its sensei in order to incorporate a new *ryuha* (school, style). And he further points out that the latter happened permanently on mainland Japan: at the end of the Edo Period (i.e., in the mid-1860s), there were around *seven hundred* styles practiced in the Japanese way of the sword.

But, again, that development of basically unlimited creation of new styles appeared in the *budo* art ken-*do* and not in the preceding martial art *kenjutsu*. It took place during the most stable and peaceful period in Japan's premodern history, in the Tokugawa (or Edo) Period, which was a more than two-hundred-year-long period of lasting peace without any widespread need for combat swordsmanship. This period contrasts with the centuries before, when *kenjutsu* was constantly needed and in hands-on use in local and in regional battles. Somewhat matching the development of *jiu-jutsu's* reinterpretation as judo, and, later, karate-jutsu's reinterpretation as karatedo, in the peaceful Edo Period, *kenjutsu* was changed and reinterpreted as what was later called kendo.

Real swords were substituted with wooden training gear, and practice became the kind of self-perfection we find in all Japanese *budo* arts which all were in peaceful times, when their martial application was no longer needed or wanted, changed from their *koryu bujutsu* (original warrior skills) into new fine arts of self-expression and self-actualization. "The martial arts began to develop this emphasis on personal spiritual growth in the sixteenth century, when the need for fighting skills in the Orient diminished" (Hyams 1979, p. 10).

A related reason for turning the combat version of Japanese swordsmanship into a Zen-based path of personal growth may have its root in the change of weaponry used in battle. The first firearms entered Japan in 1543 and, thereafter, they became the main instrument in waging war. Based on all these socio-cultural facts, "experts in the art of swordsmanship realized that, as *bushi*, their expertise in swordsmanship would have to be deployed in a different way for it to maintain social value" (Nakajima 2018, p. 73), and thus turned *kenjutsu* into kendo as an educational and character-building path of "sublimation of violence" (ibid. p. 71) where "martial artists also utilized the virtues of Confucianism to sugarcoat the techniques. Hence, today, discussions that claim some kind of moral or educational value in martial arts practice have been colored by Confucianism" (ibid. p. 64).

Whether the branching out into seven hundred kendo styles on mainland Japan at the beginning of the Meiji Period, and into two hundred styles of karatedo after WWII, was impacted by the nation's opening to the West, thus allowing Western approaches and thought systems entering and impacting the Japanese society and its culture, sounds plausible but remains speculation. What seems to be the case, though, is that this kind of breaking away from sensei and styles always took place when a martial art's combat or self-protection purpose was changed to self-perfection, when it moved away from its original purpose to become a formalized and systematized fine art that allows its practitioners to express themselves individually, as is the case for artists in other nonmartial fine arts. During the times of that kind of change, when the need for combat skills diminished, "the martial arts were transformed from a practical means of combat-to-the-death to spiritual educational training that emphasized the personal development of the participant" (ibid.). Related to our subject, such transformation represents the change from prioritizing the result when using a martial art—i.e., success in combat, which is essential on the battlefield or in civilian self-defense on the streets—to prioritizing the way or path of executing the art, i.e., perfecting or creating a form, which becomes an essential means of self-actualization. Self-perfection and self-expression now become the main purpose, and the style-unifying focus on the outcome (success in a fight) is superseded by the style-fragmenting new ways of execution.

Since a Japanese value like *giri* and a social mechanism like the *senpai/kohai* system maintain traditions, I suppose this modern and widespread notion of "breaking away" from a style and its sensei in karate is not a traditional Japanese approach but could indeed have been impacted by Western values of peculiarity and individualism, so that "due to the incomplete transmissions of the original intent of karate … this phrase [of *Shu Ha Ri*—my addition] has become the genesis for the creation of 'new' system after 'new' system" (Hayes 2018, p. 92).

That *Shu Ha Ri* was actually needed, or at least came in handy, for Japanese martial artists and their officials to legitimize the creation of their own new, non-Okinawan karate styles on the mainland, seems plausible but cannot be verified.

Chapter 4
The Application of a Truncated Shu Ha Ri Concept in Modern Management

Interestingly enough, when I did my internet research for *Shu Ha Ri* in early 2024, it was not martial arts sites that popped up at first; instead, the vast majority of listed sites were, and still are, business- and management-related ones; they deal with consulting and coaching concepts, and they aim at developing project management skills, leadership capabilities, and software engineering skills.

In the business world, it all began in the mid-1990s, when a publication about "performance zones" contextualized performance with socio-psychological findings and introduced the relation of risk-taking, fear, entitlement, and performance into management theory. Thereafter, the phrase of "leaving one's comfort zone," which is today firmly embedded in cultural discourse, became popular. The term "comfort zone" itself was coined by management thinker Judith Bardwick (1991), and it refers to a person's behavioral limits within emotional comfort zones in modern society. Within a specific zone, one operates in emotional safely without any need to take on much of a risk or face fear, though using only a reduced set of one's behavioral options to deliver steady but at most mediocre performance. To encourage employees and their managers to deliver higher performance would mean that they would have to leave their comfort zones and take risks, deal with emotional challenges, face and overcome their fears, and thereby advance into their individual learning and growth zones, as illustrated in image 9.

Though the model is not above critique—especially for its view of a limited fear zone instead of the need to overcome potential fear in all new challenges and specifically in the growth zone too—countless business consultants, coaches, and trainers jumped at the chance to use the model and came up with ideas for how to push managers, leaders, teams, and individuals out of their comfort zones and to get them to enter their learning and growth zones.

Image 9: Bardwick's Model of Comfort, Learning, and Growth Zones

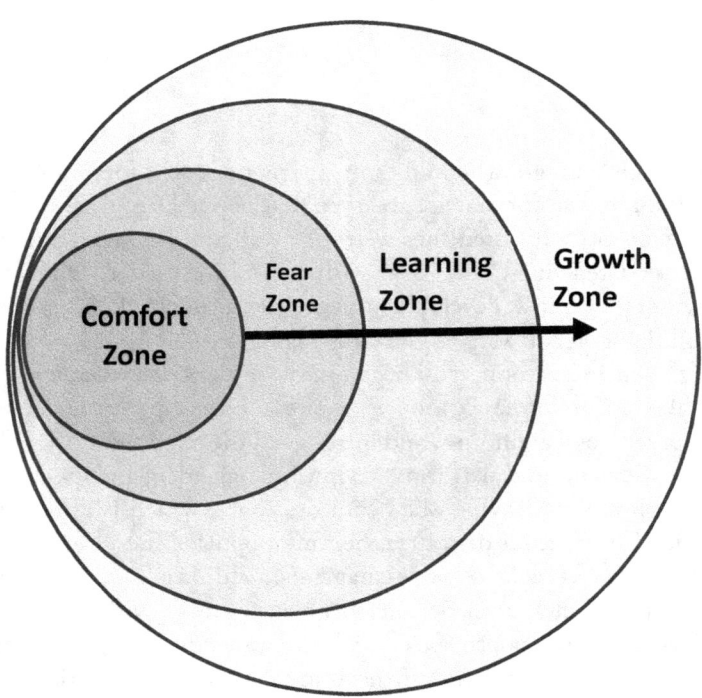

Business Consultants Discover Shu Ha Ri

It is not exactly clear which of those consultants first came up with the idea of connecting such Western developmental models with the Japanese developmental *Shu Ha Ri* principle. However, since those consultants who refer to *Shu Ha Ri* call it an ancient Japanese martial arts principle (which is incorrect) and not an ancient Japanese fine-arts principle (which it actually is), it seems safe to assume that such a connection was introduced by someone who either practices some kind of a modern Japanese *budo* art or at least knows a bit about it.

During my own professional career in the business world, I personally experienced the decades-long fascination with, and the success of, Japanese business philosophies, models, and strategies. Starting in the mid-1980s, certain concepts—like TQM (total quality management), which called for management to focus on enterprise-wide, consistent strategies instead of segmented approaches, and its *kaizen* (continuous improvement); JIT (just-in-time-production), which reduces warehousing cost, and its *kanban* (scheduling system); LM (lean management) that needs fewer supervisors and managers, and its *ikigai* (aligning activities with one's passions, values, and skills)—actually revolutionized traditional Western ways of management and production. Japan's rapid growth after WWII, in some markets almost miraculous, and its new economic significance with considerable influence on global trade, has not gone unnoticed. The Japanese way of achieving lasting success became the newly established and accepted benchmark for Western managers.

Hence, any addition of "something Japanese" to a management philosophy became a good idea, and the arguments of consultants and coaches about selling their services, even if they were just simple exercises in rhetoric, could never go too far when they included a Japanese concept. So it does not come as a surprise that over the last two decades new consulting schemes have popped up that rely on an almost mystical conception of *Shu Ha Ri*, which then spread amongst coaches and consultants like wildfire. The common denominator of related training and professional development is based on the smart concept of agile pedagogy (Höhne et.al. 2017) and the corresponding "agile mindset" that is needed to come up with creative solutions, and that—so goes the idea—can be achieved by growing through the phases of *Shu*, *Ha*, and *Ri*. Hence, in the business world the concept was understood as a pattern of development that led to greater agility.

Following its implementation into software development around 2001, we find *Shu Ha Ri* today embedded in all kinds of skill development, as image 10 shows. This list is a random overview illustrating *Shu Ha Ri's* widespread use; it is not a complete one, as my first unspecified internet searches came up with more than fifty business-related *Shu Ha Ri* entries.

Image 10: Examples* of Shu Ha Ri Use in the Business World

Management	Management 3.0 Leadership Training for Managers (n. d.). *Building learning organizations and Agile adoptions always starts with Shu Ha Ri.* https://management30.com/blog/shu-ha-ri-agile-leadership/.
Organizational Development	DiBartolomeo, Milvio (n. d.). The Shu Ha Ri mindset. https://www.praxisframework.org/en/resource-pages/dibartolomeo-shu-ha-ri..
Software Engineering	Fowler, Martin (2014). Shu Ha Ri. https://martinfowler.com/bliki/ShuHaRi.html. Gaurav, Menon (2020). Shu Ha Ri—Disciplined Learning and Problem Solving Approach. An Agile approach to learning and how to correlate it with design thinking. https://medium.com/agileinsider/shu-ha-ri-disciplined-learning-and-problem-solving-approach-91266593824b.
Coaching	Kudinov, Alex (2020). Shu-Ha-Ri of Professional Coaching. https://www.scrum.org/resources/blog/shu-ha-ri-professional-coaching. Goncalves, Louis (2023). Shu Ha Ri Agile A Fantastic Tool For Agile Coaches. https://agilemastery.org/en/blog/shu-ha-ri-agile-coaches.
Team Development & SCRUM **	Novack, Jason (2021). Shu Ha Ri: An agile adoption pattern. https://www.accenture.com/us-en/blogs/software-engineering-blog/shuhari-agile-adoption-pattern. Angel, Skip (n.d.) The Art of Shu Ha Ri in Scrum—Scrum from Student to Master. https://resources.scrumalliance.org/Article/art-shu-ha-ri-scrum.
Project Management	Ivan, F. (2015). Becoming Agile with Shuhari. United States: Project Management Institute. https://www.pmi.org/learning/library/becoming-agile-with-shuhari-9649.
* All sites retrieved on 02/13/2024	
** SCRUM is a term from the game of Rugby that denotes a cooperative play of several players.	

Misunderstandings of Shu Ha Ri in Business Applications

Unfortunately, however, hidden in *Shu Ha Ri* business applications are some essential shortcomings that reveal how the concept is gravely misunderstood there. A first misconception manifested itself when *Shu Ha Ri* was linked to Bardwick's model of developmental zones, which was introduced at the beginning of this chapter. *Shu* was allied with the comfort zone, *Ha* with the learning zone, and *Ri* with the growth zone, thus representing an attribution that reveals gross misunderstanding, not only because all three phases of the Japanese *Shu Ha Ri* concept are learning phases but because learning in the *Shu* phase has nothing to do with mediocracy or entitlement, nor with comfort, i.e., with emotional safety, as it is understood in the zones model. Hence, I will not even try to link the conceptions in image 9 above.

Evidently, misunderstandings like that do not reduce the magical attraction of being "something Japanese" for businesses, and *Shu Ha Ri* still seems to hold out the hope that this new Japanese solution will overcome the limitations of Western thought and lead businesses to new success. Today, you can even get a certification in *Shu Ha Ri* based project management from a distinguished organization, a certification that nicely sums up common misunderstandings when it is advertised as an "adopted *Shu Ha Ri* strategy for this certification program. *Shu Ha Ri* is an old martial arts concept that represents the stages of someone's learning."[44] Here are those misconceptions listed in their order of being mentioned in the quote:

a) *Shu Ha Ri is not a strategy or method that can simply be adopted*; it is a way of seeing things, a developmental principle that is inherent in the development of every skill, and its activation requires in the Western culture a "cultural translation" and assimilation of Asian values that form behavior there and which are usually not included in Western socialization.
b) *Shu Ha Ri is not an old "martial arts concept"*; it is an old fine-arts concept that was later used in the martial arts too but only after the latter's conversion from *koryu bujutsu* into their fine arts versions of *budo* some decades ago with all its related formalizing, systematizing, and standardizing.
c) *Shu Ha Ri does not represent "stages" of learning*; it represents connected, circular phases of increasing independence from forms; those phases exist in parallel, simultaneously, and holistically. Practitioners are never completely finished with a previous phase after entering the next one.

The widespread use of *Shu Ha Ri* in the business world today is understandable though, as it indeed relates to agility and creativity, and the idea of connecting this Japanese concept with skill growth in that area is of course a very good one. It just has to be is used in accordance with its true meaning and not just as a rhetorical phrase to boost consultants' sales of their services.

---

44 https://www.pmi.org/disciplined-agile/our-philosophy. Retrieved 01/15/2024.

The advantage of introducing any new process in the business world is that the consequences of the related change can be shown as measurable business outcomes. For instance, a new process for leading teams needs to either save money or to save time, which is money too, as they correctly say, in order to replace the previous one. The outcome of the implementation of the new concepts can be measured and shown in terms of hard facts; hence, it seems plausible to assume that using *Shu Ha Ri* in the business world indeed improves how things are done; otherwise, the concept would not have survived in this world of utilitarian pragmatism.

Mastery, however, as pursued by implementing *Shu Ha Ri*, is more than simple perfection, and that *Shu Ha Ri* the way it is used by utilitarian business pragmatists—in a truncated version of its initial philosophy—would achieve that kind of mastery remains questionable.

Chapter 5
Misinterpretations of Shu Ha Ri May Allow Excuses for Laxity

Since karate-jutsu and its predecessors have been practiced for centuries, it seems safe to assume that there is not one single move that would not have been used by somebody else during all that time, because in delving into the mechanics of the human body, we realize that there's a finite number of ways to move the arms and legs. And since the biomechanical and physiological basis of human movement did not change much over those centuries, supposedly nothing is really new in karate-jutsu, except those things that have been forgotten over the course of its transformation into a *budo* art, or those things that were deliberately not taught to non-Okinawans. But seemingly forgotten aspects of the art may be still included in those classic moves and authentic kata some of us practice today, and serious efforts were and still are undertaken to discover those inclusions. Important research in that sense is conducted and published on the internet as well as in print.

In other words, the claim by some karateka to having invented or created something completely new is most certainly invalid. Their creations were only new to them until they figured something out that somebody else had already figured out a long time ago. What to some extent may distinguish karate styles are the principles of application and their significance in various fighting scenarios. Beyond those differences, as our earlier tree metaphor illustrated, the main branches of the tree, i.e., the karate-jutsu umbrella styles, are united in its trunk of universal self-protection. And eventually, as mentioned earlier as well, every karate-jutsu system with its purpose of universal self-protection is—at least in my opinion— comparable to a language. It is complete as it is and based on identical fundamentals, just as all languages are based on comparable linguistic fundamentals.

A karate-jutsu system does not need new components to be added by individual karateka, just like a language does not need new grammars added by individual speakers. Instead, all different languages can be used alike, as they are, to perfectly articulate the same thing; and if indeed some new words or phrases are added, that would not change the language as it is. To continue the language metaphor, there is enough room for countless masterly poets to use the same language without the need to create a new language to compose their masterpieces. Likewise, all karate-jutsu systems can be successfully used, as they are, for self-protection, and there is enough room for countless masters within the same system without the need to break away from it. To continue the language metaphor even further, modern changes to a language usually do not increase its complexity and rather alter the nature of its proper use, as the introduction of slang phrases and grammar simplifications into American English shows. That introduction is a regrettable development that matches the simplification of karate-jutsu's complexity through karate-do inventions and creations.

The view presented here, however, will not be shared by everyone, but perhaps we can all find some common ground by looking at the seemingly undisputable fact that everything completely changes for karate when money becomes involved—when, for instance, sensei need to earn a living through teaching the art and must therefore separate themselves from competitors. Comparably, that is the case as well when karate associations need to recruit paying members to be able to disburse their leaders and hire full-time officials.

Karatedo's Commercialization May Encourage Interpretations of Shu Ha Ri as Breaking Away

If karate is a sensei's only source of income in a competitive market, it becomes essential for that sensei to find a market niche, a USP (unique selling point), that allows him to point out how his own karate approach, in addition to the general benefits of practicing the art, is different, perhaps even superior, to the one offered by competitors. This is no different than for every other small business, and in the USA an entire industry of marketing consultants has developed over the last two decades around this market necessity with promises of supporting a dojo in doing exactly this in a better way.

Whereas in the old days on Okinawa cultivating karate-jutsu and earning a living were separate areas of a sensei's life, in modern times we see these areas often melted together. It was Sensei Chibana Chosin who pointed out the necessity of a separation between earning money and teaching karate, because "a martial person must make their living away from the martial arts so as not to contaminate it through the influence of 'making money' in order to 'make a living.' This is the Okinawan way" (quote in Chambers et al. 2020, p. 45). Hence, in and before Sensei Chibana's time, the related fee was more a donation to a sensei (instead of payment for a service) to help sustain the operation of the dojo and show gratitude to the teacher. In those days, sensei were not competing in a market, so there was no "market choice" for a student to pick a teacher or a dojo out of an array of alternatives like today, where you have in every American town several dozen kickboxing, MMA, karate (in at least two or three style variations), tai chi, taekwondo, jiu-jitsu, and other "martial arts studios," all competing with each other in need for customers.

In my last book, I analyzed how postwar Japanese karatedo was deliberately turned into a worldwide business whose development followed the same track of industrialization as other arts and crafts, and how the initial "manufacturing process" of karate-jutsu, as an individually created scarce good for selected recipients on Okinawa, was, within fifty years, transformed into the production of a mass product delivered to as many customers as possible worldwide. That way, the supplier-driven market structure of Okinawan masters transferring their art to a limited number of selected followers turned into a demand-driven market in search of a recreational product (Bayer 2023a, pp. 136ff). To secure business and to distinguish products in such a competitive context, sensei need to find their market niche. They need to find a way to change their dojo from being just one non-distinguishable offer, among many others in a "fully competitive" market. To put it in economics terms, the goal is to create a situation of "monopolistic competition" where comparable but not identical products are sold, and where sensei can differentiate their products from others and thus set themselves apart from the competition.

For that purpose, breaking away from a style and creating one's own style looks like a successful business strategy because now this new style stands out as something special and becomes a clearly distinguishable offer in the karate market. Furthermore, from a business perspective, *Shu Ha Ri* comes in handy as a way to legitimize such breaking away and create one's own thing when it can be rationalized as surpassing one's teacher's capabilities. And, in difficult economic times (every small business owner will understand my doubt that there actually are, or ever will be, easy ones), it is only a short and tempting step from the need to make a living off a karate business to becoming lenient in promoting students in order to get and keep paying customers.

This is the economic or market-related reason for breaking away from a sensei or a style, but another reason can be found for such a development as well, and that is an ego-related one. Whereas breaking away and creating one's own style may even be supported and legitimized in Western cultures by their values of individualism and self-actualization, a pitfall is hidden in the possibility that karate practice may become no longer about self-protection, self-perfection, or a way of life through preserving a cultural heritage at all, but may instead be used to support some practitioners' egos and their neurotic tendency toward narcissism.

Individualism May Turn into Self-Absorption and Narcissism if Shu Ha Ri Is Interpreted as Breaking Away

In karate, as in other martial arts, the role of the ego is a complex and often debated topic. In relation to the subject of this text, ego is an important factor that impacts how *Shu Ha Ri* is interpreted by individual karateka, as it can both positively and negatively influence a practitioner's journey and performance. In a positive sense, a certain level of ego contributes to confidence, which is an individual's belief in one's own capacity to act in the ways necessary to reach specific goals (Bandura 1997) and which is essential for effective performance in all areas of life. An ego marked by self-confidence can furthermore help individuals bounce back from setbacks and failures and provides the mental fortitude needed to persevere through challenges, to overcome obstacles, and to continue to progress. But it also holds true for everything in life that "too much of a good thing" can turn something positive into a negative.

Thus, "too much ego" leads to arrogance, causing practitioners to become complacent in their training or to disregard instructions. This mindset is often accompanied by emotional reactions (especially, it seems, when opportunities for improvement are being pointed out) like anger, frustration, or defensiveness. This hinders growth and prevents karateka from realistically recognizing where they are at in their journey through *Shu Ha Ri*.

In its negative aspect, ego interferes particularly with humility, that is, with one of the most important virtues in the martial arts. Through humility and reduced egoism practitioners may learn that they themselves are their own biggest enemy in the "fight within" and that giving your best every time will only get you so far. The path never ends and getting feedback about how to improve is necessary. This path of continuous learning and maintaining a "beginner's mindset" no matter what they think they've achieved is not shared by those personalities who are overly focused on their own accomplishments, and, consequently, not only neglect opportunities for learning and self-improvement but may overestimate their own skills in general.

Such personalities are, in psychological terms, overcompensating (Dreikurs 1981, pp. 30ff) and drifting into narcissism, vanity, and a never-ending urge to be the center of attention and importance in the eyes of others (Rattner 1983, pp. 57ff). Those narcissistic personalities cannot tolerate equals close to them without hidden or open conflicts. Hidden conflicts may articulate themselves emotionally, for instance, as envy and jealousy, or even as wrath and hate. The resulting open conflicts may manifest themselves in their mildest form as avoidance or actively as degrading the one who threatens the narcissist's self-proclaimed social status by means of patronizing, badmouthing, or scheming—just to name the most common patterns.

Practitioners must strive to cultivate a balanced ego that promotes humility, respect, and self-awareness. There is a good chance that karate training, in its quasi therapeutic function of forming healthy personalities, helps to overcome over-compensatory pre-neurotic tendencies, but that requires the persistence to attend training for a long period of time and a certain degree of what psychologists call frustration tolerance (Kretch et al. 1969, pp. 757f). Karateka are permanently fighting their above-mentioned "fight within," and feedback, mirroring, and guidance constantly confront them with their own shortcomings and opportunities for improvement. This is too much to deal with for some, especially in an age of widespread spoiled attitudes, with little persistence or resilience. Consequently, more than a few karateka give up and don't continue their training anymore after having reached the edge of their comfort zone. Others, although continuing to work hard physically, may choose to remain in their emotional comfort zone, which in this context means avoiding the risk that comes with realizing their shortcomings and hence rising above their ego, which may well be (hopefully mildly) neurotic. They rather avoid the person (sensei or senpai) and the environment that place before them challenges to improve and prefer instead to break away.

This goes both ways, of course: both students and sensei may have too much ego—and both conditions may lead to inappropriate interpretations of *Shu Ha Ri* as well as to avoidance, i.e., to breaking away. But "there is no break with tradition, unless the master's or student's ego get in the way," as Sensei Bill Hayes pointed out to me on the phone. And finally, too much ego is of course not restricted to the world of karate and martial arts; it is found everywhere, and especially in our Western societies that are based on extreme individualism, where the necessity to express oneself is spoon-fed from the cradle to the grave and may in our art easily result in those kinds of exaggeration and misinterpretations of *Shu Ha Ri*.

Generally speaking, with this kind of ego-centered personality, karateka may feel that they are more advanced than they really are, overestimating the breadth and depth of their knowledge, and self-defining their skills as excelling those of their teachers; they may, thus, break away to form their own organization. Interestingly enough, narcissistic personalities, like all other character traits, attract what one may call "supplementary" personalities; i.e., they attract personalities that show the opposite traits, which serves the purpose and desire of the opposite personality both ways: narcissists "tend to attract people who desire to be infantilized," as Dr. James Hatch put it;[45] they attract admirers and unquestioning followers rather than strong and independent personalities.

---

45 Email sent to me on 10/04/2023.

Transcending in the Ri-Phase and Some Possible Misinterpretations

(with contributions by Thomas E. Ward)

For something to be seen as a "misinterpretation," there has to be something else that is correct for it to be compared to. This thought brings us back to our earlier considerations about a yardstick that measures the adequacy of karate-move interpretations. The benefit of a reasonable yardstick, or at least of a meaningful benchmark, cannot be overestimated. As long as we only deal with individual interpretations of forms, those personal interpretations are all "individually correct" and thus not measurable in an objective way. Everything along the lines of "what this move means to me is …" is a personal interpretation in the first place. It is only measurable with a neutral yardstick when it is applied to defend oneself or others in a real fight, and when it is pressure tested or examined by combat experienced sensei and other karateka in the dojo, who are qualified to judge based on their own realistic fighting experience. If it seems to be a personal interpretation that is irrelevant to realistic fighting, it still can be an instrument of self-expression, called a "fantasy move" below.

Shu Ha Ri May Be Used to Sell Fantasy Moves as Genuine Techniques

Hence, a down-to-earth way of measuring the adequacy of moves for protecting others and oneself can be best applied to karate's *jutsu* version. Such a yardstick gives transparency when the *Shu Ha Ri* concept is not used as a route to better self-protection but as an excuse for laxity and to avoid digging deeper into the system to discover hidden fighting applications. That way, when karateka come up with personal interpretations of moves and start selling those individual fantasies as genuine techniques, they may claim personal *Shu Ha Ri* transcending as their easy-way-out argument that veils their cluelessness about logic and reality of a fight, and allows them to promote their "personal insight" instead. And indeed, in the karate market we often find that there is little real-world fighting experience in some new systems the "proven effectiveness" of which was established only in the safety of the gym. In spite of that shortcoming, inadequate "new lethal street techniques" are advertised as "reality-based martial arts" and pop up in social media quite often. Their doubtful effectiveness is subject of much debate among martial artists as they are only based on the vivid imagination of their creator, with only limited benefit in the real world. Those kinds of "new martial systems" come and go; most enjoy a brief and heavily marketed period of popularity, and then quickly fade into oblivion.

In training camps, the logic and reality of real combat as a yardstick makes it pretty easy to measure the adequacy of any new moves and techniques presented by evaluating whether they work if their application is countered with *kihon* fundamentals. We have examples of instructors promoting their newly created fancy joint manipulations that left lower belts in awe but did not work when higher belts locked their joints. We have examples of instructors demonstrating how to free oneself from choke holds by massaging an opponents' wrists, which actually succeeded for controlled "partner-exercise holds" but did not work when an opponent fully focused on merciless clawing, which would be what an attacker in real life would do. We have examples of instructors teaching to absorb an attack in a way that turns the attacker to the defender's inside, which looked nice and elegant but did not work because that move left the latter completely open for a quick and devastating strike to his lower body, and so on and so forth.

Shu Ha Ri May Be Used to Reinvent the Wheel

The *Shu Ha Ri* principle may not just be (mis-)used to legitimate the above and other fantasy moves but also for reinventing the wheel, so to speak, when karateka leave a dojo as brown belts or as low black belts, open up their own school, train on their own, and now discover "new" insights, which are only new to them and which they would have gained anyway if they'd stayed. Developing into one's *Ri* phase cannot be achieved within the few years it takes to grow into the brown belt rank, nor within the roughly one decade of growing into low black belt competency; it takes much longer, actually several decades, of continuous guided practice. Most karateka who continuously trained for a decade are still learning in the *Shu* phase. In aikido, where *Shu Ha Ri* is more commonly talked about, it is suggested that *Shu* (keep the form) be practiced while growing through *kyu* ranks; *Ha* (break the form) should be practiced in *Shodan* (1st Dan) and *Nidan* (2nd Dan) ranks; while *Ri* (transcend the form) may start at *Sandan* (3rd Dan) and *Yondan* (4th Dan) qualification (Kessler n. d.). That means, in terms of time, approximately up to ten years for the *Shu* phase, up to fifteen years for the phase of *Ha*, and more than twenty years to enter *Ri* (Davis 2014). These suggested timelines apply to the rigorous; daily, many-hours-long practice of the past in Japan and may today in the West still be too short because the majority of karateka training here these days do not come close to spending as much time training in the dojo as their Asian counterparts used to.

"New" Karate Styles May Not Be New at All but Rediscovered Traditional Techniques

However, on a positive note, at times it may seem appropriate for individual teachers to transcend the style they originally trained in, perhaps for decades, and enhance their own system of fighting. There are those examples of karateka whose dedication to their style were duly noted and recognized, and who then seek instruction in some different but related approach to gain a new perspective. Students of a primarily striking style may study grappling and how to use open hands rather than clenched fists, and the resulting fusion of these two or three perspectives allows them to develop an enlarged view of their original style.

The question here, however, remains: is this actually the creation of a "new style"? Maybe not, because in more than a few cases it is simply a matter of the rediscovering of original and traditional applications within their system, which were deliberately no longer taught beginning in the early 1900s after karate's initially secret practice was opened up to the public and therefore disarmed by changing it from a fighting art into a recreational activity. A prominent example of such a development is the loss of the knowledge of grappling and limb-manipulation *(tuite)*, which is still deliberately not taught to non-Okinawans even today. Another example is the alteration of offensive open-hand moves into clenched-fist moves, where the latter are associated with defensive instead of offensive applications. *Nukite* (spear-hand) thrusts to the eyes while simultaneously receiving an attack with the same arm was initially a technique for quickly ending a fight, though one that, obviously, cannot be taught to children. In a combat kata like *Passai*, where spear-hand moves were extensively used (Nagamine 1976, p. 195), Sensei Itosu Anko replaced many of the open-hand *nukite* with closed fists when introducing karate into the physical education program of kids, and *Passai* "was changed from a combat kata to a physical education kata based on defensive movements" (Ballardini, *Bugeisha* issue #11, p.

8f). The bottom line here is that what may be seen as the creation of a new style by some is nothing new but only the correct interpretation of the original style.

In terms of creating a new style, a practitioner may train with more than one teacher in similar arts and, after years of study, combine all the perspectives offered by his different instructors. The "new" style or system developed would reflect all the included styles and the resulting creation would be more than their sum. While we commend and appreciate the insights gained on such a path, we have to raise questions here again about whether such an evolution actually gives birth to a new style instead of having merely dug out neglected components of the original one, and why such a supposedly new style has to be created at all. Initially, there was *Ti* and civilian karate-jutsu on Okinawa and nothing but Ti and civilian karate-jutsu; everything was, to appeal once again to our metaphor in Chapter 1, integrated into the "trunk of the tree" as the shared purpose of universal protection, and, as expressed by the title of Chapter 2, "There Were No Styles in Classic Okinawan Karate-jutsu." And when we look at the modern development of branching out into what is called by many the "transcending and creation of a new style," at the end of the day this is nothing but the creation of a new organization or association that is still based on the initial system with one or the other modification. In other words, it is, again, not the creation of a new style, but the creation of a new branch within the initial style to establish a USP (unique selling position) in the karate market—a new branch that often creates a copyrighted and trademark-protected new business.

This is not a negative assessment of such developments, it is just an analysis of the reality of modern karate because the answer to the above question about why a new style should be created at all apparently lies in the combination of those components that were presented earlier in this text: first, the conversion of Okinawan *bugei* karate-jutsu into the Japanese fine art of *budo* karatedo changes the original universal principle of protecting oneself and others into one of self-perfection, which now allows the promotion of self-expression and self-actualization. Against the backdrop of that redefined purpose, the request for styles came from mainland Japan to Okinawa as part of the "*budozation*" of Okinawan karate and gave rise to a fusion of factors: (1) the commercialization of karate that put pressure on sensei to find their market niche; (2) the rise of values like individualism in the postwar period that often devolved into self-absorption and egotism; and, as a result of both factors, (3) modern reinterpretations of the *Shu Ha Ri* principle now made to support these commercial and individualistic aims instead of aligning with *Shu Ha Ri's* role of guiding karateka in their quest for individual independence within a given karate system. A specific example of the application of *Shu Ha Ri* interpreted as breaking away, baffling in its brazenness and audacity, is the case of a brown belt who left his sensei, opened his own school, separated each Naihanchi kata into two new kata and *Passai* kata into three new kata, and started to teach a curriculum of nine (sub-)kata as a new traditional karate system.

If *Shu Ha Ri* were given its original interpretation as guiding karateka along the path to individual independence within a given karate system, the number of karate styles would remain limited, perhaps even decrease, and the art may even return to its roots as an art centered on self-protection. If, however, *Shu Ha Ri* is interpreted in it modern sense, the number of karate styles and karate associations will further increase, and the art will continue to split into competing branches.

How to Find Instructors in the Kind of Karate One Wants to Learn

In all cases, what makes karatekas' quests for independence successful or unsuccessful is the validity of their instructors and of the art they teach. This is true for students of both modern and traditional karate, whether karate-jutsu, karatedo, or sports-karate. To evaluate their validity, we ask, Where did this teacher train? Who issued his or her credentials and what parts of his or her curriculum were taught by what other sensei? Is the credentialing association connected to Okinawan or Japanese organizations? Does my sensei, when teaching black belts, explicitly promote and coach those students toward independence instead of chaining them to his or her own level of insight? Is teaching karate my sensei's only source of income, and are there enough serious students in the dojo to secure reasonable revenue? What are the ranking and testing criteria in this dojo?

If students are in search of training for sports-karate, additional clarifying questions can be answered relatively easy by seeing how successful a teacher and his or her students have been in competition. If karateka are in search of true self-defense capabilities, however, answers to clarifying questions are not as easily found. But those questions might include, Has my sensei seen combat? Did my sensei serve in the military, police, or in any other profession in the security field? Is my sensei's instruction based on the logic and reality of fighting? The last question is important because every time a defender has to think instead of successfully reacting at near-reflex speed, it takes too long to prevent a second or third damaging blow.

But in case all questions are answered satisfactory, karateka are well-advised to never break away from that sensei, and to never break away from the art he or she teaches. Instead, their best path would be (1) to mimic this teacher for years, (2) to understand the intentions behind the techniques they are taught for many more years, (3) to strive to become a model in the dojo for even more years, and then, after decades, (4) to become a teacher themselves.

Chapter 6
Parallels and Differences Between Shu Ha Ri and Western Educational Concepts and Their Probable Mutual Supplementation

(with contributions by Thomas E. Ward)

Sensei Tom Ward, 7th Dan *Shorin Ryu Shorinkan*, recalls how he, "as a martial arts instructor with a few years of experience under my black belt, became obsessed with how I could convey more advanced meanings, philosophies, and skill sets to my students. As a formally trained educator I assessed how I was being taught and what influences that had on me and my understanding of my art, and I learned about the Japanese martial arts concept of learning referred to as *Shu Ha Ri*. As a well-disciplined student I often felt caught in this description of development. When should one move from stage to stage? At what point can a student be considered to have enough understanding to accept other teachings? When is a student sufficiently grown so that he is not considered impertinent for doing such things? As I have grown, developed, and matured, I've found that those questions are only answered 'from within' [meaning by personal insights within a karateka's mind]." The notion of finding answers "within" is something of a double-edged sword in that answers may indeed be found within, but there is no measure for assessing the truth and reliability of what are essentially subjective claims. They may reflect reality in many cases but may turn out to be wishful thinking in others as well.

Therefore, it might be wise to cross-check students' personal interpretations against the insights of experienced karateka, who possess the real-life combat skills needed to distinguish effective self-defense techniques from mere illusions. The neutral yardstick (or at least benchmark) for measuring the soundness of subjective interpretations mentioned earlier was "measurable self-defense impact" (see the subsection "The Yardsticks That Measure the Adequacy of Interpretations of Karate Moves" in Chapter 1). Again, and as pointed out several times in this text, such a validation of individual moves is only possible when karate is interpreted in its *bugei* version of karate-jutsu, as an art for universal self-protection with unpretentious fighting moves. It is quite different for the fine art of karatedo, where individual karateka may express themselves through changing the purpose of moves from self-defense to self-articulation. The latter are personal moves and as such not really measurable (except, perhaps, in terms of how well they match a sensei's personal ideas), whereas moves are only measurable neutrally, in an objective way, when they are being used as means of self-protection, as in karate-jutsu.

To be in a better position to answer related questions, let us first look a bit closer at the educational methods we use in Western education to develop skills, and let us then compare these Western approaches to the Japanese developmental principle *Shu Ha Ri*.

Modern Western Educational Concepts

Acquiring a skill or learning a subject is more complex than one may first imagine, and the process of teaching a skill or a subject is even more complex. Teachers have to decide what they are trying to achieve with their students (objectives), how they are going to accomplish that objective (methodology), and then find a way of measuring to what degree they've been successful (assessment). Such an instructional design is often surprisingly difficult to put into words.

In the mid-1950s, the educational psychologist Benjamin S. Bloom chaired a committee of educators that did just that. It created a classification of six learning levels to help instructors to better structure their teaching and their students' learning (Bloom 1984). The six levels of the resulting "Bloom's Taxonomy" are:

- Remember   (recognizing and recalling)
- Understand   (interpret, exemplify, classify, summarize, infer, compare, explain)
- Apply   (execute and implement according to learned information)
- Analyze   (differentiate, organize, and attribute)
- Evaluate   (check and critique)
- Create   (generate, plan, and produce)

While the specific stages and the terminology differ between this Western model and *Shu Ha Ri*, the two approaches share the idea of progressing from a beginner's level to a more advanced and independent stage. Both frameworks emphasize the importance of building a solid foundation, of developing skills and understanding through practice, and of eventually reaching a stage where creativity and innovation can thrive.

Though the committee of educators developed approaches for all three learning areas of the cognitive, the affective, and the psychomotor, Bloom's Taxonomy is mostly used in the cognitive area, about which Bloom himself wrote and edited the first handbook out of a series of three. The model didn't fare as well, however, in the effort to describe emotional learning or the acquisition of physical skills. Other educational concepts were formulated to fill that gap and better cover psychomotor learning areas, which apparently are more difficult to put into words for Western educators than cognitive approaches.

To acquire physical skills, students first imitate actions shown to them. After repeated attempts and practice, they may move to a level of skill where they can manipulate those movements. Here they can change the rhythm of the movement, change the speed of performance, or make other adjustments to the moves without much substantial change or fundamentally altering them. As the process continues, students begin to increase the precision of their movement. In basketball, their shots become more accurate with practice. In skiing, they're able to make more acute turns. In martial arts, their movements are crisper and are performed with more focus and power. Eventually, the student begins to articulate the movements, perhaps using movements in new ways or using already-learned movements in different applications. The movements gradually become natural and are done without conscious awareness. Not only are they performed almost automatically, but they are also applied in novel situations without forethought.

Such a process is reflected, for instance, in the five stages of the "Dreyfus Model of Skill Acquisition" that was formulated about twenty-five years after Bloom's Taxonomy (Dreyfus 1980). This model for developing professional skills introduces the five stages of

- Novice   (needs instruction)
- Beginner   (needs only direction)
- Competent   (can be expected to work independently)
- Proficient   (will routinely deliver above expectations)
- Expert   (will define new standards and go beyond existing interpretations)

The Dreyfus model seems to work well for acquiring professional, work-related skills and for executing a craft; but when it comes to its application in the martial arts—though it includes some psychological adaptions and affective developments—it does not adequately integrate the underlying martial values, the mental and spiritual components, and the progress that consists in acquiring skills through repeating phases rather than by moving up a hierarchy of levels, which all are essential to the process of skill development.

In spite of several other educational concepts having been formulated in recent years (e.g., SOLO taxonomy,[46] Dee Fink's taxonomy,[47] Edys Quellmalz's framework of thinking skills[48]), Bloom's trailblazing cognitive-centered taxonomy remains by far the most used model in the US, in Europe, and in other Western educational systems.

---

46 https://www.johnbiggs.com.au/academic/solo-taxonomy/.
47 https://clt.champlain.edu/kb/dee-finks-taxonomy-of-significant-learning/#:~:text=Fink%20proposes%20that%20significant%20learning%20occurs%20when%20six,significant%20the%20learning%20will%20be%20for%20the%20student.
48 Quellmalz, Edys et.al. (1995). "School Based Reform: Lessons from a National Study; a Guide for School Reform Teams" (Reprint: University of Michigan Library).

Limitations and Advantages of Western Concepts Compared to Shu Ha Ri

It's notable that both Western models and *Shu Ha Ri* describe a process of individual development that focuses on internalization of knowledge and skills that eventually allow creativity. However, each of the Western models is hierarchical in nature and postulates that ultimately, at the end of your development, you are an expert and you are basically done. The Japanese concept of *Shu Ha Ri* is different in this sense. Recall that it was represented as a circle of revolving phases in image 1 rather than as a ladder or a stairway up to a final level of mastery. In Sensei Lara Chamberlain's words, "When *Ri* is achieved, the *Ri* phase is finished, and [a karateka] enters into a new dimension of *Shu*."[49] This view adds another dimension to our initial circle in image 1 and transforms it into something like a spiral, as shown in image 10 and as elaborated further in the next chapter.

In contrast, Western educational models are linear, imply segmented thinking, and neglect the fact that all stages may present themselves repeatedly at various times, even simultaneously, and at all skill levels, during a student's development. Even though with the addition of affective and psychomotor components, some Western models came closer to answering the question of what it actually means to have learned a martial arts subject, this neither changes the hierarchical character of all those models, nor their segmented thinking, nor the neglect of mental and spiritual components that are seen as equally important in the martial arts as physical self-defense.

One of the core advantages of Western educational philosophies, however, is their systematic approach toward learning and their sophisticated measurement of to what degree the subject matter taught is actually learned by students. This is achieved by the stringent and logical application of three related concepts to ensure successful learning: *learning objectives, instructional methodology,* and *assessment* of what has been learned. Western educational models furthermore incorporate the indisputable fact that there are different types of learner, such as visual, auditory, verbal, logical, kinesthetic, social, and solitary, who all need to be addressed differently through differing instructional methods so that each ends up with comparable skills.

---

49 Message sent to me on 03/15/2024.

Image 11: Implicit Philosophies in Japanese Shu Ha Ri and in Western Educational Concepts

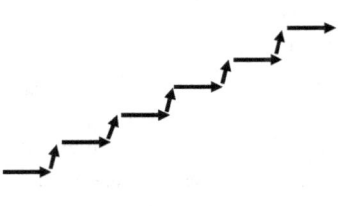

Shu Ha Ri:
Spiral of Recurring Circles

Bloom's Taxonomy:
Steps and Levels

While the Japanese concept of *Shu Ha Ri* as a holistic understanding of development as a spiral and not as a hierarchical stairway is quite different from Western models, it parallels those models in its attempt to categorize learning phases. Those categories open our eyes to a better understanding of the teaching practices our instructors use and help us choose the sensei we want to train with, namely those who help their students achieve independence.

Some teachers we encounter may teach predominantly in lower areas of Bloom's taxonomy and may rarely venture out of their comfort zone into other objectives or methods of instruction. They may, for instance, prefer to teach at the remember-understand-apply levels of Bloom's taxonomy without progressing into analyzing, evaluating, or creating. The majority of the time in such a dojo will be spent on practicing kata, move by move, in a counted setting (a student's move is the reaction to the sensei's "count," which is either a number or a word like "hop"), to master the movements exactly as presented. Such a training confined up to Bloom's third level of "apply" of course may prepare a student to individually attain into the higher levels by themselves. These higher levels cannot be taught as directly as the lower ones; they are rather to be individually discovered along a guided path and thus need a different, less instructor-centered teaching approach that includes coaching, enabling, and encouraging.

Essential questions are whether instructors may (unconsciously) prevent their students from reaching those higher levels and to instead limit their growth to their own comfort zone; whether they are equipped to use teaching methods other than the most common one of instructor-centered direct teaching; and whether instructors are thereby equipped to support their students to find their independence beyond such limitations.

The example of our own sensei may illustrate simultaneous employment of more than one teaching principle. Sensei Noel Smith's traditional, no-nonsense training approach surely reflects his priority of passing along the proper performance of kata and kihon just as they were taught to him by O'Sensei Nakazato Shugoro, who often spoke about the importance of never changing the kata movements. Sensei Nakazato's principle was reflected in his teaching methodology, which Sensei Smith continues. On the other hand, Sensei Smith teaches not just kata performance, but *bunkai* and *oyo*, and he sets tasks in his rank tests, starting at medium *kyu* rank testing, that clearly demand a student's analysis, evaluation, and creativity. Those assignments require imagining up to twenty different self-defense situations and creating individual receiving-giving sequences with one, two, and three counters, breaking free from holds, and sweep-throw counters—and all that with ever increasing and more sophisticated use of higher kata and kihon application the higher the rank to be examined for. All sequences are to be developed and shaped in detail by the student, who needs to define and visualize all kinds of attack situations, to think them through step by step, and to come up with proper receiving and giving moves—all that without any help from higher ranks, who may only serve as a "dummy," i.e., as a training partner. In this role they act per the student's instructions in partner exercises when asked for assistance by the ones who are going to be tested and who need to figure out their own personal sequences. In addition, when teaching black belt ranks, Sensei Smith encourages his students constantly, in his words, to "put your individuality" into moves and into kata execution—in keeping with the essence of a move and kata.

Sensei Eddie Bethea, 8th Dan *Shorin Ryu Shorinkan*, like Sensei Smith one of Nakazato Shugoro's "Original Seven" black belts sent to the USA to promote *Shorin Ryu Shorinkan* there, had studied karate along with Sensei Noel Smith at O'Sensei Nakazato's dojo in the 1970s and has set up his own curriculum when he began teaching after returning from his deployments to Asia. That curriculum included what he learned from O'Sensei Nakazato, as well as things he learned outside the Okinawan *honbu dojo*. Based on this combined experience, he developed self-defense techniques and training routines, codified them, and taught them as requirements for rank promotions. Though most of these techniques were found by Sensei Bethea's through his detailed study of kata, that approach was not specifically taught by his teacher in Okinawa.

The point here is that both senior US *Kobayashi Ryu* authorities accepted the curriculum they were given on Okinawa and that this rigid, and at a first glance "limited," training prepared them to move on, to become independent, and to incorporate other ways to use the forms in fighting scenarios. They created new applications and found ways of expressing one's individuality within a given karate-jutsu system. That way they "broke with traditions" in their *Ri* phase, which seems to have become common practice for more than a few modern karateka after returning home from Japan, but neither of these two senior US *Kobayashi Ryu* authorities ever left O'Sensei Nakazato, broke away from him, or broke away from their *Shorin Ryu Shorinkan* system to create their own new style. On the contrary, until O'Sensei Nakazato's passing 2016, they went each year at least once, and for many of those years more than twice, to Okinawa to train with their sensei at his *Shorin Ryu Shorinkan honbu dojo*. After his death, they continued this routine with his son, Sensei Nakazato Minoru, the new president of his father's organization.

The ability of a sensei to guide a student's *Shu Ha Ri* development depends on whether sensei themselves have left their own comfort zone at some point during their own growth and that they have developed teaching strategies beyond the direct instruction and corrections needed in their students' *Shu* phase—indirect teaching strategies to be used for another kind of instruction in their students' Ha phase. And, in our time and age, it helps a lot if sensei know something about educational philosophy and base their instruction on pedagogical principles that have proven themselves in the course of developing students into independence.

Bottom line: the first two categories of Bloom's taxonomy (remember, understand) seem close to the *Shu* phase of the Japanese developmental principle and can be taught directly and closely; the third and fourth (apply, analyze) and fifth and sixth categories (evaluate, create) seem close to the *Ha* and *Ri* phases and have to be individually discovered. The teacher's role changes in these phases from directly teaching, mirroring, and correcting to encouraging, enabling, coaching, and mentoring. After having reached *Ri*, however, the phase of evaluation and creation, the development then circles into a new phase of Shu of a higher order, where all the initial teaching and learning characteristics of that phase now come to life again.

It may well be that Asian educational concepts and Western ones can complete each other (see "Integrating a Well-Established Western Educational Concept with Established Asian Teaching Methods May Help Retain Students in Traditional Karate" in Chapter 8). The Asian concept allows a holistic understanding of developments, and the Western one supplements that with its systematic approach of ensuring that all necessary learning areas are targeted, ensuring that appropriate instructional methods are used to bring all subjects deliberately and systematically across, that all different learner styles are properly addressed, and, finally, that educational effectiveness is sufficiently measured and is not just a product of an instructor's wishful thinking.

Chapter 7

The Essence of Shu Ha Ri Is Its Coexisting "Trinity of Phases"

We now know that *Shu Ha Ri* is a universal principle that describes any type of personal growth and that it is a developmental principle in the Japanese fine arts that can be applied to many disciplines. The principle describes the natural order in which mastery can be attained, given enough effort, time, analysis, and deliberate practice. We furthermore know that it is more adequately understood as a revolving synthesis of coexisting developmental phases instead of those levels or stages we predominantly associate with Western educational concepts. And, finally, we know that the growth process is never finished.

Trinity of Coexisting Phases in Shu Ha Ri Instead of Skill Levels

After integrating the insights of Sensei Jason Perry, Sensei Lara Chamberlain, Shifu Hong Yi-Xiang, and Shifu Hong Ze-Han into my own research and conclusions, I hold that the *Shu phase of dependence* characterizes a karateka's learning as abiding by the rules; they learn the forms, the "surface appearances" or external mechanics of what they are doing, and they remember those forms bit by bit through repetition. When the time comes, they have internalized all forms and rules and can abide by them—and when *Shu* is achieved that way, the *Shu* phase is finished, and karateka enter into the *Ha phase of semi-autonomy*. They now learn the intentions behind the forms, the function of moves including the common denominators of the fundamentals underlying them, and the initially rigid rules become more flexible, applied to every case but a practitioner recognizes those cases where an exception has to be made. When the time comes, karateka apply fundamental principles automatically and competently; they see more than one aspect to every form and rule—and when Ha is achieved that way, the Ha phase is finished, and karateka enter into the *Ri phase of independence*. They now learn the dynamics of change and adaptability to naturally employ form and intent to any circumstance, and their responses become second nature. Now the *Ri* phase is finished, and a karateka enters into a new dimension of *Shu*, and so on and so forth.

In the unconscious actions and responses in the *Ri* phase, the three core components of mastery come into play, which I illustrated in my second book with the example of playing chess (Bayer 2023a, pp. 112ff). I will briefly summarize them here: beginners may think through one move, including its implications and an opponent's possible reactions. Advanced players may be able to think through two, three, or even more moves. But there are chess masters who do not analyze "sequentially," i.e., step by step, and think in detail through all possible moves. They process the information on the board differently, holistically, including its inherent patterns and all possible developments. Such a level of mastery is the combination of three core components:

1. *Holistic perception,* complete and simultaneous, comprehending the big picture, its inherent patterns, and all possible developments. This competency can be illustrated by the metaphor of climbing the highest tree in a forest to look to get oriented and gain an entirely new understanding of one's surroundings. Now "the big picture"—the forest, the "totality" of the landscape beyond the forest, and the many details close by—can be seen as a whole. Such new insight changes one's perspective irreversibly and completely.
2. *Mental storage of concepts in a complex, cross-linked hierarchy,* as an organized scheme of deep penetration and advanced understanding of the subject. The deeper the penetration and understanding, the more *the complexity of reality reduces itself into a limited number*

of constitutive fundamentals. For a master, it is obvious how the combinations of a handful of core concepts, or fundamentals, explain all the particulars of an art—just as all the countless hues of printed works of art are reducible to combinations of only four basic printing colors, blue, yellow, red, and grey.
3. *Automatic, habitual, subconscious actions and reactions rooted in the complete calmness of an "empty mind,"* honed through decades of training where moves and concepts are tested in all possible circumstances.

When *Ri* is achieved, the *Ri* phase is finished, *and karateka enter into a new dimension of Shu*. In other words, improvements and advanced skills gained in a later phase redefine what a practitioner did before in a less advanced manner, continuously changing everything in a never-ending spiral of evolution, where all phases simultaneously coexist (see image 12).

During this journey, one can achieve complete self-control of body and mind, thereby gaining master over emotions like fear and anger that often blind us to the reality of a situation. The resulting applications and concepts become a master's store house of spot-on reactions to all kinds of attacks, and the unconscious, accurate application of concepts eventually becomes habit. Moves happen automatically, at reflex speed, efficiently and unconsciously guided by an empty mind.

Image 12: The "Trinity" of the Shu Ha Ri Developmental Principle

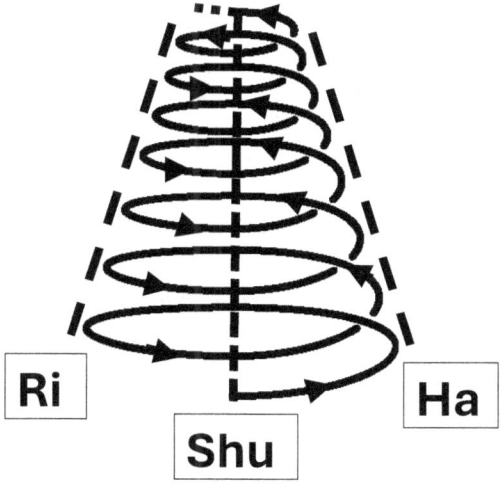

"Practice makes perfect" the saying goes, which is generally true even if more is needed than mere practice because practice alone can also lead to routine, to mere competence with mechanics instead of mastery. Practice as such does not make perfect, it makes permanent, and practicing the wrong thing only makes one a master of failure. Only perfect practice creates perfection in application. Hence, *Shu* and *Ha* phases continuously complement *Ri* phases; practice needs to be constantly double checked and compared to fundamental benchmarks to avoid practicing something incorrectly. Practice needs to be guided iteratively and repeatedly by sensei for a long time; practice needs to supersede frustration and ego, and it needs a karateka's dedication and stalwart commitment to continue on this never-ending path.

For our Western minds, which are based on linear and segmenting logic, it may seem weird to see contradictions, as with the phases of *Shu, Ha,* and *Ri,* coexisting and forming one unit, one trinity, in the way this coexistence is seen in eastern Asia. However, just as there is no day without night and vice versa, and as there is no high without low and vice versa, so also is there is no *Shu* without *Ha* or *Ri* and vice versa—and holistic thinking is needed to better grasp such a principle. Holistic thinking allows us to understand that a whole is more than the sum of its parts, that a melody is more than an assemblage of tones, that a kata sequence is more than a string of techniques.

Holistic Thinking Overcomes Assumed Contradictions

The simultaneous coexistence of contradictions that define each other by contrast and together constitute a whole is a millennia-old conception in Chinese philosophy, with roots in Taoism (see "Excurse: Japan's Cultural Roots in Confucianism and Taoism" at the end of this text), and which is graphically illustrated in the well-known symbol of yin and yang as emblems of opposite forces that together form an entity. It has to be noted that the opposing components are not completely disconnected; *there is always some yin in yang, and some yang in yin*, symbolized as the black spot in the white and the white spot in the black (see image 13).

Image 13: Coexistence of Contradictions in Chinese Philosophy

Holistic thinking based on this philosophical conception of the whole being more than the sum of its parts allows us to better understand what *Shu Ha Ri* means. In Western terms, holistic thinking can in this sense be understood as an "as well as" instead of an "either-or" approach. It constitutes itself, among other things, as the coexistence—as an "as well as"—of change and constancy, where there is an overarching unity of both, which, again, is not an easy thing to grasp with our Western brain. An example may help: understanding the flow of a river, which represents change, is only possible when standing at the riverbank, which represents a "constant" in its physics/mathematical sense as point of reference. In this sense, only with the existence of competence in *Shu*, as point of reference, can there be *Ha* (and thereafter *Ri*), while, at the same time, competence in *Ha* (and *Ri*) can only exist when there is *Shu*. All phases coexist; without *Shu*, without adhering to forms and rules, there cannot be a breaking away from and transcending of forms and rules. At the same time, *Ri* and *Ha* reinvent *Shu*, and all that creates new versions of revolving circles in a never-ending spiral of evolving competence.

When employing this line of thought in those karate-jutsu systems that aim at protection of oneself and others, there are of course contradictions at a first glance. There is, for instance, a contradiction between change and permanence, between the "principle of never-changing kata" and those distinguishable versions of the same kata that are practiced differently in the three Okinawan systems of *Shorin Ryu*, *Goju Ryu*, and *Uechi Ryu*. At second glance, however, we can see an overarching unity of similar *kihon* and a variety of *kihon* interpretations; we can see a unity of similar underlying principles and variety of their applications; we can see a unity of shared fundamentals and their wide-ranging use in those karate-jutsu systems. Hence, in taking another look, we can see those contradictions constituting mutual interdependences and forming an overarching unity as a new whole, just as the black and white of the yin-yang symbol together form the whole circle.

Now, applying this thought (that constancy and change together constitute a whole) to kata itself, I agree with Sensei Itzik Cohen, 7th Dan *Shorin Ryu Kyudokan*, who is one of those rare sensei with extensive strategic and practical combat experience in his various roles in the military and security field. He points out that "to preserve the kata's historical capsule of information we must understand the importance of the kata's DNA, and not simply change it. If a kata has changed, then valuable accumulated knowledge may be lost, and with it, the essence of the art will disappear" (Cohen 2023, p. 101). To overcome possible concerns that this would mean limiting or "freezing" a kata, it needs to be pointed out that kata preservation, in relation to the principle of never changing, does not bar but allows for a wide range of application of technique in fighting situations and all based on the same fundamentals. It permits a variety of angles, extensions, and directions of moves, and it allows a broad variety of hand, arm, foot, and leg positions that may differ by a couple of inches, which all embody change, and thus cover that wide range of possible fighting situations, serving more than just one intention when used, while the fundamental principles—the essence of the kata, or its "DNA," to use Sensei Itzik's term—is maintained.

Up to now we used this line of thought for karate-jutsu systems intended for the protection of oneself and others. Those karate-jutsu systems are united as the "trunk of the tree" in our earlier tree metaphor that unifies them in their differentiation into the three Okinawan systems of *Shorin Ryu*, *Goju Ryu*, and *Uechi Ryu*. This is due to the fact that these three systems share the identical purpose of universal protection and as such embody the unity of change and permanence, as explained above. The universal essence of traditional kata like *Naihanchi*, *Passai*, *Seisan*, *Gojushiho*, and others, is their suitability for self-protection. They were created to preserve knowledge of the optimal performance of fighting moves—although in most cases not as obvious applications—and this kata "DNA," as time capsules of the art of fighting, is preserved in all three Okinawan karate systems, in spite of their somewhat varying execution of the same kata and their different interpretation of calisthenics.

Such underlying unity, however, may not be so easily found in karatedo styles. When a karate version is stripped of its purpose of self-protection and turned into a way of self-perfection, to "find oneself" or to "express oneself," then space opens up for the creation and invention of individual, sometimes fictional moves that go beyond fighting and may serve other purposes. I can illustrate with a recent experience. In early April 2024, I had an opportunity to compare the execution of *Pinan Sandan* in an old-style Japanese karatedo system to the one in a classic Okinawan style. Though the *Pinan* kata series was created in the early 1900s, that is much later than those classic Okinawan fighting katas, which can be traced back one or two centuries before that. Moreover, though *Pinan* kata were created by Sensei Itosu Anko for the purpose of teaching kids and were thus stripped of lethal applications, some fighting moves involving receiving and giving were preserved in his versions as obvious techniques. One of these moves consists in stepping into a horse stance to close the distance with an opponent and to support an elbow move with a trunk twist (to block, or to break a grip, or to throw when gripped, or …), but the difference between karate-jutsu and karatedo when it comes to how to step is spectacular (image 14).

Image 14: Stepping into a Horse Stance in Shorin Ryu Karate-jutsu (left) and Doshinkan Karatedo (right) Versions of Pinan Sandan

[caption continued from previous page] Starting from and ending in the same positions for this move in both styles, the transitions into a horse stance with an immediately following elbow thrust are quite different between the two karate interpretations. According to the original *kata* that was created by Sensei Itosu in the early 1900s, preserved by Sensei Chibana before and during WWII, and then handed down to Sensei Nakazato Shugoro, in *Shorin Ryu Shorinkan* the karateka slides into the horse stance to close the distance to an opponent. In contrast, in *Doshinkan Karatedo* the karateka uses an exaggerated circular high leg move to close that distance. In terms of fighting applications, the latter is not a good idea as it completely opens up one's lower body to an opponent while both hands are not available for protection. Hence, the creator of this karatedo style obviously had something other in mind than a fighting application when changing the blueprint of Sensei Itosu's *Pinan Sandan*. And indeed, the intention here is health related. Sensei Ichikawa Isao, founder of this karatedo style, said many times that he focuses on stretching, extending, bending, straining, and extending limbs and body to the limit in every move in order to improve a karateka's overall health.

I think the reason for the exaggerated leg moves in image 14, for stepping in a way that makes no sense at all in a fight, is that the creator of this karatedo style had something in mind other than fighting applications when changing the blueprint for Sensei Itosu's *Pinan Sandan*. I attended many training sessions with Sensei Ichikawa Isao, the founder of this karatedo style he created to preserve O'Sensei Toyama Kanken's *Shudokan* heritage. He explained to us students his approach that included in the first place maximizing health benefits through karate training and the corresponding necessity of stretching, extending, bending, straining, and extending limbs and the body in general in every move to the limit (and then some more) for that purpose.

Sensei Ichikawa's health-related approach is supported by scientific studies, which confirm that "such techniques, although originally devised for combat and military situations, might be adapted for health research and clinical applications" (Jennings n.d.), and in this sense, "karate plays a vital role in physical healing. Through the enhancement of cardiovascular fitness and strength development, karate acts as an effective means to improve overall health and reduce the risk of various chronic diseases. The practiced movements and techniques facilitate the improvement of flexibility, coordination, and balance, benefiting individuals recovering from injuries or dealing with physical limitations" (Yadav 2023, p. 1).

Individually created new moves, like the ones introduced for health benefits (as shown in image 14), can be demonstrated to spectators, copied by like-minded fellow karateka to preserve the kata the way it was created by the style's founder, and may even work in a certain sense with compliant partners as prearranged *kumite* exercises in the secure confines of a dojo. But that they will work as fighting moves on the street can be doubted. Whether they do or not, their combat adequacy can be quite easily evaluated by karateka who have the practical experience of having dealt with violence and who thus know something about the specific logic of a "real fight" (for this term see the Excurse below).

Excurse: Real Fights in Contrast to Consensual Play

Since I use the term "real fight" or "fight on the street" multiple times in this text, a closer look at what is meant by that seems advisable. First, we are talking here exclusively about fights among civilians and not about combat among soldiers. Second, for fights amongst civilians, professionals in the security field (e.g., Miller 2011) and hoplology researchers (e.g., Acutt 2016)—hoplology is the science of human combative behavior and performance—distinguish between circumstances where there are options to control the situation versus those in which you are at mercy of others, whether there are options to avoid a fight while it is still in the making, and by varying likelihood of getting injured or killed. Fight settings include:

- Predatory attacks (nonconsensual serious fights)
- Dueling (consensual, socially sanctioned serious fights)
- Beat downs (status-seeking or group norm-driven nonconsensual serious fights)
- Brawling (biologically or socially driven consensual serious fights)
- Sparring (socially sanctioned consensual play fights)
- Tussling (biologically or socially driven consensual play fights)

Excluding the consensual play fights of sparring and tussling (even though realistic sparring in the dojo comes closest to preparing you for protecting yourself and others) leaves us with four categories of fighting scenario that carry risk of injury or even death outside of the dojo. Let's look at those categories in the order of how easy it is to deescalate or avoid a fight.

Dueling was institutionalized in past societies and is still found today in some group-specific subcultures. But dueling is rare in our time and age. In spite of the fact that dueling includes a good chance of getting severely hurt and even killed, this kind of fight can be avoided by not accepting the challenge and simply leaving the situation, which can be done if someone swallows his or her pride and prioritizes his or her own security. Prioritizing your own safety over others' perceptions is not easy, I admit; but because avoidance is possible—and, by the way, is an option in light of the genuine Okinawan principle of self-protection—we'll exclude dueling from the type of "real fight" requiring the *bugei* that is the focus of this book.

So, predatory attacks, beat downs, and brawling come into focus. Some versions of the last type, like a punch-fest in a bar, are essentially consensual and are thus perhaps avoidable either by leaving the scene, by de-escalating with an apology, or by simply not reacting to provocations. Instead, you can stay calm, swallow your pride, and prioritize your own security over emotion and the judgment of others. Such avoidance is, as mentioned, consistent with how the universal principle of protecting oneself and others was and is interpreted in Okinawan karate-jutsu, which calls for prioritizing your own safety over hurt feelings and wisely factoring in how pride and cockiness can blind you to your options for de-escalation.

The remaining types of fight are rarely avoidable. These are *brawling* (when there is no way out of the fight), *predatory attacks* (if someone takes something by force that someone else has, or if an attacker simply wants to hurt and degrade a victim), *status-seeking beat downs* (if someone is physically punished for, perhaps unknowingly, threatening the status of a violent individual in front of their peers, or if someone is simply chosen to be beaten up as an example or to make a statement), as well as *educational beat downs* (if someone is physically punished for, perhaps unknowingly, violating an important rule of a group). One or the other of those situations can perhaps be deescalated but that cannot be taken for granted, and if de-escalation does not work, effective self-protection capabilities are urgently required. These are the "real fights" or the "fights on the street" I refer to when using those terms in this text. Predatory attacks may every now and then not end so badly if the predator receives what he or she was looking for, be it money, jewelry, a car, or whatever. But in the many cases where a predator is angered, irritated, frustrated, or annoyed, things can get ugly. The same is true for beat downs that cannot be de-escalated and for cases where an individual or an entire group wants to make a statement by bashing their victim.

All those fights follow the logic and reality of a world, other than the noncriminal world, with its own norms, values, and rules. Rules, values, and norms like sportsmanship, fairness, mercy, humanity, and kindness mark the character of individuals who usually do not have to deal with violence and perhaps never had to face violence in their lives. The rules, values, and norms that regulate behavior in the other world are quite the opposite. There is no fairness in real fights, no clemency, and no rules in place other than the imperative to win by all means.

Attacks will come unannounced, and you will, with absolute certainty, get hit in such a fight. Thus, methods for absorbing blows, or cuts if knives are involved (i.e., "receiving" techniques in the terminology of Okinawan karate), are as important as "giving" techniques (i.e., counters and attacks). Any technique used by the defender, be it an offensive or a defensive one, needs to create enough damage or surprise to interrupt the attack long enough for escaping the scene—or, if escape is not possible, to end the fight altogether. On a side note: in the latter case it is strongly advisable for all karate-jutsu practitioners to know about the legal interpretations of self-defense and all its consequences, which may differ by state.

Realistic karate-jutsu training in this sense needs to prepare practitioners not just physically but also psychologically to immediately overcome the shock of being hit (hard!) and to counter efficiently in a way that may even contradict their own values. In the words of Sensei Noel Smith: "If your opponent cannot see [e.g., because of damaged or tearing eyes], he cannot fight efficiently for a second and you may have a chance. If your opponent cannot breathe [e.g., because of an effective strike to his airway], he cannot fight efficiently for a second and you may have a chance. If your opponent cannot move freely [e.g., because of a damaged or locked joint], he cannot fight efficiently for a second and you may have a chance [remarks in parentheses were added by me]."

Chapter 8
Conclusion and Consequences

Shu Ha Ri is a concept that first appeared in the Japanese fine arts several centuries ago. As a way of understanding personal growth, the model suggests that karateka move through three phases: learning the forms and fundamentals of the art (*Shu*); over comprehending the intentions behind the forms and focusing on (experimenting with) applications (*Ha*); into transcending the initial forms and creating their own ways of preserving fundamental traditions (*Ri*). Since the three phases are of a repetitive character, improvements and advanced skills that are gained in a succeeding phase trickle back into what a practitioner did before, optimizing executions continuously in a never-ending spiral of evolvement. In other words, all phases coexist simultaneously and form a trinity of revolving phases, which allows karateka to continuously deepen their understanding and mastering of the art.

With a Western mindset, many may see such a development as a karateka's path through ranks and belts up to mastership, to the top-level of a stairway of skills and status. "Although it's not impossible for Westerners to grasp such concepts [like *Shu Ha Ri*—my addition]," says Sensei Michael Clarke, "it is made more difficult by the world we grew up in and the 'values' ingrained into us over time. In the end, we're talking about something we can either see in someone, or not. We're talking about human values that can't be measured in terms of 'status' without killing the value of what we saw. Once we assign status to the various stages of *Shu Ha Ri*, the concept becomes meaningless … but the more a person believes (holds on to) the notion of *Shu Ha Ri*, the less likely they are to get beyond the early stages of learning." *Ri* competence cannot be grasped through the Western concept of status; it embodies something different, a holistic personal evolution, where all three phases together form a trinity and coexist simultaneously.

Though keeping in mind that "when dealing with foreign philosophies we are often at a disadvantage because there is nothing that we can readily compare them to" (Waterfield 2014, p. 1), we do not want to "mystify" the *Shu Ha Ri* concept, especially its *Ri* phase, or label it as "incomprehensible" for outsiders. *Ri* competence is achievable (and to be found) in areas other than the martial arts as well, and not only in Japan. The *Shu Ha Ri* principle has become widespread, for instance, in today's business world within the context of agile learning after it was introduced about two decades ago in software engineering, project management, and general leadership skills development.

Since considerations about *Shu Ha Ri* in karate are primarily found after WWII, it could well be that the Japanese interpretation of karate as a fine art—as the *budo* art of karatedo with the purpose of achieving self-perfection, which contrasts with the Okinawan interpretation of karate-jutsu as an art for protecting oneself and others—opened up Japanese karatedo for *Shu Ha Ri* application. Based on Japan's self-acclaimed racial and cultural superiority at that time, the Okinawan way of self-protection embodied backwardness in the eyes of mainland Japan's political and martial arts officials. They redefined karate-jutsu as the *budo* art of karatedo for self-perfection and integrated it into the mainland's system of *budo* along with the latter's philosophical undergirding. This new concept of karatedo allowed for the application of mainland Japan's *Shu Ha Ri*, Zen meditation, and Buddhism, which differ considerably from anything in Okinawa's socio-cultural traditions and from the Okinawan universal principle of protecting oneself and others that guided karate's practice and application there. The pragmatic, outcome-focused Okinawan fighting approach that prioritizes results over the way to get there is now converted into a Japanese fine art that prioritizes the execution of forms over their effectiveness in a fight.

The Japanization of Okinawan karate is accompanied by the mainland's introduction of and request for karate styles (initially, there were no styles in Okinawan karate, there was only the unifying principle of protecting oneself and others). Japanization is accompanied further by the redefinition, labelling, and standardization of techniques (there were originally no terms for moves in Okinawan karate; the latter was not taught intellectually but through modelling and imitating a sensei). Japanization destroyed the original fluid and flexible art through "freezing" every move and position into techniques and stances (there are no "stances" in Okinawan karate, only fluid positions to support a specific move or technique). Finally, Japanization led to the introduction of formal attire, a ranking system, and a militaristic training etiquette. All this substantially contrasted with the original laid-back and outcome-focused Okinawan way of practicing karate-jutsu and transformed karatedo into a fine art.

This transformation allows the values of self-expression and self-articulation to be included in karatedo's purpose of self-perfection or, in other words, to end up with the same purpose that characterizes all fine arts and constitutes an essential component of them. In light of the value placed on individual interpretation and self-expression—values important to painters, poets, and other artists in the fine arts—it makes sense to emphasize the *Shu Ha Ri* interpretation that aligns with Western individualism, allowing the karateka to convey a personal interpretation of a kata or technique. This interpretation of the art and of *Shu Ha Ri* can be found in the West and in some Japanese karatedo variants, where individual interpretations represent a means of self-actualization rather than creating effective combat applications.

Based on the varying philosophies and purposes of today's karate versions, namely self-protection in karate-jutsu, self-perfection in karatedo, and winning in sports-karate, we can distinguish at least two conceptions of how the *Shu Ha Ri* principle is used today. One approach explains a karateka's development within a karate-jutsu system, which means to continuously develop skills while practicing within the traditions of a classic system without switching it to another one. That understanding was previously presented as phases in a process of gaining independence from forms and rules and involved moving from a state of dependence, to a phase of semi-autonomy, and then into independence, where the art itself becomes the source of growth. *Ri*-transcending within a karate-jutsu system would then mean to neither transcend the system as such, nor to break away from a sensei. The other view, common these days mostly in the West, understands the phase of *Ri* as breaking away from a style or from a sensei, primarily to create a new style. The first interpretation understands *Shu Ha Ri* as perfecting one's capabilities within the tradition of a classic fighting system; the second one understands mastery as an evolutionary process that aims to surpass a sensei and to perhaps invent something new. The first conception seems philosophically closer to its Eastern Confucian roots, the second one to Western individualism.

"Is the *Shu Ha Ri* as currently in vogue not simple wishful thinking by Westerners (especially those from heavily individualistic societies) who want to believe they are ready for *Ha* and *Ri* when they have not truly grasped *Shu?* Is *Ri* not ultimately about respect for the lesson (i.e. *giri*), which our teachers wanted for us?" asks Dr. James Hatch, who pinpoints here one among many possible Western misunderstandings. Other researchers go even further, holding that "distancing oneself from the organization because they feel they have outgrown their teacher or the style is a fool's endeavor" (Waterfield 2014, p. 8). Whether and how Western values of individualism, self-expression, and self-actualization impacted postwar karatedo cannot be established here. However, it could well be that these values first impacted the Japanese culture after the nation opened itself up to Western ideas during the Meiji Period and especially after WWII during the American occupation of Japan, paralleling the adaption and transformation of Japanese philosophies in the West. The combined impact of those socio-cultural interpenetrations is definitely to be seen in some interpretations of the *Shu Ha Ri* principle today.

In *bugei* karate-jutsu, *Ri* is not understood as transcending your style or breaking away from your sensei, as we have noted at length. This is not needed to achieve karate-jutsu's essential purpose of universal self-protection, of neutralizing an attacker as quickly and as efficiently as possible. Karate-jutsu styles were introduced as systems that are complete in themselves, equipping their practitioners with everything necessary to succeed in a fight. To illuminate the fact that every karate-jutsu system that was created for self-protection is complete as it is, I have used the metaphor of a language, which is also complete as it is and possesses linguistic fundamentals comparable to any other language, and which does not need innovative additions or a new grammar to fulfil its purpose. This understanding of a karate-jutsu style as an optimized fighting system for self-protection that includes everything it needs to work efficiently—just as every language is complete as it is and is thus able to express the same thing as any other language— illustrates a karateka's evolvement in terms of *Shu Ha Ri* as individual adaptations of unchanged fundamentals. It excludes all those fight-inefficient innovations and fantasy moves that have even been used to create completely new karate styles that aim at new purposes beyond self-protection.

Ri-transcending *within* a karate-jutsu system then means to gain independence from narrow guidance and to transcend one's own limitations but not to transcend the system as such, not to break with traditions or breaking away from the sensei. From this perspective, *Ri*-phase competency allows individual avenues for gaining full bodyweight power in every application based on relaxation, harmony, and the complete openness of an empty mind—and all of that within the existing karate-jutsu system. Transcending in the *Ri* phase *within* a karate-jutsu system would then also mean becoming independent from narrow guidance and naturally, often called intuitively, applying form and intent to any circumstance. In summation, transcending *within* a karate-jutsu system would not mean transcending the system as such but to mimic the teacher, then to understand the intentions of the teachings, to become the model, and finally to become the teacher.

This understanding differs from the one used in some versions of the *budo* art karatedo oriented toward self-actualization to achieve self-development. Martial arts applications may turn here into personal interpretations, into individual expressions of the art, and they may be more or less fit or unfit for the reality of fighting. Such interpretations transform *Ri* into "transcending styles" and reinterpret a self-defense craft as a scholarly fine art of self-development. There, karateka may reach their full potential in the psychological sense of self-perfection by following individual paths of self-expression toward self-actualization. Thus, the door is now wide open for the creation of "new styles" as well.

However, since karate-jutsu and its predecessors have been practiced for some centuries, it seems safe to assume that there is not one single move that would not have been used by somebody else during all that time, especially due to the fact that there's a finite number of ways to move the body, the arms, and the legs. In other words, the claim by some karateka to having invented or created something completely new, a genuinely "new style," is most certainly invalid. Their creations are probably not new; they were only new to them until they figured something out that somebody else had already figured out a long time ago. What is called "new" is often the rediscovering of original and traditional interpretations within their system, which had been deliberately no longer taught since the early 1900s, at least not to non-Okinawans, after karate's originally secret practice was opened up to the public and disarmed. And, when we look closer at the modern developments that involved branching out into what may be called the transcending of a style and creation of a new style, this is more often than not really just the creation of a new organization or association that is still based on the original system, just with one or the other modification. In other words, it is not the creation of a new style, but the creation of a new branch jutting off from the original style to establish a USP (unique selling point) in the karate market as a new copyrighted and trademark-protected business.

My considerations here are not meant as a negative critique of such developments; it is a socio-economic fact that most of today's karate is fully commercialized (Bayer 2023, pp. 133ff). What I mean to offer is a neutral acknowledgment of the reality of modern karate. It is a marketable commodity that has arisen as a consequence of (a) the necessity to create something distinguishable in the karate market (styles), (b) karate's commercialization, and (c) the related challenge for sensei to find their market niche to make a living. Related Western (and some Japanese) *Shu Ha Ri* interpretations grew out of this need on the part of sensei to establish a market advantage by inventing and teaching a "new" system.

There is another trap sensei have often fallen into (and I am not only talking about Western sensei here). Interpretations of *Shu Ha Ri* based on Western individualism may not only turn the value of that individualism into a justification for crude commercialism; those interpretations may also be the result of narcissistic self-absorption. Such personality-driven takes on karate may promote interpretations of *Shu Ha Ri* as breaking away from a system or a sensei that have not much to do with the art itself but help practitioners avoid the demands of deeper levels of learning and the kind of *Ri* "enlightenment" that would demand a karateka's modesty, which a narcissist has no desire for.

Whereas today's two karate versions of "*jutsu*" and "*do*" both show the unity of their practitioners' physical, mental, and spiritual development, and thus allow the implementation of the *Shu Ha Ri* principle in its holistic sense, in sports-karate there is no integrated spiritual evolution either toward collectively oriented Confucian values or toward Western self-actualization. Personal ambition, hopefully controlled by ideals of nonviolent sportsmanship and (perhaps) of learning how to lose, seems to be the driving value of progression here, which leads to a possible understanding of *Ri* in sports-karate as "breaking the form," often involving the invention of spectacular fantasy moves and athletic performances not suited for combat but breathtaking to behold, as well as insertions of interruptions to the flow of kata, which would be counterproductive in a fight but serve the purpose in sports of emphasizing positions and of demonstrating control of the body to judges and spectators.

Physical, Mental, and Spiritual Development Covers the Totality of Karate Today

After turning *Ti*, the centuries-old fighting system for professional Okinawan aristocratic security circles, into karate-jutsu for civilians as a means of protecting oneself and others (starting in the 1800s), karate was (after 1910) opened up to the public and "disarmed" for its use in the Okinawan educational system. Then, after being introduced to mainland Japan in the mid-1920s, it was integrated into the mainland's martial arts, further altered, and redefined. No one can better summarize this development than karate authority Sensei Patrick McCarthy, 9th Dan *Koryu Uchinadi:* "During a period of intense military escalation, Japan experienced distortions in her spiritual beliefs, widespread political propaganda, and a strong surge of nationalism. Adapting to societal norms, and with its Chinese foreign origins concealed, karate was shaped into a challenging competitive activity and a popular social recreation. Such transformation catered not only to the youth of that era but also aligned with the prevailing social pressures of military conscription and Japan's culture of conformity. Within this historical backdrop, karate underwent an evolution that resulted in excessive ritualization and dysfunctionality as an effective method of self-defense. This shift reflects the complex interplay between cultural adaptation, societal pressures, and historical circumstances that reshaped not only the original Okinawan art of karate, but also of Japanese *budo* in general" (McCarthy in a Facebook post on 04/26/2024). A few years later, karate's further evolution led to the almost complete loss of all realistic fighting applications during the rise of its sports-karate versions that began in the mid-1950s.

Hence, though we find a mixture of all those sources (*jutsu*, *do*, sports) in today's karate versions, classic Okinawan karate-jutsu, let alone *Ti*, is rarely to be found in its genuine form in our modern time and age. It can still be found, though, in some places on Okinawa, as well as in the West, albeit only practiced by few and only shared with selected students; it has been carefully maintained in its genuine version, and up to this day is still not taught to everyone in all its physical, mental, and spiritual components.

The different forms of karate that arose, which were already "announced" by Sensei Matsumura Sokon in the late 1800s as *bugei no bugei*—the *true martial arts (karate-jutsu)*, the *martial arts of scholars* (karatedo), and *martial arts in name only* (sports-karate)—represent different purposes and philosophies. Different purposes in karate-jutsu (universal protection of oneself and of others), karatedo (self-perfection and an entire way of life), and sports-karate (competition) suggest differing understandings of *Shu Ha Ri* in those three variations, and, as explained in Chapter 1, differing underlying values, purposes, and philosophies in today's main karate versions did indeed lead to different ways of understanding *Shu Ha Ri* in karate-jutsu and karatedo. In sports-karate, it seems that this Japanese developmental principle is basically not used.

I mentioned earlier that I do not see the two karate versions of *bugei* (karate-jutsu) and *budo* (karatedo) as a "transformation" of the genuine Okinawan "craft" of karate-jutsu into the Japanese "fine art" of karatedo; I rather see the creation of the latter as a newly constructed *budo* version in addition to its classic *bugei* or *jutsu* version. This represents, not an evolution or maturation, but embodying the conscious and deliberate generation of a different Japanese thing with a different purpose, and newly created in parallel to the still-existing classic Okinawan version.

Although the two versions of karate-jutsu and karatedo, which are closer to the origins of the art than sports-karate, may not completely overlap with each other, they may as well together form the whole of karate in modern times through their parallel coexistence, where there is always some *jutsu* in *do*, and there is always some *do* in *jutsu* (image 15). Both karate versions include both aspects, the one of fighting (*jutsu*) and the other of spiritually maturing (*do*), albeit with differing priorities. The two paths and their associated karate styles prioritize one purpose over the other without completely excluding the other one. *Do* and *jutsu* cannot be completely separated, for physical, mental, and spiritual growth are intertwined. The body cannot go where the mind has not yet been, and the mind cannot grow if it remains limited by egoism, anger, or fear, all of which in turn influence the fluid adaption of physical techniques.

Image 15: Karate-jutsu and Karate-Do Together Constitute the Whole of the Art in Modern Times

The contention that *do*-philosophy of spiritually maturing is found in all karate-jutsu versions today as well is supported by an empirical study. Looking at the biggest impact martial arts training had on the life of long-term practitioners revealed a result that united karatedo and karate-jutsu versions: independently of the system they studied, all practitioners pointed out that "their training revealed hidden character traits, helping them discover something positive in themselves they did not know existed prior to beginning their journey" (Kane/Wilder 2022, p. 303). This result is obviously related to their path, to their *do*, and goes beyond the acquisition of fighting skills in a narrower sense.

Further, the mental and spiritual facets of karate are in general based on "mind over matter" philosophies and on nonreligious philosophies of enlightenment that postulate the superiority of mind and spirit over the physical and thus encourage the addition of nonphysical components to karate practice. In karatedo styles those components are prioritized. In making those nonphysical, noncombat components of karatedo into its sole purpose, some executions of the art may approximate esoteric or religious rituals.

After the explosion of popularity of karate in the West, which often resulted in a dilution of quality, something seriously changed over the last decade for classic karate-jutsu and old-style karatedo. Traditional dojos, those teaching classic karate-jutsu and old-style karatedo, not only lost, and still lose, students at an alarming rate, they also fail to attract enough new students to maintain themselves. This contrasts completely with the development of sports-karate, where student numbers steadily increase. Such trends have of course a multitude of reasons. Whether and why one of those reasons may be related to how the art is taught deserves a closer look. That is because we see a growing contrast between teaching the art in an unmodified way in traditional dojo and significantly changed socio-cultural conditions in the West. There, the art is still taught in ways that completely contrast with present students' learning and leadership experience in other social institutions.

Integrating a Well-Established Western Educational Concept with Established Asian Teaching Methods May Help Retain Students in Traditional Karate (with contributions by Thomas E. Ward)

All sensei throughout history have taught and teach their art based on some kind of educational concept—either consciously and explicitly, or unconsciously and intuitively applied. Some educational concepts in East Asia may well have arisen from the training traditions within a sensei's family that owns, curates, and transmits a system, or from methods that were related to the customary training for military or security personnel at that time. Other educational approaches may have been based on their own fighting experience or on observations of animals. The bottom line is, however, that there is no teaching that does not follow some "educational theory," though that theory may not be a systematized pedagogy but an intuitive one that comes from applying the lessons of personal experience.

In every culture, those conscious or unconscious educational concepts are molded by the basic values and norms of that very culture. Hence, the karatedo versions most karateka practice today were Japanized fine arts, based, on the one hand, on Japanese Confucian philosophies and their related educational concepts, on the other, on Japanese *budo* philosophy, initially with all its prewar militaristic undertones. That all fitted well within that culture and made it easy for East-Asian students to adhere to the Japanese training regimen in an old-style dojo. Such a training regimen appealed as well to Western military personnel. Marines and other soldiers were attracted by the fighting components of Okinawan karate-jutsu and old-style karatedo, and, when becoming karate teachers in the USA themselves, mirrored how they were taught, relying upon mimicking and modeling as their predominant method of education.

All this worked quite well in the West for a long time. Combined with increasing Western fascination with everything Oriental, when Western youth went in search of a different way of finding their purpose in life than their parents' generation did (Bayer 2021, pp. 29ff), and with the redefinition of *budo* in Japan from its prewar way of understanding it in terms of the warrior spirit to its postwar understanding in terms of character-building, there was a boom in karate for at least five decades, attracting new social groups that practiced the karate version they saw fit for either self-perfection or self-protection. Then something changed dramatically.

Classic Karate-jutsu and Old-Style Karatedo Dojo Are Losing Students at an Alarming Rate

After the postwar "inflation" of karate dojo and instructors, many traditional dojo as a whole not only lost but continue to lose students; they also fail to attract enough new students to maintain their student body. Thus, as dojo membership shrinks and ages, the remaining older students, continuing their training with as much dedication as before, become representatives of a past era. Another example of such a downward trend is declining attendance at training camps. In well-established annual camps we regularly attend, attendance has shrunk over the last one or two decades from several hundred excited participants to less than one or two dozen.

We want to stress again that we are talking, in the first place, about classic karate-jutsu and, in the second, old-style karatedo as the karate versions losing students in many Western dojos, because developments in sports-karate look quite different. We want to point out as well that this decline is not true for *all* traditional schools, since we do know personally of some who are successfully maintaining their student body. Whether and why that may be related to modern Western educational methods that were adapted will be looked at in a moment.

The usual explanation in traditional dojo for shrinking student numbers is an assumed lack of dedication and will in "entitled youths" and "spoiled generations." However, while changed values and attitudes may play a role, there is no problem in this world for which only one side can be blamed. How about the part played by the other side? How about looking at unchanged teaching routines in a changed world with a dramatically changed culture? As with any evolutionary process, if an organization does not adapt to change, it may well begin to fade away until it vanishes altogether. It is no different for traditional dojos that resist change. But fortunately we are familiar with examples of other traditional dojos that successfully try out something new and maintain a student body of sufficient numbers to sustain a sensei's living.

Though traditional karate may still attract prospects temporarily, if a dojo does not adapt, it only retains those (rare) students who already know about the martial way, are ready to unquestionably accept its underlying values, have dedicated themselves to a path of ever deepening understanding, are prepared to bear frustration, pain and soreness, and already know that they have to sacrifice a lot of time and energy on such a path. But this is not the majority of new students. The majority of prospects do not come mentally prepared to a traditional dojo; they need to be carefully guided in facing new physical, mental, and spiritual challenges, and they need to be coached, mentored, and encouraged to pull through. From a psychological perspective, their attitudes need to be changed, and their resilience has to be built up, which are not easy things to do, and which definitely cannot be achieved by means of an instructor-centered, authoritarian approach to education.

"So, what?" one may say. Why not focus on the minority of dedicated students and forget about the rest? The answer is simple but unpleasant: this group is getting older and smaller by the year. Not only do new students quit their training, but longer-term students, who once trained seriously, give up at an alarming rate as well. Knowing the physical, mental, and spiritual benefits of traditional karate, however, makes it imperative for all of us who love our art to convey it to as many folks as possible.

We are convinced that in traditional dojo more prospects can be reached, and that more "deserters" can be retained than is currently the case. The justification for our view was briefly introduced in Chapter 6 as the possible mutual enrichment of Asian and Western teaching concepts. Here is the thought: it may well be that one of the reasons traditional karate is losing so much ground in the socio-culturally changed West is that it is still exclusively taught based on diluted Asian concepts, while sports-karate versions, which are taught differently, boom. Western societies and their cultures have changed dramatically over the last few decades, including exchanging traditional values for new values, and moving from authoritarian, instructor-centered teaching (and leadership) models to new ones. Whether that change is seen as for the worse or for the better is not as relevant as the fact that it is the new socio-cultural reality. Social change requires that organizations adapt or vanish. However, in many traditional dojo not one single modern educational method ever gets incorporated, and the majority of instructors there still bank on how they were taught, based solely on their interpretation of Asian concepts. If anything has changed over the last decade, it might be loosening some etiquette, e.g., turning a respectful bow into a disrespectful and sloppy one, but the educational approach may not have been updated. Instead, routines may have been kept in place that now grossly contradict what Western karate students experience in other educational and social contexts. *We are not suggesting abandoning the traditional values and training routines of traditional karate*—the opposite is true, as we are convinced of their unchanged benefit for today's togetherness. Likewise, we are in favor of maintaining respectful training etiquette. What we are suggesting is *the addition of tested and proven Western educational concepts to the Asian training routines in the dojo*, concepts that align with the kind of learning and leadership that students experience in school, college, and at their workplace, and that, because they are tailored for Western minds, would support the learning of Eastern approaches.

Sports-karate may serve as an example to illustrate this suggestion. Sports-karate has included seasoned Western educational concepts in its training approach during its decades-long professionalization in order to better develop local, regional, national, and international athletes. Learning objectives for kata and *kumite* competition were created for that purpose, knowledge was systematically transferred, and athletes' abilities were improved both through proper instructional methods and through assessments and tests that assess achievement of those learning objectives (Mehrenberg, 2013, Chaabene et al. 2019, and Sepotri et al. 2022 present related examples). Moreover, initiated and supported by UNESCO, teaching concepts were developed for the integration of karate training into physical education programs in schools (Gomez/Fabinai 2022) as well as for youth development in general (UNESCO 2019).

Utilizing sound Western educational concepts when teaching traditional karate in a Western dojo would help significantly in the transmission of knowledge from teacher to student in our Western culture, and such an approach would probably better conserve the art's genuine intentions than those marketing incentives and awards we see today, or the loosening of requirements to keep customers. If modern educational concepts amenable to a young Western student's mindset were to be given as much attention in the dojo as bastardized versions of Eastern concepts, fewer students may give up and others currently on the fence may join.

Again, we are not suggesting replacing the current teaching approach in traditional karate, which is based on Eastern teaching concepts; this approach has proven itself successful at having produced many remarkable karateka in the East and in the West over the decades in the postwar era. We merely suggest adding a Western educational concept that is tailored to Western minds to help retain more younger students in traditional karate who otherwise would not keep up their training.

"You cannot use the runway behind you" goes a saying for pilots, which expresses a sentiment similar to Albert Einstein's famous maxim that "you cannot solve a problem with the same mind that created it." So let's consider something new.

Instruction Alone Is Not Sufficient for Advanced Learning

A coherent Western educational model in addition to the Asian concepts in traditional karate training systematically aims at overcoming the "pedagogue's fallacy." This is a term used in the field of professional education that, in essence, points to the misconception that instructing

CONCLUSION AND CONSEQUENCES 145

alone is sufficient for learning to occur. It can lead educators to fail to take the time to determine whether students are actually engaging with and understand the material. A prominent example of such a gap shows itself when we hear the phrase "we told you a thousand times that ... " in the dojo, which simply proves that simply stating a thing is not usually sufficient for successfully teaching it.

Many karate teachers in the West teach classic karate-jutsu and old-style karatedo as they were taught themselves long ago and in another culture. As with their East Asian teachers, they rely upon mimicking and modeling as their predominant educational methodology. Occasionally, a sensei will introduce some new method of instruction, but in general instructors of traditional martial arts in the Western world have limited background in education and have even less formal training in how to teach. On the other hand, and increasingly over the last decade, we find younger students insisting that they need explanations of what they are ordered to do in the dojo; we find them wanting to discuss their practice, and to figure out the reasoning behind it. Such demands can seem unreasonable to sensei who simply transfer the knowledge and skills they have learned in the instructor-centered, direct, and only-one-right-way approach they learned in Japan and perhaps in the military. This approach is often not appealing to Westerners. Students will unconsciously compare the teaching approach they encounter in the dojo with teaching they encountered in high school, trade school, or college that is based on Western educational concepts and that matches their Western minds. The contrast they see and feel may be one of the reasons why many don't continue their training, which then would constitute another reason for giving up than their assumed lack of dedication or willpower: dedication and willpower needs to be taught in the dojo and be built up, perhaps even from scratch; they cannot be demanded as preconditions that students have already developed and bring to the dojo.

Kata training, at least under all my instructors and in all the styles I trained in, represents the lion's share of training and may illustrate another possible gap between teaching and learning. If karateka are not explicitly guided to distinguish between general concepts and specific applications when they are learning kata, all moves get mixed into a mish-mash of techniques that make more or less sense to a student (e.g., is pulling one's fist to the side or hip a grabbing technique on its own or is it a reinforcing move? And if it can be both, when is it one or the other? Is the open-hand receiving move in *Passai* a middle block like the closed-fist moves in *Pinan* or something different? And if it can be both, when is it one or the other?). Moreover, if the meanings of the moves that constitute a kata are not transparent for karateka, the kata becomes a series of actions that will seem more or less reasonable to a student. (Why would someone stand on one leg while fighting? Is every kata move tailored for individual fighting or are there moves in a kata intended for security personnel—at that time, royal security guards and police officers—working together as a team, as Sensei Itzak Cohen points out in his books?) Those examples and perspectives are pointing us to a handful of general learning objectives for kata instruction, which are not yet in written form, at least not to my knowledge. They need to be deliberately formulated and properly pursued through adequate instructional methods.

To avoid the pedagogue's fallacy, especially when addressing a Western mindset, we must ensure that our teaching methods actively engage students by encouraging them to analyze and respond to questions like those mentioned above. This may involve double-checking their understanding by having them demonstrate and present the results of their analyses and evaluations. It could also involve encouraging feedback, challenging their present level of understanding, and employing other interactive and reflective educational techniques. Furthermore, *bunkai* and *oyo* training can be systematically taught for all kata rather than sporadically. Techniques can be taught at various levels beyond formalized *kumite* exercises. They could, for instance, be pressure tested in simulations of real combat scenarios: a first step would be the explanation of *omote* (surface-level) application of movements using the traditional instructor-centered method that aims at developing a student's understanding of a subject matter and its application. Thereafter, depending on students' competency, small-group assignments could involve figuring out potential *ura* (hidden) applications of those moves, which would be another instructional method that encourages evaluating and analyzing. Group findings could then be presented to the other groups of fellow students and to the instructor. This would be the assessment of what the groups came up with and requires higher level instructional methods like feedback, encouraging, and mentoring.

For advanced learning to occur, the mental and spiritual components of karate could also be delivered systematically rather than sporadically. The core values of traditional karate could be formulated as a list of learning objectives to be achieved through student-centered teaching methods that ask learners to evaluate equivalent or similar values in Western societies and identify the benefit of those values in their lives. In summation, the learning process would be greatly improved by employing educational methods beyond instructor-centered lecture—methods that challenge students' creativity and critical thinking by encouraging them to see connections between traditional karate values and their everyday experiences with peers, family, and friends. This could extend to areas such as dojo etiquette, kata training, kumite, self-protection, resilience, persistence, stamina, discipline, humility, respect, and more.

In this way, a well-structured educational approach can foster advanced learning, expanding students' understanding beyond what is gained through repetition and modeling. Such an approach not only stimulates deeper learning but also guides students meaningfully into the higher levels of Bloom's Taxonomy (analyzing, evaluating, creating). Lastly, it provides the framework to mentor and coach the most advanced students through the *Ha* and *Ri* phases.

In a Traditional Western Dojo, Western Educational Concepts Can Support Established Asian Teaching Routines

In socio-cultural terms, teens and young adults in the West do not directly encounter Asian philosophical concepts in the way preceding generations did in Japan, Indonesia, Korea, or Vietnam. They have no idea of *Do*; they are not used to following the path of *do* at home, at school, or at their workplace like many Asian karateka do. Such a philosophical concept needs to be broken down and explained to Western students because they learn cognitively as a first step and not intuitively like their Asian fellow karateka generally do. Appropriate learning areas, the proper approach to them from an instructional standpoint, and what it is to be student-centered instead of instructor-centered should be determined, defined, and developed.

Secondly, teens and young adults in the West are not familiar with the Confucian values on which karatedo training is based. These values guide adherence to traditions, prioritize social harmony, shape relationships based on mutual obligations, and emphasize the implicit expectation of unquestioningly following the directives of elders, teachers, *senpai*, and sensei. Western students may not immediately grasp this philosophy, as its authentic Eastern interpretation—rooted in Confucian ideals—often contradicts the way they were raised. Therefore, an educational bridge must be built to connect these Eastern concepts with the students' Western mindsets. To achieve this, socio-cultural contexts should be explained, enabling students to analyze potential adaptations in the West by identifying parallel values and assessing their personal significance. Additionally, appropriate learning areas and instructional approaches—focusing on student-centered rather than instructor-centered methods—should be identified, defined, and developed.

For instance the path of *Shin Gi Tai*, which provides the systematic integration of mental and spiritual development *(Shin)* with techniques *(Gi)* based on physical fitness *(Tai)* (Clarke, M. 2011a), is one that most advanced karateka still need to discover in the course of an unguided personal journey, without a sensei's mentoring support. Our own training experience may give an example for that: for over forty years, our training, like that of many others, has focused predominantly on the lower levels of Bloom's Taxonomy, i.e., on remembering, understanding, applying, and occasionally analyzing. Any progress beyond that was left for us to discover on our own through unguided personal efforts, and whether we achieved anything in that sense or not is for others to judge. However, since karate-jutsu and karatedo together form the complete art, instruction should aim to develop all three elements—physicality, technique, and mind/spirit—equally and systematically, and not only focus on the lower levels of learning. Those lower levels are perfect for learning in the *Shu* phase, while developing students through *Ha* into *Ri* requires those different, non-instructor-centered, methods of guidance into independence that not all sensei are familiar with.

As Clarke (2011b) notes, "Practicing karate with an *instructor* only provides tuition in the physical techniques of karate; it will do little else. Where a sensei will guide, point, and serve as an example to those they teach, an *instructor* will drill, dictate, and can only offer coaching." True growth can only occur when these three components are given equal emphasis, allowing for a deliberate pursuit of developmental principles like *Shu Ha Ri*. Without this balanced approach, it becomes nearly impossible for a student—after decades of intense and continuous study—to be mentored through the phases of *Ha* and especially *Ri*. The higher stages of learning cannot be taught in the same direct, instructor-centered manner as the foundational levels. They require a more individualized and indirect approach, one that involves guided self-reflection, mentoring, empowerment, and encouragement.

Hence, we suggest adding the core components of modern Western education to proven Eastern concepts in traditional karate training. We are not suggesting that the current teaching approach be replaced. We suggest instead an approach of "as well as" instead of "either/or" in the Western dojo by combining established Japanese educational concepts with a tested Western one.

The major components of Western educational philosophy are *learning objectives*, *instructional methodology*, and *assessment* of what has been learned. Learning objectives are desired outcomes of instruction, which might include how you want your students to have changed as a result of your teaching. These objectives should be clearly stated and shared with students from the beginning. The second component, instructional methodology, refers to the techniques of instruction a teacher uses to impart their objectives and reach different learner types (some examples of instructional methods are open, structured, and pro-con discussions; projects; group assignments to figure out something cognitively or to apply something physically; modeling; individual and group practice; lectures; and pyramiding parts of overall objectives). Assessments, the third component, are ways to determine the effectiveness of instruction and whether learning objectives have been met (conversational interviews, written tests, performance reviews, peer-to-peer evaluations, presentation of projects, applications, and students' demonstrations of what they have figured out in their assignments are some examples of assessments). The phrase "any questions?" commonly heard after a round of instruction is not a good assessment of teaching effectiveness. Many students at that point are unable to put their questions into words; often, only the most advanced are. The others first need to consciously link what they have learned with their background knowledge. They have to measure new information against what they already know, reanalyze it while trying it out (to see that, for example, a different angle when using a *tuite* move may not lead to the intended effect), and "digest" all this, so to speak. This psychological process takes time. That is why questions on the subject will often be asked later, perhaps even in a later training session, but not right away when the "questions?" shot is fired by the instructor. A better assessment of "lessons learned" would be one that gives students time to think about, to discuss among themselves, and to evaluate what they have learned, determine how well they understand it, identify what is still not clear to them, and report all that back to the instructor, who can thereby assess instructional effectiveness and clarify further if needed.

In Western public and private school systems across America, Europe, and much of Oceania, we ask our teachers to have clear, written objectives for each class. They are expected to present the material using effective methods, encourage critical thinking, and guide students in forming their own ideas. We also aim to measure learning with accurate and fair assessments. Why shouldn't martial arts instructors be held to a similar standard? While it would be overkill to impose the same rigorous requirements as those we place on professional educators, a simplified and down-to-earth educational approach could easily complement traditional karate training to better engage Western students. Such an approach would help instructors systematize and effectively convey their teachings. It would also give students a clearer understanding of key concepts, such as physical, mental, and spiritual development, form and function, principle and application, receiving and giving, the universal principle of self-preservation, self-perfection, and other elements of traditional karate.

Moreover, adopting a more grounded educational method would acknowledge that students have different learning styles—visual, auditory, verbal, logical, kinesthetic, social, and solitary—each requiring different instructional techniques to achieve similar outcomes. A one-size-fits-all, instructor-centered teaching model simply doesn't address this diversity.

Incorporating modern Western teaching methods into the time-honored traditions of East Asian karate training also emphasizes the need for a reliable yardstick to assess the accuracy of karate techniques. In such an educational framework, measuring the effectiveness of instruction and the achievement of learning objectives becomes essential.

The Necessity of a Yardstick to Formulate Meaningful Learning Objectives

What is important for a student to learn? What is unnecessary? What aspects of the subject should be taught and developed? What should my students be able to achieve after attending my class? These questions can be addressed through the development of educational objectives. Creating these objectives requires instructors to have a clear understanding, early on, of the specific version of karate they are teaching. Only with a solid grasp of the differing philosophies underlying karate-jutsu, karatedo, and sports-karate can instructors craft a stringent and robust hierarchy of learning objectives and establish corresponding benchmarks to measure student progress effectively (see "The Yardsticks That Measure the Adequacy of Karate Move Interpretations" in Chapter 1). The value for instructors of clarifying for themselves what is to be achieved, what to do to achieve it, and the best way to teach to enable students to achieve it, cannot be underestimated. It clears the mind, centers attention on what is relevant, and defines each training session in terms of its specific role within the total hierarchy of learning objectives and overarching purpose.

Hence, a teacher owes it to their students to consider objectives before ever stepping onto the dojo floor. Once determined, these objectives should be clearly stated and shared with the students. Instructors should also make transparent what the student should be able to do after receiving instruction and at what level of competency they should be performing. Objectives should be presented in a logical and constructive fashion, each building upon the last until a final objective is met.

Not only should there be meaningful learning objectives in place, but all components of good teaching—clear educational objectives, methods of instruction, and assessments—should cohere with one another and be fair. We bring this up because it is not uncommon in rank testing, and especially in black belt tests, to spring something entirely new on students, like breaking boards, a written test, or a test of fitness (e.g., a run of several miles), that was completely absent in all the training leading up to the test. It would be better to have the assessments match the teaching methods, and the teaching methods match the educational objectives. Otherwise, students become confused about what exactly is expected from them, which may result in frustration—often concealed and unmentioned—and, in turn, dropping out of training. Of course, we can never completely avoid frustrating students when we take developing them seriously, but we can lay before them a fair and coherent path and perspective for them to meet expectations.

The Symbiosis of Eastern and Western Teaching Concepts

Many traditional karate schools in the West, particularly those that profess to have a lineage or legacy of some kind, are losing younger students and aging overall. Yet, many resist evolving their training methods or integrating new concepts. This reluctance carries risks—it can lead to stagnation or, worse, to the fading of traditional karate into oblivion. In terms of *Shu Ha Ri*, this hesitance to embrace successful Western educational approaches alongside traditional Eastern training concepts in the dojo actually hinders the deliberate and systematic progression of Western students through the phases of *Shu, Ha,* and *Ri.* In some cases, it may even prevent this evolution entirely.

A potentially illuminating perspective on how to successfully teach classical karate-jutsu and old-style karatedo in Western dojos may lie in blending both Eastern and Western teaching concepts, rather than relying solely on traditional Japanese methods. The simultaneous use of these two seemingly contradictory educational approaches—each defined in contrast to the other—can together form a more effective method for teaching traditional karate, as illustrated in image 16. We propose leveraging the mutually beneficial relationship between these two approaches. Our idea is to add modern Western methods to support, rather than replace, the established Eastern ones. This addition would better engage the younger Western mindset of today without losing the essence of traditional karate.

Image 16: Eastern and Western Concepts Together May Constitute the Whole of Teaching Traditional Karate in the West

CONCLUSION AND CONSEQUENCES 153

Excurse: Japan's Cultural Roots in Confucianism and Taoism

Since this text discusses *Shu Ha Ri* adaptions in the art of karate, shedding some light on the socio-cultural background in which that developmental principle is embedded seems like a good idea. This will (hopefully) help to distinguish possible modern Western misconceptions from the principle in its classic Japanese form.

Such a philosophical excurse can only be a brief overview, and I trust that our learned readers accept that I will not present every aspect of the philosophical background here, which would lead us way beyond the purpose of in this text. The following paragraphs portray the most basic understanding of millennia-old ideas and belief systems that are useful for today's karateka to know—without the necessity for them to study philosophy in order to comprehend the cultural background of their practice.

Two ancient thought systems are of utmost importance for today's east-Asian cultures, and these are the philosophies of Daoism (Taoism) and Confucianism. Both were developed around 2,600 years ago. They present two somewhat opposed understandings of society and two different but complementary ways of understanding human well-being.

Daoism (Taoism) is based on the thought of Laozi and developed into an ancient Chinese philosophy and later into an indigenous religion as well (the latter representing a form we are not looking at in this Excurse). Philosophical Daoism teaches how to exist in harmony with nature and with the entire universe by understanding the way of nature as a whole, the *Dao*, of which human life is only a small part. In philosophical Daoism the Dao postulates the natural and favors the spontaneous and the simple, and humans are enjoined never to do anything unnatural, meaning something out of keeping with the *Dao*. Related to this so-called "doctrine of non-action"—better characterized as the doctrine of not acting against the way of nature—was the notion that no one should have excessive desires because they are bound to cause injury to oneself and to others. Since philosophical Daoism seeks harmony between the individual (or human) way and the natural order by letting things happen naturally, it tends to dismiss human society as artificial and constrained. Out of the pure Dao energy, called *ch'i* or *qi* in Chinese and *ki* in Japanese, emerges as the dynamic force that causes yin and yang, which in turn create everything, or "the ten thousand things", as Laozi worded it in his time (Lao Tsu 1972). Yin and yang, the concept of balancing forces, carries the implication that everything in the universe is connected, that contraries coexist, and that nothing makes sense by itself, separated from its counterpart.

Confucianism is not a religion, though it is sometimes labelled as such. It is rather an ethical/ philosophical system based on the teachings of Confucius, who lived in the 6th–5th centuries BCE and is regarded as China's "first teacher." Confucianism represents an all-encompassing way of thinking and living. Confucians used the concept of the Dao to describe the way humans ought to behave in society. For them, Dao was a human ethical or moral way, which is a narrower concept than the Dao as conceived of in philosophical Daoism. Postulating that human beings are innately good, Confucianism assumes that humans understand the difference between right and wrong, and are inclined to choose what is right. They only engage in immoral behavior because of a lack of a strong moral standard or ethical code. But devotion to such an ethical code, in combination with rituals to reinforce it, helps everyone to live a productive and tranquil life of peace that will eventually translate into a strong, ethical, and prosperous state. The necessary moral quality for that is achieved, manifested, and cultivated by the honorable behavior of an individual in the social institutions of family, school, community, and state. When people interact and live together based on these ethics, their relationships result in corresponding gives and takes, it leads to reciprocal responsibilities, mutual contribution, and hence to shared aims of all parties involved, i.e., to harmonious goals of individuals, groups, organizations, and states.

The philosophy of Daoism influenced Confucianism through its concepts of the Dao (Tao) and its inherent dynamic force or energy (*ki*). Derivatives from these concepts impacted Japanese culture as *do*, as the idea of unending improvement and spiritual enlightenment, as well as through the theory of universal energy, *ki*, through which everything that lives is connected and into which it transforms back after its material existence.

Confucian thought impacted Japanese culture by calling for individuals to pursue moral and intellectual perfection, for families to seek harmony and order, and for the polity to work for peace and prosperity.

Generally speaking, philosophical Daoism embraces nature and all that is natural, joyful, and spontaneous; that way postulating non-action, or "letting it happen." Confucianism views morality, performance of duty, and conformity to virtue in both the individual and in human institutions—family, school, community, and the state—as essential to human flourishing. Rules and regulations that aim at maintaining such virtues help encourage people to do the right thing, but these rituals as well as social systems and institutions need to be created; they don't form spontaneously through inaction. These two somewhat opposed thought systems can be symbolized by yin and yang, which work together to form an integral whole with a corresponding way of life that is in harmony with nature and carrying with it a moral system, a social order, and a political system.

The resulting social order, maintained by the Chinese people for more than two millennia, spread into other East-Asian countries as well and greatly impacted Japan's socio-cultural development. Although it underwent transformation over time, Confucianism is still a major source of Japan's values and the basis of the nation's social code. While it does emphasize the importance of learning, virtue, and self-cultivation, it does not have a direct equivalent to *Shu Ha Ri*. Confucianism places strong emphasis on ethical conduct, familial respect, and social harmony, and its teachings focus on general moral and social principles rather than on individual skill development. But Confucianism definitely helps explain the stability of social structures and the durability of socio-cultural traditions in Japan, and as such harmonizes with the interpretation of *Shu Ha Ri* in this text as a path of growth that maintains traditions without breaking them and without breaking away from a teacher.

LIST OF ABBREVIATIONS

AAU	Amateur Athletic Union.
CFA	*Classical Fighting Arts* magazine.
et al.	Latin, meaning "and others"; used to shorten a list of coauthor names when referencing.
ibid.	Latin, meaning "same location"; used to reference a source immediately quoted before.
i.e.	Latin, meaning "that is."
JKA	Japan Karate Association.
JKF	Japan Karate Federation (aka Japan Karatedo Federation).
MMA	Mixed Martial Arts.
n. d.	"No publication date available"; used when referencing (internet) publications.
n. p.	"No page numbers available"; used when referencing (internet) publications.
ODKS	Okinawa Dentou Karatedo Shinkokai.
OKIC	Okinawa Karate Information Center within the Okinawan Karate Kaikan.
OPG	Okinawan Prefectural Government.
publ.	"Publishers"; used to distinguish authors from publishers in references.
sic	Latin, meaning "thus"; used to indicate that something unconventionally written is intentionally being left as it was in the original.
SKIF	Shotokan Karate-Do International Federation
UNESCO	United Nations Educational, Scientific, and Cultural Organization.
USP	Unique Selling Point, also called a unique selling proposition
USKK	United States Karate-Do Kai Inc.
WKF	World Karate Federation.
WWI	First World War 1914–1918.
WWII	Second World War 1939–1945.

LIST OF PHOTOS AND GRAPHS

Title	P	T	G	Page
Image 1 *The Shu Ha Ri Developmental Principle*			X	14
Image 2 *Unity of Constant and Change in Okinawan Karate-jutsu*			X	20
Image 3 *Tuite Move to Damage Joints in Traditional Passai Sho versus Arm Circle without Martial Purpose in Modern Passai Sho*	X			31
Image 4 *Swastika Is A Religious Symbol in Many Asian Cultures*	X			42
Image 5 *Tentative Shu Ha Ri Interpretation for Today's Three Main Karate Variations*			X	44
Image 6 *Today's Three Non-Japanese Umbrella Karate Styles on Okinawa*			X	55
Image 7 *Ferocious Warriors (Nio) Protect the Buddha*	X			78
Image 8 *Sensei Frank Hargrove and Sensei Noel Smith in the Late 1970s*	X			83
Image 9 *Bardwick's Model of Comfort, Learning, and Growth Zones*			X	92
Image 10 *Examples of Shu Ha Ri Use in the Business World*		X		94
Image 11 *Implicit Philosophies in Shu Ha Ri and in Western Educational Concepts*			X	114
Image 12 *The Holistic Trinity of the Shu Ha Ri Developmental Principle*			X	121
Image 13 *Coexistence of Contradictions in Chinese Philosophy*			X	123
Image 14 *Stepping into a Horse Stance in Shorin Ryu Karate-jutsu and Doshinkan Karatedo Versions of Pinan Sandan*	X			126
Image 15 *Karate-jutsu and Karate-Do Together Constitute the Whole of the Art in Modern Times*			X	139
Image 16 *Eastern and Western Concepts Together May Constitute the Whole of Teaching Traditional Karate in the West*			X	152

EXPLANATIONS OF EAST ASIAN TERMS IN DR. HERMANN BAYER'S BOOKS

- *Analysis of Genuine Karate — Misconceptions, Origins, Development, and True Purpose*
- *Analysis of Genuine Karate 2 — Socio-Cultural Development, Commercialization, and Loss of Essential Knowledge*
- *Analysis of Shu Ha Ri in Karatedo — When a Fighting Art Becomes a Fine Art*

Especially for our readers not familiar with karate and martial arts, I have listed the explanations of East Asian terms I used in my books here alphabetically for your quick orientation. Explanations are focused on a term's connotation as referred to in the text.

B

Bo	Staff, about six feet long, used as a weapon in *kobudo*.
Bubishi	Name of an ancient Chinese work on martial arts and traditional medicine.
Budo	Japanese term for modern Japanese sports martial arts derivatives from *bu-jutsu*.
Bugei	Martial arts, military arts, arts of war
Bu-jutsu or jujutsu	"Warrior skills"; term for traditional martial arts on ancient mainland Japan.
Bunkai	Application of kata moves and concepts in combat.
Bushido	Moral code for a samurai's attitudes, behavior, and lifestyle.

C

Ch'üan fa	Ancient term for traditional Chinese empty hand martial art.
Chi	See *Ki*.
Chudan	Solar plexus level; often called "middle" in a karate move.
Chudan-uke	"Middle block"; in karate, a defending arm move using a forearm's radius bone.

D

Dachi	Stance/position in karate.
Daimyo	Feudal vassals of a Shogun in ancient Japan.
Dan	Ten black-belt ranks in martial arts; used to designate levels of proficiency.
Deshi	Student of an art.
Dento	Genuine, original.
Do	Never-ending "way" or "path" of continuous improvement.
Dojo	Training hall.
Doriyoky	Hard work with total commitment.
Doshinkan	"Hall to study the way of the heart"; a Japanese karate style created by Ichikawa Isao in the 1960s based on the teachings of Toyama Kanken's *Shudokan* (around 1930).

E, F

Eku	Often used term for an oar, about six feet long, used as a weapon in *kobudo*.
Fukyu (kata)	"Something to be spread and shared"; in karate a "*Fukyu* kata" is a basic kata of a style.

G

Gaijin or gaigene	Non-Japanese foreigner; has somewhat negative connotations.
Gedan	Lower-body level; often called "low" in a karate move.
Gedan-barai (uke)	"Low block"; an arm technique in karate to block the lower part of one's body.
Gi	Martial arts uniform worn during training and performance, traditionally white in karate.
Goju Ryu	Officially recognized umbrella karate style in Okinawa; created by Miyagi Chojun around 1930 based on the teachings of Higaonna Kanryo around 1870; literally "hard-soft-style."
Gojushiho	Name of a kata practiced in Okinawan and Japanese karate.

H

Hachiji-dachi	"Natural stance"; an upright position in karate with feet shoulder-width apart and angled naturally.
Haito	"Knife-hand"; cutting move in karate with the edge of the hand at its thumb side.
Hanshi	Honorary title meaning "master," "most senior teacher," and "teacher of teachers"; used in many martial arts for the top few instructors of that style, sometimes translated as "Grand Master"; in many karate styles awarded to tenth Dan; in some styles to 9th Dan as well.
Hara	Energy center and spiritual center of the body, located in the abdomen.
Heian	Name of a kata series in Japanese *Shotokan* karate created by Funakoshi Gichin as a modification of the Okinawan *Pinan* kata series.
Heiko-dachi	Comparable to *jigo-dachi,* "horse stance"; a karate position like riding a horse with feet set wide apart, knees bent, but feet parallel, not angled, and pointing forward.
Heisoku-dachi	An upright position in karate with feet placed parallel together; in some styles this is the "bow position."
Hiki	Ryukyu Islands' royal government organization under King Sho Shin in the 16th century.
Hojo undo	Physical conditioning and strengthening practices as a discipline of genuine karate-jutsu.
Honbu dojo	Martial arts style's administrative headquarters and central training hall.
Honto	"Real," "true"; here, essence of kata concepts.

I, J

Ichidan	See *Shodan.*
Ichigeki hissatsu	The martial arts ideal of killing with a single blow.
Ikebana	The Japanese art of arranging flowers.
Isshin Ryu	Karate substyle of *Shorin Ryu* in Okinawa (with considerable *Goju Ryu* elements); created by Shimabuku Tatsuo in the 1950s.

Jigo-/Jigotai-dachi	"Horse stance"; a karate position like riding a horse with feet set wide apart, knees bent, and feet pointing outward, angled in line with thighs.
Jo	Mid-sized staff up to five feet long, used as a weapon in *kobudo*.
Judan	Head-level; often called "high" in a karate move.
Jutsu	"Science of an art"; general Japanese term for combat martial arts.
Jujutsu	"Warrior skills"; traditional martial arts on ancient mainland Japan focused on grappling, pinning, joint locks, and throws, using attackers' energy against them.

K

Kado	The Japanese art of formal flower arrangement
Kakedameshi	Challenge match resembling a real fight setting in traditional Okinawan *karate-juts*u
Kama	Sickle used as a weapon in *kobudo*.
Kamaete	"Get ready" or "in position"; a command used in karate.
Karate	Japanese martial art, created and developed in Okinawa as the renaming of *Te* and *Tode*, the genuine fighting arts of the Ryukyus; initially meaning "China-hand," to be altered later to "open-hand."
Karatedo	Path of continuously practicing karate to combine physical, mental, and spiritual development.
Karateka	Karate practitioner (singular and plural).
Kata or gata	Standardized series of defending and attacking moves; literally meaning "form."
Kenpo	"Fist method"; traditional Okinawan martial art related to Chinese boxing.
Ki	Japanese term for the natural energy of the universe flowing through everything. Also spelled *chi* or *qi*.
Kiai	Focusing all energy, e.g. into the application of a technique by combining body movement with breathing. The result may be a shout, or it can be done silently.
Kiba-dachi	"Straddled leg stance" in Japanese karate, comparable to *heiko-dachi*.

Kihon (kata)	"Basic"; in karate a "*Kihon* kata" is a combination of fundamental moves.
Kiko	Techniques for the development of internal energy as a module in genuine karate-jutsu
Kyusho (Jutsu)	Striking vital points as a discipline of genuine karate-jutsu
Kyoku	Name of a kata series in *Doshinkan* karatedo.
Kobayashi Ryu	Other word for the karate style of *Shorin Ryu*; created by Chibana Choshin in Okinawa around 1930 based on the teachings of Matsumura Sokon (around 1840) and Itosu Anko (around 1900).
Kobudo	Using everyday tools and trade equipment as extensions of the body in karate.
Kohai	"More junior student"; in this context, seniority refers to membership in the same organization, not to age.
Kokusaidori	Main street in central Naha, Okinawa, Japan.
Koryu	"Old school"; a Japanese term for any kind of traditional arts.
Kuchibushi	Literally "mouth warrior" used in the text as "time to talk through things."
Kumite	Partner exercises; used in karate as formal drills or as sparring or free-fighting combat.
Kung-fu or gongfu	Modern term for Chinese empty-hand martial art.
Kyogi or Kyougi	Game, match, contest.
Kyoshi	Honorary title meaning "polished senior teacher"; in some karate styles awarded to 7th and 8th Dan; in others awarded to sixth Dan and above.
Kyu	Ten colored (initially all white) belt ranks below the ten black-belt Dan ranks in karate and other martial arts to designate various levels or degrees of proficiency or experience.

M

Maai	Martial arts term for the space between two opponents in combat; the "engagement distance."
Machi dojo	Privately owned dojo in Okinawa where traditional martial arts are taught and preserved.
Mae-geri	Forward kick; foot/leg technique used in karate.

Makiwara	Strong but flexible tapered wooden board, anchored to the ground and hit by karateka for hand, arm, foot, and leg conditioning.
Matsubayashi Ryu	Karate substyle of *Shorin Ryu* in Okinawa created by Nagamine Shoshin after WWII; the term is derived from kanji of *Shuri-Te* and *Tomari-Te* masters Matsumura/Matsumora.
Morote	Using one hand/arm to support the other one in a karate technique.
Mushin	Fully alert mind neither distracted by thoughts or emotions.
Musubi-dachi	An upright position in karate with heels together and feet open at a 45-degree angle; in many styles this is the "bow position."

N

Naihanchi	Name of a traditional Okinawan kata series that today has three forms.
Naihanchi-dachi	"Straddled leg stance" in Okinawan karate.
Naore	"Return to the starting position"; in some karate styles used as a command at the end of a kata performance.
Nekoachi-dachi	"Cat stance"; a position in karate with most of the weight on the back leg and bent knees.
Nukite	"Spear-hand"; a thrust move in karate with extended fingers tightly compressed together.
Nunchaku	String- or chain-connected short wooden pieces used as a weapon in *kobudo*.
Nunte Bo	Harpoon/boathook used as a weapon in *kobudo*.

O, P, Q

Obi	Belt worn by martial arts practitioners.
Okuden	A high level of advanced training in Japanese arts.
Omote	"Outside" or "surface" of something. Here, the obvious application of a kata concept.
Oyo	Application, practical use of a concept
Pangainun Ryu	Initial name of an Okinawan karate style later renamed *Uechi Ryu*. Created by Uechi Kanbun in the early 1920s based on Okinawan *Te* and Chinese martial arts.

Pinan	"Peaceful (mind) and (stay) safe"; name of a karate kata series of five forms created by Itosu Anko around 1900 for educational purposes in the public school system.
Qi	See *Ki*.

R

Rei	"Bow and show respect"; used as a command in martial arts ceremonies.
Renshi	Honorary title meaning "polished Instructor." Skilled or expert teacher. Awarded in karate to fourth Dan and above.
Ryu, Ryuha	"School" or "system," "flow of thoughts"; term used when naming martial arts styles.

S

Samurai	Military nobility and officer caste of medieval and early modern Japan from the twelfth century until their abolition in the 1870s.
Sanchin (kata)	Basic kata in some karate styles representing the most important fundamentals to synchronize breathing, focus, conditioning, moves, and body-weight transfer.
Satsuma	Southern Japanese former province led by the Shimazu clan that increased its feudal domain by invading and occupying the Ryukyus in 1608.
Seibukan	Karate substyle of *Shorin Ryu* in Okinawa created by Shimabukuro Zenryo in the 1960s.
Senpai	"Senior student"; in this context, seniority refers to membership in the same organization, not to age.
Sensei	General term for "teacher," "mentor"; not reserved for teachers of a particular Japanese art; doctors, lawyers, and certain other professionals may receive this designation too.
Shima	A millennium-old form of Okinawan wrestling/grappling.
Shihan	Honorary title meaning "chief instructor." In some Japanese karate styles used as 9th Dan rank below Hanshi, in others it is not related to rank.

Shitei/seitei (kata)	Form/kata created in the early 1980s by JKF, based on traditional Okinawan forms as a prerequisite for karateka to qualify for JKF-facilitated tournaments. Used until 2013.
Shito Ryu	Officially recognized karate style on mainland Japan created by Mabuni Kenwa around 1935.
Shobayashi Ryu	"Small Forest Karate," a substyle of *Shorin Ryu* in Okinawa created and named by Shimabukuro Eizo around WWII.
Shogun	Historical term for Japan's military commander.
Shodan	First level; used to name a kata or rank level in karate.
Shomen	"Font"; in karate the dojo wall where symbols, flags, and sensei portraits are displayed
Shorin Ryu	Officially recognized umbrella karate style in Okinawa based on the teachings of Matsumura Sokon around 1840, *Shuri-Te*, and Itosu Anko around 1900; literally "small forest style."
Shotokan	Officially recognized karate style on mainland Japan created by Funakoshi Gichin in the mid-1920s; named by Funakoshi's students sometime later as *Shotokan Ryu*.
Shudokan	"Hall to study the way"; a Japanese karate style created by Toyama Kanken in the 1930s.
Shu Ha Ri	Japanese martial arts concept that describes the stages of learning to mastery. In this context, used to explain individual training variances within an acceptable range of possible interpretations.
Shodo	The art of traditional Japanese handwriting
Shoshin	Attitude of openness and eagerness when studying a subject, even when studying it at an advanced level, just as a beginner would.
Shuto	"Knife-hand"; cutting move in karate with the edge of the hand below the pinky finger.
Soto-deshi	Student of an art who lives outside of a dojo.
Soto-uke	"Outside block"; in karate, a "middle" defending arm move using the forearm's ulna bone.
Suikendo	"Fists flowing like water"; a karate fighting style created by Yamashita Tadashi.
Sundome	Stopping before contact; today light contact in sports-karate

T

Tai Chi	A so-called "internal" Chinese martial art, having spiritual, mental, and qi-related aspects, practiced for defense training, health benefits, and meditation. An "external" martial art focuses more on physical aspects.
Tanbo	Short staff, about four feet long, used in *kobudo*.
Taikyoku	Name of a kata series used in several karate styles.
Te or Ti or Ti'gwa	Traditional Okinawan weaponless fighting art; literally meaning "hand."
Tekki	Name of a kata series in Japanese *Shotokan* karate created by Funakoshi Gichin as a modification of Okinawan *Naihanchi* kata.
tegumi	A form of grappling dating back to the 11th century in Japan which became a module of genuine karate-jutsu.
Tekko	Net-hauling tool or modified horseshoes used as weapons in *kobudo*.
Tichiki / tijiki	Term in *Uchinaguchi*, the Okinawan language, meaning "hands show what I do."
Tichikun / tijikun	Term in *Uchinaguchi*, the Okinawan language, meaning "use your hands like this."
Tode, Todi, Toudi	Renaming of "*Te*"; literally meaning "China hand."
Tonfa	Wooden handle used as weapon in *kobudo*.
Torite or Tuite	The method of seizing and restraining an opponent, which was used by law enforcement officials, security agencies and correctional officers in the Ryukyu kingdoms and Japan.
Tsuki	Fist strike, punch; attack move in karate.

U, V, W

Uchi deshi	Full-time live-in student of an art at a dojo; literally "inside student."
Uchinaguchi	Native language on the Ryukyu islands.
Uechi Ryu	Officially recognized umbrella karate style in Okinawa created by Uechi Kanbun around 1900 based on Okinawan ^and Chinese martial arts.

Uechi-Hachiji-Dachi	"Inward natural stance"; an upright position in karate with feet less than shoulder-width apart, toes pointing inward, and knees bent inward.
Uke	"Receive," a defensive concept in Okinawan karate-jutsu using the forearm bones; often somewhat inaccurately expressed as "to block" in modern karatedo.
Ura	"Back" or "behind." A side that is hidden from view; here, the hidden aspect of kata concepts.
Wado Ryu	Officially recognized karate style on mainland Japan created by Otsuka Hironori around 1935.
Waza	Technique; e. g. *Kihon-Waza* means basic technique in karate.

Y

yakusoku	In the karate context used here it means "arrangement," "engagement," and, more specifically, "partner exercises" or "partner drills."
Yin / yang	East Asian concept of dualism, describing how opposite or contrary forces may be complementary and interconnected in the natural world, defining each other by contrast and thus creating an overarching entity of mutual interdependence.
Yudansha	Martial artists holding Dan (black belt) ranks in karate or in other martial arts. (Singular and plural.)
Yumaru	Spirit of caring and helping one another in Okinawa.

Z

Zanshin	In karate the state of awareness and of relaxed alertness. In other martial arts it may also refer to a posture after the execution of a technique.

REFERENCES

Acutt, Jamie (2017*). Fight-Logic: Recording Martial Arts as Disembodied Knowledge. A Method for Statistical Analysis of Martial Arts.* https://www.academia.edu/37583919/Fight_logic_Recording_martial_arts_as_disembodied_knowledge_A_method_for_statistical_analysis_of_the_martial_arts. Retrieved 04/20/2024.

Acutt, Jamie (2016). *Contexts of Violence: A Typology of Combat as a Predicate for a Typology of Martial Art.* https://www.academia.edu/111943017/Contexts_of_Violence_A_Typology_of_Combat_as_a_predicate_for_a_Typology_of_Martial_Art. Retrieved 04/20/2024.

Ambrozy, Tadeuz and Juliusz Piwowarski (2013). *Modernity, Tradition, and Security in Budo Karate. The Security Dimensions.* Krakow: International & National Studies Higher School of Public and Individual Security, "APEIRON," pp. 42–60. https://www.academia.edu/35854094/Modernity_Tradition_and_Security_in_Budo_Karate. Retrieved 12/27/2023.

Asato Anko (1914). *Die Kampftechniken aus Okinawa Parts I, II, III—Asato Anko Spricht über Karate.* [Interviewed by Funakoshi Gichin supposedly in 1902 and published in *Ryukyu News* 1914]. In: Wittwer, Henning (2007). *Shotokan:* Überlieferte *Texte & Historische Untersuchungen.* © Henning Wittwer; pp. 9–26.

Ballardini, Bruno (div. years). *Karate Archeology.* Standing rubric in *Bugeisha* magazine. Diverse Issues (Quoted as *"Bugeisha*, Issue#, page#.")

Bandura, A. (1997). *Self-Efficacy: The Exercise of Control.* New York, NY: W. H. Freeman and Company.

Bardwick, Judith (1991). *Danger in the Comfort Zone: From Boardroom to Mailroom—How to Break the Entitlement Habit That's Killing American Business.* New York, NY: American Management Association, AMACOM.

Bayer, Hermann (2021). *Analysis of Genuine Karate—Misconceptions, Origins, Developments, and True Purpose.* Wolfeboro, NH: YMAA Publication Center, Inc.

Bayer, Hermann (2022). *Japan's Assertion of Okinawan Karate—How a Subcultural Intangible Heritage Was Converted into a National Cultural Symbol.* Research paper I presented to the International Martial Arts Studies Conference in Lausanne/Switzerland on June 30, 2022.

Bayer, Hermann (2023a). *Analysis of Genuine Karate 2—Socio-Cultural Development, Commercialization, and Loss of Essential Knowledge.* Wolfeboro, NH: YMAA Publication Center, Inc.

Bayer, Hermann (2023b). *Okinawa Is More than the Birthplace of Karate—Okinawa Is a Mindset.* https://ymaa.com/articles/2023/12/okinawa-more-birthplace-karate-okinawa-mindset. Retrieved 12/29/2023.

Bellah, Robert N. (1965). *Japan's Cultural Identity—Some Reflections on the work of Wasutsji Tetsuro*. Journal of Asian Studies, Volume 24, Issue 4, pp. 573–594. http://read.dukeupress.edu/journal-of-asian-studies/article-pdf/24/4/573/1704413/s002191180010854x.pdf. Retrieved April 29, 2023.

Bellina, Christian (2018). *Toyama Kanken—The Heritage of Shudokan*. Klagenfurt/Austria: © Christian Bellina. Limited edition.

Benesch, Oleg (2011). *Bushido: The Creation of a Martial Ethic in Late Meiji Japan*. Thesis submitted in partial fulfillment of the requirements for the PhD degree at the University of British Columbia. Vancouver/Canada. http://www.unterstein.net/nn/OB2011-*bushido*-creation-of-a-martial-spirit-in-meiji-japan.pdf.

Bloom, Benjamin S. (1984). *Taxonomy of Educational Objectives, Handbook 1: Cognitive Domain*. 2nd Edition. Boston: Addison-Wesley Longman Ltd.

Bowman, Paul (2010). *Theorizing Bruce Lee: Film—Fantasy—Fighting—Philosophy*. Amsterdam, NL & New York, NY: Editions Rodopi B.V.

Brown, David H. K., George Jennings, David S. Contreras-Islas, Jungjoo Yun, and Simon Dodd (2022). *Sacred Imagery and the Sacralisation of Violence in the Martial Arts. IM@GO, A Journal of the Social Imaginary*, Volume 10, Issue# 19, pp. 35–66. (Quoted as "Brown et al. 2022").

Chaabene, Helmi, Yassine Negra, Laura Capranica, Prieske Olaf, and Urs Granacher (2019). *A Needs Analysis of Karate Kumite with Recommendations for Performance Testing and Training. Strength and Conditioning Journal*, Volume 41, Issue #3, pp. 35–46. (Quoted as "Chaabene et al. 2019.")

Chambers, David, Taku Ikemiyagy, and Robert Dohrenwen (2020). *Okinawa Karate—The Exquisite Art*. Naha/Okinawa: Dragon Associates, Inc. & Ikemiya Shokai Co., Ltd. © *Classical Fighting Arts*. (Quoted as "Chambers et al. 2020.")

Carria, John M. (2022). *Uechi Ryu: Instructor's Edition*. Coppell, TX: Carria.

Cohen, Itzik (2023). *Karate's Genetic Code—Rukyu-di—The Pragmatic Facet. Perception of Techniques Over Time*. Middletown: Independently published. © Itzik (Itzhak) Cohen.

Clarke, Christopher M. (2012a). *Okinawan Karate–A History of Styles and Masters, Volume 1: Shuri-Te and Shorin Ryu*. Huntington, MD: Clarke's Canyon Press.

Clarke, Christopher M. (2012b). *Okinawan Karate–A History of Styles and Masters, Volume 2: Fujian Antecedents, Naha-Te, Goju Ryu, and Other Styles*. Huntington, MD: Clarke's Canyon Press.

Clarke, Michael (2011a). *Shin Gi Tai—Karate Training for Body, Mind, and Spirit*. Wolfeboro, NH: YMAA Publication Center.

Clarke, Michael (2011b). *Shin Gi Tai—Karate Training for Body, Mind, and Spirit.* https://ymaa.com/articles/shin-gi-tai-karate-training-for-body-mind-and-spirit. Retrieved 05/09/2023.

Cynarski, Wojciech J. (2017). *The Traditionally Understood Karate-Do as an Educational System: Application of the Martial Arts' Pedagogy.* Center of East Asian Studies at University of Gdansk: East Asian Studies, Volume 12, pp. 7–20.

Dale, Peter N. (2011). *The Myth of Japanese Uniqueness.* New York, NY: Routledge.

Davis, Cath (2014). *Shu Ha Ri: The Aikido Journey: The Metamorphosis of Form.* Portland: OR: Shoshin Press.

Dawes, James (2013). *Evil Men.* Cambridge: Harvard University Press.

De Mente, Boye Lafayette (2009). *Why the Japanese Are a Superior People—The Advantages of Using Both Sides of Your Brain.* Phoenix Books/Publishers.

Doi, Takeo (1973). *The Anatomy of Dependence.* Tokyo, New York, London: Kodansha International.

Dreikurs, Rudolf (1980). *Grundbegriffe der Individualpsychologie.* 4th Edition. Stuttgart/Germany: Klett-Cotta.

Dreyfus, Stuart E. and Hubert L. Dreyfus, (1980). *A Five-Stage Model of the Mental Activities Involved in Directed Skill Acquisition.* Research Paper Operations Research Center, University of California, Berkeley. https://apps.dtic.mil/sti/pdfs/ADA084551.pdf. Retrieved 02/13/2024.

Endo, Seishiro (2005). *An Interview with Endô Seishirô Shihan.* Aiki News, Dou, Issue# 144. *https://web.archive.org/web/20101204035427/http://www.aikidojournal.com/article?articleID=674.* Retrieved 12/02/2023.

Feldmann, Thomas (2021). *Anko Itosu. The Man. The Master. The Myth. Biography of a Legend.* Self-published through Lulu Press.

Franz, Steven (2016). *The Problem with Christian Karate.* The Dojo Shorinkan, n.p. https://thedojoshorinkan.wordpress.com/2016/02/10/the-problem-with-christian-karate/. Retrieved 04/05/2024.

Funakoshi, Gichin (1983). *Karatedo—Mein Weg.* 1st German edition. Tokyo & Weidenthal: Kodansha Int. & Werner Kristkeitz Verlag.

Funakoshi, Gichin (1973). *Karate-Do Kyohan—The Master Text.* Tokyo: Kodansha International Ltd.

Fukurai Hiroshi/Yang, Alice (2018). "The History of Japanese Racism, Japanese American Redress, and the Dangers Associated with Government Regulation of Hate Speech." *Hastings Constitutional Law Quarterly,* Volume 45, Issue 3, pp. 533–575.

Gomes, Mariana/Fabiani, Débora (2021). *Martial Arts Applied at School as Physical Education: Creating a Learner Centered Environment.* Publication International Centre of Martial Arts for Youth Development and Engagement under the auspices of UNESCO, Volume 5, pp. 33–39.

Haitani, Kanji (1990). "The Paradox of Japan's Groupism." *Asian Survey.* Volume 30, Issue# 3, pp. 237–250.

Hein, Laura E. and Mark Selden (eds.) (2003). *Islands of Discontent—Okinawan Responses to Japanese and American Power.* Lanham, MD: Rowman & Littlefield Publishers, Inc.

Hasegawa, Yoko and Yukio Hirose (2005). "What the Japanese Language Tells Us about the Alleged Japanese Relational Self." *Australian Journal of Linguistics.* Volume 25, Issue# 2, pp. 219–251.

Hayes, William ("Bill") R. (2018). *My Journey with the Grandmaster—Reflections of an American Martial Artist on Okinawa.* Kearney, NE: Morris Publishing.

Herbert, Wolfgang (2024a). "Practice According to Funakoshi." *SKM Shotokan Karate Magazin*, Issue# 160, pp. 32–34.

Herbert, Wolfgang (2024b). "Karate-jutsu, Karatedo, und Sports-Karate." *SKM Shotokan Karate Magazin*, Issue #159, pp. 14–17.

Herbert, Wolfgang (2023). *Zen—Psychotechnik oder Religion? / Zen in den Kampfkünsten—oder wie verhält sich Religion zum Krieg?* Speeches at OAG, Tokyo, and Universität Wien, Institut für Ostasienwissenschaften/ Japanologie. https://www.academia.edu/105029760/Zen_Psychotechnik_ oder_Religion_Mit_Exkursen_zu_Zen_im_Krieg. Retrieved 15/12/2023.

Herbert, Wolfgang (2021). "Miszellen zum Thema 'Karate, Zen und Meditation." *Toshiya Magazin für Karate, Kampfkunst & Kultur*, Edition 90, pp. 12–21.

Höhne, Benjamin P., Sandra Bräutigam, Jörg Longmuß, and Florian Schindler (2017). *"Agiles Lernen am Arbeitsplatz—Eine neue Lernkultur in Zeiten der Digitalisierung.* Zeitschrift für Arbeitswissenschaft." Volume 71, pp. 110–119. (Quoted as "Höhne et al.").

Holt, Jason (2023). "Physical Philosophy: Martial Arts as Embodied Wisdom." *Philosophies*, Volume 8, Issue #14, pp. 1–7. https://doi.org/10.3390/ philosophies8010014

Hong, Ze-han (2023). *Blurred Boundaries. A Martial Arts Legacy and the Shaping of Taiwan.* Translated by Christopher Bates. Wolfeboro, NH: YMAA Publication Center, Inc.

Hokama, Tetsuhiro (2000). *History and Traditions of Okinawan Karate.* Hamilton, Ontario, Canada: Master Publication.

Hyams, Joe (1979). *Zen in the Martial Arts.* New York: Penguin Putnam Inc.

Japan Karate Association (n.d.). https://www.jka.or.jp/en/. Retrieved 12/02/2023. Cited as "JKA."

Jennings, George (nd). *Pursuing Health through Techniques of the Body in Martial arts.* Essay. https://www.academia.edu/33985467/ESSAY_Pursuing_Health_Through_Martial_Arts_docx. Retrieved 02/14/2024.

Johnson, Noah C.G. (2012). "The Japanization of Karate? Placing an Intangible Cultural Practice." *Journal of Contemporary Anthropology*, Volume 3, Issue #1, pp. 60–78.

Kane, Lawrence A. and Kris Wilder (2022). *Martial Arts and Your Life. The Story of Us. What We Do and Why.* Seattle, WA: Stickman Publications, Inc.

Kane, Lawrence and Kris Wilder (2005). *The Way of Kata: A Comprehensive Guide to Deciphering Martial Applications.* Wolfeboro, NH: YMAA Publication Center, Inc.

Karpov, Aleksei (2021). *Shaolin Kung Fu: From Practice to Enlightenment.* Master of Arts Thesis in Chinese Philosophy at Beijing University Graduate School. https://www.academia.edu/50451840/Shaolin_Kung_Fu_From_Practice_to_Enlightenment. Retrieved 05/22/2024.

Kessler, Miles (nd) *Shu-Ha-Ri: 3 Stages of Mastery in Aikido.* https://theintegraldojo.com/shu-ha-*Ri*-3-stages-of-mastery-in-*aikido*/. Retrieved 02/08/2024.

Kerr, George H. (2000). *Okinawa—The History of an Island People.* Rutland, VM & Tokyo & Singapore: Tuttle Publishing. Revised edition.

Kotek, Ruthie (2016). *What Is so Japanese about Shotokan Karate-Do?: Protection of Cultural Identity and Economic Rights in the Global Sphere.* Thesis submitted in partial fulfillment for the master's degree to the University of Haifa, Department of Asian Studies.

Krech, David, Richard S. Crutchfield, and Norman Livson (1969). *Elements of Psychology.* New York: Alfred A. Knopf, Inc. 2nd edition (quoted as "Krech et al. 1969").

Langley, Scotty (2018). *Shu-Ha-Ri—Evolving Karate Thoughts.* Dublin: Mason Press.

Lao Tsu (1972). *Tao Te Ching. A New Translation by Gia-Fu Feng and Jane English.* New York: Random House Vintage Books.

Latella, Matthew (1994). "Rethinking Groupism: An Alternative to the Postmodern Strategy." *Dalhousie Journal of Legal Studies* 137, CanLIIDocs 7. https://canlii.ca/t/289g. Retrieved 01/02/2024.

Lee, Yongsun (2022). *Unpacking Martial Arts Pedagogy in Sport-Based Youth Development.* Dissertation at the University of North Carolina at Greensboro in Partial Fulfillment of the Requirements for the Degree Doctor of Philosophy. https://libres.uncg.edu/ir/uncg/f/Lee_uncg_0154D_13690.pdf. Retrieved 01/15/2024.

Lloyd, Henry M. (2014). "The Martial Arts as Philosophical Practice." In G. Priest and D. Young eds., *Philosophy and the Martial Arts: Engagement.* Routledge: New York, NY, pp. 68–86.

Lloyd, Henry M. (2014). *Philosophy as a Way of Life and the Practice of Martial Arts.* Draft Paper. https://www.academia.edu/4914897/Philosophy_as_a_Way_of_Life_and_the_Practice_of_Martial_Arts. Retrieved 01/12/2024.

Maslow, Abraham H. (1943). "A Theory of Human Motivation." *Psychological Review,* Volume 50, pp. 370–396.

Matayoshi, Masaharu and Joyce Trafton (2000). *Ancestors Worship—Okinawa's Indigenous Belief System—A Traditional View of Ideal Family Relationships.* Toronto, Canada: University of Toronto Press Incorporated.

Matsumuro Sokon (2020). *The Seven Virtues of Martial Arts.* Translated and published by Andreas Quast. Self-published in Düsseldorf, Germany. 2nd Printing.

McCarthy, Patrick (2016). *Bubishi—The Classic Manual of Combat.* Rutland, VT: Tuttle Publishing. Revised and expanded edition.

McCarthy, Patrick (1987). *Classic Kata of Okinawan Karate.* Burbank, CA: Ohara Publications, Inc.

McCarthy, Patrick (2023). *Kensei Kyan Chotoku. The Man & His Art.* Las Vegas, NV: The International Ryukyu Karate Research Society. www.koryu-uchinadi.com.

McCarthy, Patrick (1994). "The World within Karate and Kinjo Hiroshi." *Journal of Asian Martial Arts,* Vol. 3 No. 2, pp. 90–99. In DeMarco, Michael, ed. (2017). *Okinawan Martial Traditions, Vols. 1–2: te, tode, karate, karate, karatedo, kobudo.* Santa Fe, NM: Via Media Publishing Company. https://zoboko.com/text/9jo38134/okinawan-martial-traditions-vol-1-2-te-tode-karate-karatedo-*kobudo*/4. Retrieved 12/02/2023.

Mehrenberg, Richard L. (2013). "Pedagogical Inspiration through Martial Arts Instruction." Journal of Pedagogic Development, Volume 13, Issue# 2. https://www.beds.ac.uk/jpd/volume-3-issue-2/pedagogical-inspiration-through-martial-arts-instruction/. (Retrieved 01/05/2024).

Meissl, Walter (2021). *Many Kinds—Zur Kunst von 10. Dan Isao Ichikawa Gründer von Karatedo Doshinkan.* Vienna, Austria: edition thetis.

Meyer, Stanislaw (2020). "Between a Forgotten Colony and an Abandoned Prefecture: Okinawa's Experience of Becoming Japanese in the Meiji and Taishō Eras." *The Asia Pacific Journal: Japan Focus.* Volume 18, Issue 20. https://apjjf.org/2020/20/Meyer.html. Retrieved 12/10/2023.

Meyer, Stanislav (2007). *Citizenship, Culture, and Identity in Prewar Okinawa.* Thesis submitted for the degree of doctor of philosophy. University of Hong Kong.

Mijatov, Nikola (2014). "Eastern Mysticism in Judo, Karate, and *Aikido.*" *Sport-Science and Practice,* Vol. 4, Issue#2, pp. 83–92.

Miller, Rory (2011). *Facing Violence—Preparing for the Unexpected.* Wolfeboro, NH: YMAA Publication Center, Inc.

Motobu, Naioki (2024). *Kiai (Short Shout)—Was There Originally Kiai in Karate?* https://medium.com/@motobu715/kiai-short-shout-8a2f212dc616. Retrieved 02/13/2024.

Nagamine Shoshin (1976). *The Essence of Okinawan Karate-do.* Rutland, VT, Tokyo: Charles E. Tuttle.

Nakajima, Tetsuya (2018). *"Japanese Martial Arts and the Sublimation of Violence: An Ethnographic Study of Shinkage-Ryu."* Martial Arts Studies, Volume 6, pp. 62–74.

Noble, Graham (2019). "Gichin Funakoshi's Exquisite Art." *Classical Fighting Arts Magazine*, Vol. 3, Issue# 57, pp. 33–51.

Noble, Graham (2020). "Gichin Funakoshi's Exquisite Art Part II." *Classical Fighting Arts Magazine*, Vol. 3, Issue# 58, pp. 43–51.

Okinawa Dento Karatedo Shinkokai (n. d.). https://www.odks.jp/en/. Retrieved 1/15/2024. Quoted as "ODKS."

Park, Charles (2020). "An Inconvenient History—Japan's Dark Shadow on Asia." *East Asian History and Peace Institute.*

Perry, Jason S.D. (2018). *An Old Man's Way. Doug Perry's Unlikely Journey Through Karate, War, and Life.* Pennsylvania, USA: Apsos, LLC.

Quast, Andreas (2023). *Shingitai—Mind | Technique | Body (1).* https://ryukyu-*bugei*.com/?p=10868. Retrieved 12/02/2023.

Quast, Andreas (2021). *Style Sheet.* https://ryukyu-*bugei*.com/?p=9559. Retrieved 01/26/2024.

Quast, Andreas (2012). *Kinjo Hiroshi: From Karate to Karate. 2011.* https://ryukyu-*bugei*.com/?p=1060. Retrieved 01/04/2024.

Rabson, Steve (2012). *"Being Okinawan in Japan: The Diaspora Experience." The Asia-Pacific Journal: Japan Focus*, Volume 10, Issue 12. https://apjjf.org/-Steve-Rabson/3720/article.pdf. Retrieved 08/19/2023.

Rattner, Josef (1983). *Menschenkenntnis und Charakterkunde.* Hamburg/Germany: Hoffmann und Campe. 1st Edition.

Raudino, Giuseppe (2007). "Karate: Martial or Performing Art?" *Art Times*, Vol. 24, Issue# 5, p. 5.

Sanchez-Garcia, Raul (2018). "An Introduction to The Historical Sociology of Japanese Martial Arts." *Martial Arts Studies*, Volume 6, pp. 75–88.

Septri, Sonya, Hendra Nelson, Syahrial Kurniawan, Anton Bakhtiar, Kadek Komaini, and P. L. Yogi (2023). "Karate in the Digital Age: Augmented Reality for Enhanced Learning and Performance." *Journal of Physical Education and Sport* (JPES), Vol. 23, Issue #12, pp. 3235–3245. (Quoted as "Septri et al. 2023.")

Staller, Mario S., Sven Körner, and Andrew Abraham (2020). "Beyond Technique—The Limits of Books (and Online Videos) in Developing Self-Defense Coaches' Professional Judgement and Decision Making in the Context of Skill Development for Violent Encounters." *Acta Periodica*

Duellatorum, Volume 8, Issue #1, pp. 157–171. (Quoted as "Staller et al. 2020.")

Steinbrecher, Olaf (2017). *Mastering Karate: "The Third Precept of Karate-Do" by Anko Itosu*. https://www.thekaratepage.com/mastering-karate-the-third-precept-of-karate-do-by-anko-itosu. Retrieved 02/09/2024.

Swennen, Filip (2006). *The Creation of the Myth of "Traditional Japanese" Karate under the Pressure of Pre-War Nationalism*. Thesis for a licentiate in Japanology at Katholieke Universiteit Leuven, Belgium. Academic year 2005–2006. Faculteit Letteren TAAL En Regiostudies.

Swift, Charles Joseph (2019). *Itosu Anko. Savior of a Cultural Heritage*. Tokyo: Self-Published with Lulu Press. © Charles Joseph Swift.

Tan, Kevin S. Y. (2004). "Constructing a Martial Tradition: Rethinking a Popular History of Karate-Do." *Journal of Sport and Social Issues*, Volume 28, Issue #2, pp. 169–192.

Toyama, Kanken (2007). "Karate Styles—Translated by Mario McKenna." *Classical Fighting Arts Magazine*, Vol. 2, Issue #12, pp. 56–59.

Ueshiba, Morihei (1992). *The Art of Peace—Teachings of the Founder of Aikido*. Boston & London: Shambhala Pocket Classics. Compiled and translated by John Stevens.

UNESCO (2019). *Youth Development through Martial Arts: an Evaluation Framework for Youth Activities*. UNESCO Office Bangkok and Regional Bureau for Education in Asia and the Pacific, International Centre of Martial Arts for Youth Development and Engagement https://unesdoc.unesco.org/ark:/48223/pf0000371559. (Retrieved 1/10/2024).

Van Wolferen, Karel (1990). *The Enigma of Japanese Power: People and Politics in a Stateless Nation*. New York: Vintage Books.

Waterfield, Marc (2014). "*SHU HA RI the Process of Human Development.*" Paper submitted to the International Chito-*Ryu* Karate-do Federation as a component of the Renshi go grading requirements. https://www.academia.edu/41846357/SHU_HA_RI_the_Process_of_Human_Development . Retrieved 04/20/2024.

Wittwer, Henning (2014). *Karate Kampfkunst Hoplologie*. Niesky, Germany: Self-published. © Henning Wittwer.

Wittwer, Henning (2007). *Shotokan: Überlieferte Texte—Historische Untersuchungen*. Niesky, Germany: Self-published. © Henning Wittwer.

World Karate Federation (2024). *Karate Competition Rules*. https://www.wkf.net/structure-statutes-rules. Retrieved 01/17/2024. (Quoted as "WWK.")

Yadav, Pradeep K. (2023). "The Power of Karate: Exploring Its Healing Potential." *International Journal of Research and Analytical Reviews*, Volume 10, Issue #4, pp. 604–606.

INDEX

agile mindset 93
agile pedagogy 93
Ancestor Worship 5
art of peace 2
Asato Anko 6
athletes create an impression 35
athletic gymnastics 22
athletic kata dance xxv
avoidance 101, 102
backwardness 75
become the model 17, 59, 108
become the teacher 17, 59, 108
big picture 120
bird metaphor 15
Bloom's taxonomy 111, 112, 114, 116
body-weight power 27, 31, 32
break away from your sensei xxvii, 12
breaking the form 43
breaking with tradition 26, 56
Bubishi 159, 174
Buddhism 35, 39, 41, 78
budo 75, 76
budo karatedo xxv, 27
bujutsu 75
bushido 75, 77
calligraphy xxv, 22
center of gravity 31, 32
character development 77
ch'i 153, 167
Chibana Chosin 19, 69, 99
Christianity 39
classic Okinawan karate-jutsu 78
codifying 7
cognitive xxvii, 111, 112
competition showmanship 22
concept of self-protection 77

Confucianism 62, 78, 122, 153, 154
Confucian roots xxvii, 25
contradiction between change and preservation 124
cross-linked concepts 120
culture of conformity 25
Dai Nippon Butoku-Kai 76
development within a karate-jutsu system xxvi
Dreyfus Model of Skill Acquisition 112
ego 26, 100, 101, 102, 107, 122
emotional learning 111
empty-hand self-defense craft xxv
empty mind 40, 121
Endo Seishiro 36
enlightenment 28, 36, 37, 38, 41, 154
esoteric 35, 40
essence of a traditional kata 125
fantasy moves 21, 26, 27, 43
fine art xxv, 4, 19, 23, 27, 33, 43, 65
fine art of self-development 27, 33, 43
frustration tolerance 102
Fukyu kata 61
Funakoshi Gichin 21, 75
fundamentals 121
giri 62, 64
Gorin kata 61
groupism 25
hidden applications 25
Hiroshi Kinjo 10, 36
holistic concept 14
holistic perception 120
Holistic thinking 123
holistic understanding xxvii
Hong Yi-xiang 13, 56, 60
humility 19, 77, 101

ikebana 65
individual expression of the art 16
individual innovations 21
individual interpretations of forms 103
individualism 25, 102
individually differing interpretations 31
industrialization 99
inherent patterns 120
intellectual comprehension xxvii
invent a new fighting system xxvii
Isshin-Ryu 56
Itosu Anko 78
Japanese business philosophies 93
Japanese cultural values 26
Japanese fine arts principle xxiii, xxvi, 65
Jeet Kun Do 24
JKA 34, 77
kado 65
karate as a fine art 3
karate as a self-defense art xxv
ki 153, 167
kumite 35
learning objectives 113
Lee, Bruce 24, 25, 29, 170
lethal encounters 23
logic and reality of fighting 31
long-standing protocol 59
Mainstream karate 18
market niche 98, 99
martial art in name only 24
martial art of scholars 24
martial arts in name only 23
martial arts of scholars 23
mass product 99
Matsumura Sokon 23, 35
meditative philosophy 19
Meiji Period 72
mimic the teacher 17, 59, 65, 108

mind over matter 38, 41
modern karate reality 106
monopolistic competition 99
moral standard 154
mysticism 35, 37
Nakazato Shugoro 60, 69, 115
narcissism 100, 101
national cultural symbol 76
nationalism 73
nerve strikes 77
never change kata 124
occupation of Southeast Asia 73
Okinawan Karate-Jutsu 77, 78
Okinawan sub-cultural symbol 76
Original Seven 115
outcome is prioritized over the form 7
overarching unity 123, 124
Passai 15, 30, 105
path towards self-perfection xxv, 28
personal interpretations 33, 43, 58, 103
physical and non-physical harm 4
physiology of the human body 23
Picasso, Pablo xxv, 23
pressure points 77
psycho-motoric learning 111
qi 153, 167
racial superiority 72, 74
real fight 16, 103, 162
recreational athletics 19, 29
re-inventing the wheel xxv, xxvi, 27
relationship between student and teacher xxvii
resilience 102
second class citizens 71
self-absorption 107
self-acclaimed superiority 73
self-actualization xxiv, 4, 18, 27, 28, 33, 36, 37, 40, 43, 65, 75, 100, 106
self-control 121

self-perfection xxii, xxvi, 3, 4, 19, 29, 33, 36, 43, 76, 77
self-protection xxvi, 4, 6, 7, 16, 19, 23, 29, 33, 42, 58, 60, 61, 76, 98
senior karate authorities xxv, xxvi
senpai/kohai system 26, 62
Shimabukuro Eizo 56, 57
Shimabukuro Tatsuo 56
Shin Gi Tai xxvi, 18
Shudokan 36, 160, 166, 170, 188
simultaneous existence of phases 15
socio-cultural background 153
sports-karate xxii, xxv, 2, 24, 29, 30, 34, 35, 42, 43
standardization 7
state of dependence xxvii
state of independence xxvii
state of semi autonomy xxvii
subcultural identity 77
supplier driven market structure of Okinawan masters 99
systemizing 7
Taoism 62, 153, 154
three-phased growth path 11
time capsule of fighting information 125
Tomaya Kanken 36, 60
totality 120
transcend the system xxvii, 17, 42
true martial arts 23
trunk of the tree 106, 125
Uchinaguchi 5, 8
Ueshiba Morihei 2
underlying concepts 8
understand the intentions of the teachings 17, 59, 65, 108
universal self-protection 6, 55, 59, 78, 98, 110
USP 98, 106
warrior spirit 76
Western educational concepts 14, 119
Western individualism xxvii, 18, 43, 64
Yzong Tangschou 13
Zen 19, 29, 36, 37, 77, 78
Zen meditation 37, 38, 40

ABOUT THE AUTHOR

Hermann Bayer, PhD
Hermann is a long-time karate practitioner, scientist, and author, who holds degrees in economics, sociology, psychology, and business administration. He worked in German and US universities for eighteen years as a researcher, professor, campus dean, and multi-site dean. For another twelve years, Hermann was the CEO and executive coach of a German coaching and consulting  firm. In addition, he had ten successful years of self-employment, nine years working in the manufacturing industry, and two years of serving in the (West) German army's corps of engineers. He immigrated to the USA in 2005, where he later on changed his life priorities to practicing and studying karate and kobudo (weapons) full-time.

The author of several books and numerous articles on industrial relations and on coaching and consulting, Hermann today publishes on karate-jutsu's and karatedo's socio-cultural roles and their development. With YMAA Publication Center, he authored *Analysis of Genuine Karate—Misconceptions, Origin, Development, and True Purpose* in 2021 and, in 2023, *Analysis of Genuine Karate Volume 2—Sociocultural Development, Commercialization, and Loss of Essential Knowledge*, in addition to numerous articles. These publications shed light on the political reasons and arguments Japan used to redefine the Okinawan self-protection system (karate-jutsu) into a fine art and a path toward self-perfection (karatedo), and later into recreational sports-karate, with the related loss of essential knowledge through this socio-cultural development, and by Americanization, industrialization, and commercialization of the art.

Hermann started to train and to study karate—including its historical and socio-cultural development—in 1981. His experience covers old-style (non-sports) Japanese *Shudokan-Doshinkan* karatedo as well as classic Okinawan *Shorin Ryu* karate-jutsu. In addition, Hermann studies *Suikendo*, meaning "the art of fists flowing like water," one of today's most advanced karate fighting systems. Over the years he has spent considerable time with renowned Japanese, Western, and Okinawan teachers, all the while researching the socio-cultural backgrounds and the core essence of the styles they represent. Hermann holds black belt ranks in all those empty-hand and kobudo systems he studies.

Today, in his upper seventies, Hermann is still training hard; he practices karate daily and attends several weekly empty hand and kobudo trainings, completed by annual training camps in the USA and in Okinawa. To make a point about combining (not to be confused with "integrating") traditional karate-jutsu and today's sports karate, he continues to successfully compete in martial arts tournaments.

BOOKS FROM YMAA

- 101 REFLECTIONS ON TAI CHI CHUAN
- 108 INSIGHTS INTO TAI CHI CHUAN
- A WOMAN'S QIGONG GUIDE
- ADVANCING IN TAE KWON DO
- ANALYSIS OF GENUINE KARATE
- ANALYSIS OF GENUINE KARATE 2
- ANALYSIS OF SHU HA RI IN KARATE-DO
- ANALYSIS OF SHAOLIN CHIN NA 2ND ED
- ANCIENT CHINESE WEAPONS
- ART AND SCIENCE OF STAFF FIGHTING
- THE ART AND SCIENCE OF SELF-DEFENSE
- ART AND SCIENCE OF STICK FIGHTING
- ART OF HOJO UNDO
- ARTHRITIS RELIEF
- BACK PAIN RELIEF
- BAGUAZHANG
- BRAIN FITNESS
- CHIN NA IN GROUND FIGHTING
- CHINESE FAST WRESTLING
- CHINESE FITNESS
- CHINESE TUI NA MASSAGE
- COMPLETE MARTIAL ARTIST
- COMPREHENSIVE APPLICATIONS OF SHAOLIN CHIN NA
- CONFLICT COMMUNICATION
- DAO DE JING: A QIGONG INTERPRETATION
- DAO IN ACTION
- DEFENSIVE TACTICS
- DIRTY GROUND
- DR. WU'S HEAD MASSAGE
- ESSENCE OF SHAOLIN WHITE CRANE
- EXPLORING TAI CHI
- FACING VIOLENCE
- FIGHT LIKE A PHYSICIST
- THE FIGHTER'S BODY
- FIGHTER'S FACT BOOK 1&2
- FIGHTING THE PAIN RESISTANT ATTACKER
- FIRST DEFENSE
- FORCE DECISIONS: A CITIZENS GUIDE
- HOMECOMING
- INSIDE TAI CHI
- JUDO ADVANTAGE
- JUJI GATAME ENCYCLOPEDIA
- KARATE SCIENCE
- KEPPAN
- KRAV MAGA COMBATIVES
- KRAV MAGA FUNDAMENTAL STRATEGIES
- KRAV MAGA PROFESSIONAL TACTICS
- KRAV MAGA WEAPON DEFENSES
- LITTLE BLACK BOOK OF VIOLENCE
- LIUHEBAFA FIVE CHARACTER SECRETS
- MARTIAL ARTS OF VIETNAM
- MARTIAL ARTS INSTRUCTION
- MARTIAL WAY AND ITS VIRTUES
- MEDITATIONS ON VIOLENCE
- MERIDIAN QIGONG EXERCISES
- MINDFUL EXERCISE
- MIND INSIDE TAI CHI
- MIND INSIDE YANG STYLE TAI CHI CHUAN
- NORTHERN SHAOLIN SWORD
- OKINAWA'S COMPLETE KARATE SYSTEM: ISSHIN RYU
- PRINCIPLES OF TRADITIONAL CHINESE MEDICINE
- PROTECTOR ETHIC
- QIGONG FOR HEALTH & MARTIAL ARTS
- QIGONG FOR TREATING COMMON AILMENTS
- QIGONG MASSAGE
- QIGONG MEDITATION: EMBRYONIC BREATHING
- QIGONG GRAND CIRCULATION
- QIGONG MEDITATION: SMALL CIRCULATION
- QIGONG, THE SECRET OF YOUTH: DA MO'S CLASSICS
- ROOT OF CHINESE QIGONG
- SAFEST FAMILY ON THE BLOCK
- SAMBO ENCYCLOPEDIA
- SCALING FORCE
- SELF-DEFENSE FOR WOMEN
- SHIN GI TAI: KARATE TRAINING
- SIMPLE CHINESE MEDICINE
- SIMPLE QIGONG EXERCISES FOR HEALTH, 3RD ED.
- SIMPLIFIED TAI CHI CHUAN, 2ND ED.
- SOLO TRAINING 1&2
- SPOTTING DANGER BEFORE IT SPOTS YOU
- SPOTTING DANGER BEFORE IT SPOTS YOUR KIDS
- SPOTTING DANGER BEFORE IT SPOTS YOUR TEENS
- SPOTTING DANGER FOR TRAVELERS
- SUMO FOR MIXED MARTIAL ARTS
- SUNRISE TAI CHI
- SURVIVING ARMED ASSAULTS
- TAE KWON DO: THE KOREAN MARTIAL ART
- TAEKWONDO BLACK BELT POOMSAE
- TAEKWONDO: A PATH TO EXCELLENCE
- TAEKWONDO: ANCIENT WISDOM
- TAEKWONDO: DEFENSE AGAINST WEAPONS
- TAEKWONDO: SPIRIT AND PRACTICE
- TAI CHI BALL QIGONG: FOR HEALTH AND MARTIAL ARTS
- TAI CHI BALL QIGONG
- THE TAI CHI BOOK
- TAI CHI CHIN NA
- TAI CHI CHUAN CLASSICAL YANG STYLE
- TAI CHI CHUAN MARTIAL APPLICATIONS
- TAI CHI CHUAN MARTIAL POWER
- TAI CHI CONCEPTS AND EXPERIMENTS
- TAI CHI DYNAMICS
- TAI CHI FOR DEPRESSION
- TAI CHI IN 10 WEEKS
- TAI CHI PUSH HANDS
- TAI CHI QIGONG
- TAI CHI SECRETS OF THE ANCIENT MASTERS
- TAI CHI SECRETS OF THE WU & LI STYLES
- TAI CHI SECRETS OF THE WU STYLE
- TAI CHI SECRETS OF THE YANG STYLE
- TAI CHI SWORD: CLASSICAL YANG STYLE
- TAI CHI SWORD FOR BEGINNERS
- TAI CHI WALKING
- TAI CHI CHUAN THEORY OF DR. YANG, JWING-MING
- FIGHTING ARTS
- TRADITIONAL CHINESE HEALTH SECRETS
- TRADITIONAL TAEKWONDO
- TRAINING FOR SUDDEN VIOLENCE
- TRIANGLE HOLD ENCYCLOPEDIA
- TRUE WELLNESS SERIES (MIND, HEART, GUT)
- WARRIOR'S MANIFESTO
- WAY OF KATA
- WAY OF SANCHIN KATA
- WAY TO BLACK BELT
- WESTERN HERBS FOR MARTIAL ARTISTS
- WILD GOOSE QIGONG
- WING CHUN IN-DEPTH
- WINNING FIGHTS
- XINGYIQUAN

AND MANY MORE . . .

VIDEOS FROM YMAA

- ANALYSIS OF SHAOLIN CHIN NA
- ART AND SCIENCE OF SELF DEFENSE
- ART AND SCIENCE OF STAFF FIGHTING
- ART AND SCIENCE STICK FIGHTING
- ART AND SCIENCE SWORD FIGHTING
- BAGUA FOR BEGINNERS 1 & 2
- BEGINNER QIGONG FOR WOMEN 1 & 2
- BEGINNER TAI CHI FOR HEALTH
- BREATH MEDICINE
- BIOENERGY TRAINING 1&2
- CHEN TAI CHI CANNON FIST
- CHEN TAI CHI FIRST FORM
- CHEN TAI CHI FOR BEGINNERS
- CHIN NA IN-DEPTH SERIES
- FACING VIOLENCE: 7 THINGS A MARTIAL ARTIST MUST KNOW
- FIVE ANIMAL SPORTS
- FIVE ELEMENTS ENERGY BALANCE
- HEALER WITHIN: MEDICAL QIGONG
- INFIGHTING
- INTRODUCTION TO QI GONG FOR BEGINNERS
- JOINT LOCKS
- KUNG FU BODY CONDITIONING 1 & 2
- KUNG FU FOR KIDS AND TEENS SERIES
- MERIDIAN QIGONG
- NEIGONG FOR MARTIAL ARTS
- NORTHERN SHAOLIN SWORD
- QI GONG 30-DAY CHALLENGE
- QI GONG FOR ANXIETY
- QI GONG FOR ARMS, WRISTS, AND HANDS
- QIGONG FOR BEGINNERS: FRAGRANCE
- QI GONG FOR BETTER BALANCE
- QI GONG FOR BETTER BREATHING
- QI GONG FOR CANCER
- QI GONG FOR DEPRESSION
- QI GONG FOR ENERGY AND VITALITY
- QI GONG FOR HEADACHES
- QIGONG FOR HEALTH: BETTER DIGESTION
- QIGONG FOR HEALTH: HEALING QIGONG EXERCISES
- QIGONG FOR HEALTH: IMMUNE SYSTEM
- QIGONG FOR HEALTH: JOINT REHABILITATION
- QIGONG FOR HEALTH: MERIDIAN EXTREMITIES
- QIGONG FOR HEALTH: SITTING QIGONG EXERCISES
- QIGONG FOR HEALTH: SPINE AND BACK
- QI GONG FOR THE HEALTHY HEART
- QI GONG FOR HEALTHY JOINTS
- QI GONG FOR HIGH BLOOD PRESSURE
- QIGONG FOR LONGEVITY
- QI GONG FOR STRONG BONES
- QI GONG FOR THE UPPER BACK AND NECK
- QIGONG FOR WOMEN WITH DAISY LEE
- QIGONG FLOW FOR STRESS & ANXIETY RELIEF
- QIGONG GRAND CIRCULATION
- QIGONG MASSAGE
- QIGONG MINDFULNESS IN MOTION
- QI GONG—THE SEATED WORKOUT
- QIGONG: 15 MINUTES TO HEALTH
- SABER FUNDAMENTAL TRAINING
- SAI TRAINING AND SEQUENCES
- SANCHIN KATA: TRADITIONAL TRAINING FOR KARATE POWER
- SCALING FORCE
- SEARCHING FOR SUPERHUMANS
- SHAOLIN KUNG FU FUNDAMENTAL TRAINING: COURSES 1 & 2
- SHAOLIN LONG FIST KUNG FU BEGINNER-INTERMEDIATE-ADVANCED SERIES
- SHAOLIN SABER: BASIC SEQUENCES
- SHAOLIN STAFF: BASIC SEQUENCES
- SHAOLIN WHITE CRANE GONG FU BASIC TRAINING SERIES
- SHUAI JIAO: KUNG FU WRESTLING
- SIMPLE QIGONG EXERCISES FOR HEALTH
- SIMPLE QIGONG EXERCISES FOR ARTHRITIS RELIEF
- SIMPLE QIGONG EXERCISES FOR BACK PAIN RELIEF
- SIMPLIFIED TAI CHI CHUAN: 24 & 48 POSTURES
- SIMPLIFIED TAI CHI FOR BEGINNERS 48
- SPOTTING DANGER BEFORE IT SPOTS YOU
- SPOTTING DANGER FOR KIDS
- SPOTTING DANGER FOR TEENS
- SUN TAI CHI
- SWORD: FUNDAMENTAL TRAINING
- TAEKWONDO KORYO POOMSAE
- TAI CHI BALL QIGONG SERIES
- TAI CHI BALL WORKOUT FOR BEGINNERS
- TAI CHI CHUAN CLASSICAL YANG STYLE
- TAI CHI FIGHTING SET
- TAI CHI FIT: 24 FORM
- TAI CHI FIT: ALZHEIMER'S PREVENTION
- TAI CHI FIT: CANCER PREVENTION
- TAI CHI FIT FOR VETERANS
- TAI CHI FIT: FOR WOMEN
- TAI CHI FIT: FLOW
- TAI CHI FIT: FUSION BAMBOO
- TAI CHI FIT: FUSION FIRE
- TAI CHI FIT: FUSION IRON
- TAI CHI FIT: HEALTHY BACK SEATED WORKOUT
- TAI CHI FIT: HEALTHY HEART WORKOUT
- TAI CHI FIT IN PARADISE
- TAI CHI FIT: OVER 50
- TAI CHI FIT OVER 50: BALANCE EXERCISES
- TAI CHI FIT OVER 50: SEATED WORKOUT
- TAI CHI FIT OVER 60: GENTLE EXERCISES
- TAI CHI FIT OVER 60: HEALTHY JOINTS
- TAI CHI FIT OVER 60: LIVE LONGER
- TAI CHI FIT: STRENGTH
- TAI CHI FIT: TO GO
- TAI CHI FOR WOMEN
- TAI CHI FUSION: FIRE
- TAI CHI QIGONG
- TAI CHI PRINCIPLES FOR HEALTHY AGING
- TAI CHI PUSHING HANDS SERIES
- TAI CHI SWORD: CLASSICAL YANG STYLE
- TAI CHI SWORD FOR BEGINNERS
- TAI CHI SYMBOL: YIN YANG STICKING HANDS
- TAIJI & SHAOLIN STAFF: FUNDAMENTAL TRAINING
- TAIJI CHIN NA IN-DEPTH
- TAIJI 37 POSTURES MARTIAL APPLICATIONS
- TAIJI SABER CLASSICAL YANG STYLE
- TAIJI WRESTLING
- TRAINING FOR SUDDEN VIOLENCE
- UNDERSTANDING QIGONG SERIES
- WHITE CRANE HARD & SOFT QIGONG
- YANG TAI CHI FOR BEGINNERS
- YOQI: MICROCOSMIC ORBIT QIGONG
- YOQI QIGONG FOR A HAPPY HEART
- YOQI:QIGONG FLOW FOR HAPPY MIND
- YOQI:QIGONG FLOW FOR INTERNAL ALCHEMY
- YOQI QIGONG FOR HAPPY SPLEEN & STOMACH
- YOQI QIGONG FOR HAPPY KIDNEYS
- YOQI QIGONG FLOW FOR HAPPY LUNGS
- YOQI QIGONG FLOW FOR STRESS RELIEF
- YOQI: QIGONG FLOW TO BOOST IMMUNE SYSTEM
- YOQI SIX HEALING SOUNDS
- YOQI: YIN YOGA 1
- WU TAI CHI FOR BEGINNERS
- WUDANG KUNG FU: FUNDAMENTAL TRAINING
- WUDANG SWORD
- WUDANG TAIJIQUAN
- XINGYIQUAN
- YANG TAI CHI FOR BEGINNERS

AND MANY MORE ...

more products available from ...

YMAA Publication Center, Inc. 楊氏東方文化出版中心

1-800-669-8892 • info@ymaa.com • www.ymaa.com

www.ingramcontent.com/pod-product-compliance
Lightning Source LLC
Chambersburg PA
CBHW070136080526
44586CB00015B/1713